Contents

Behind the Box

The Hidden System of Freight Forwarding and the Global Flow of Goods

This book assumes no prior knowledge of logistics or trade. It is written for curious readers, small business owners, and early career professionals who want a clear, practical explanation of how freight really works, without jargon.

Publisher: Cirvie LLC Bellaire, Tx, USA

Book Design & Production: Cirvie LLC

Ordering Information: For details, contact the publisher at publisher@cirvie.com or visit www.cirvie.com for more information.

First Edition: 2025

ISBN: 978-1-971042-01-5

Published by Cirvie LLC in the United States of America

Dedication

To the curious minds who look past the box and ask how the whole system works.

"Every product carries a journey. Freight forwarders are the ones who make sure that journey finishes in the right place, at the right time, and with the right people."

Acknowledgments

The author is grateful to the many people who shaped my path in logistics. Most of what I learned came from working alongside experienced professionals who opened doors long before I understood their full value. To the mentors who shared their craft, asked hard questions, and quietly created opportunities: thank you.

I also owe deep thanks to my family: my wife, children, and extended relatives, whose patience, encouragement, and steady support made it possible to write this book while building a career. Finally, to the many friends, colleagues, and readers who believed in the project and offered help in ways large and small, your support has mattered more than you know.

Prologue: Why This Hidden System Matters

If you are holding this book, you have already met global logistics, even if you did not notice.

The screen you are reading on, the chair you are sitting in, the food in your kitchen, and the medicine in your cupboard all travelled through a web of farms, factories, trucks, ships, planes, warehouses, ports, and border checks. That web is the supply chain. Freight forwarding is one of the crafts that keeps it moving.

Most of the time this system is invisible. Shelves are stocked, parcels arrive, fuel appears at gas stations, and supermarkets quietly refill overnight. As long as everything works, few people ask how. The people who plan routes, book containers, clear customs, and fix problems in the background rarely appear in headlines or television shows.

When something breaks, the system suddenly comes into view. During the COVID-19 pandemic, container ships waited outside ports for weeks. Supermarkets limited purchases of basic goods. Factories paused production because one missing part was stuck on the wrong side of an ocean. A ship called the *Ever Given* wedged itself across the Suez Canal and held up billions of dollars of cargo per day. For a time, freight rates multiplied, delivery dates blurred, and everyone from small shop owners to national governments was reminded that physical goods do not move by magic.

This book exists because that reminder should not arrive only in a crisis.

Understanding how freight forwarding and supply chains work is useful even when the world is calm. It helps a small business owner negotiate better contracts. It helps a student see real applications for math, geography, and economics. It helps anyone reading the news connect a story about a drought in Panama or a strike in Rotterdam to prices and products in their own life.

It also opens a door into a wide range of careers. The highest paid people in this field are not always the ones driving the trucks or packing the boxes. Often they are planners, problem solvers, and negotiators who understand how the whole system fits together and who know how to use rules, data, and relationships to keep goods moving.

This book is not a legal manual or a set of exam notes. It is a guided tour built from stories, mental models, and practical examples. You will follow a single mug from a factory in Asia to a kitchen in North America, watch a small exporter in Ohio learn a hard lesson about customs and Incoterms, see how ports and carriers react to real crises, and look inside the offices and control rooms where freight forwarding decisions are made.

Along the way you will meet a handful of core ideas:

- What freight forwarders, carriers, brokers, and ports actually do and how they fit together.
- How international shipments really move, step by step, from factory to final customer.
- Why concepts like **LCL and FCL**, **Incoterms**, **HS codes**, and **total landed cost** quietly decide who makes money and who takes the risk.

Who This Book Is For

This book is for several overlapping groups of readers.

- Curious readers who have noticed ships on the horizon, empty shelves, or "supply chain" headlines and want a clear explanation of what is happening behind the scenes.
- Small and mid sized business owners who buy or sell physical products and need to understand freight well enough to negotiate, budget, and spot avoidable risks.
- Early career professionals and students who are considering logistics, freight forwarding, or supply chain roles and want to see what the work really involves, day to day.
- People who already work in operations, customer service, or finance and want a practical bridge between their current responsibilities and the mechanics of global trade.

It is not written as an exam prep manual or a legal commentary. Lawyers, regulators, and veteran logistics professionals may still find useful mental models and examples, but the primary goal is to give non specialists a solid, working understanding of the system.

How to Use This Book

You can read the book straight through, as a narrative that moves from a single mug to ports, costs, rules, special cargoes, careers, and crises. That is the best route if the topic is new to you.

You can also treat it as a reference.

- Use Chapters 1 to 3 when you want story driven explanations of how shipments and networks work.
- Dip into Chapters 4 to 7 when you need specifics on hardware, ports, costs, and rules for a real shipment you are planning.
- Turn to Chapters 8 to 12 when you face specialized challenges such as cold chain freight, trucking capacity, or major disruptions.
- Use Chapter 13 when you need to think about decarbonization, automation, and other longer term trends in freight.

At the end of each chapter you will find a Field Guide and an "If You Only Remember Three Things" section. Those pages are designed as quick refreshers before a meeting or when you are trying to explain an idea to someone else.

Chapter 1: The $5 Coffee Mug That Crossed Three Oceans

1.1 The Mug With More Miles Than You

Alex was already ten minutes behind.

The laptop was half open, the inbox was filling up, and the shirt for an important meeting was still damp because the washing machine had finished five minutes too late. The one steady comfort in the middle of this clumsy morning was the mug. Thick white ceramic, chipped on the handle, but exactly the right size. It fit under the espresso machine without needing to be held at an angle.

Alex pressed the button and watched the coffee stream down. One hand reached for the mug, and then there was a soft, slightly wrong sound.

A hairline crack ran across the bottom. The coffee hit the crack, seeped through, and within a few seconds it was everywhere. Brown liquid pooled under the machine, slid down the cabinet front, and soaked the clean socks that were supposed to make it to the meeting.

A very specific kind of morning anger showed up. Not full rage, more like a tired disbelief: *Not today. Come on.*

Alex grabbed paper towels, saved what little could be saved, and did what millions of people do when something cheap breaks.

Opened a shopping app.

Ceramic coffee mug.

Scroll, scroll, scroll. A plain white mug for $5. Simple, unbranded, nothing to think about. Under the price, in bright letters: "Free shipping. Delivery in 2–3 days."

Tap.

Buy Now.

In Alex's mind, the problem was finished. The cracked mug went in the trash. The meeting started. The new mug became a mental box that was already checked.

Outside that screen, the story of the $5 mug was only at the opening scene.

That new mug has already traveled more miles than many people do in a year. It has probably moved through more countries than show up on most vacation plans. None of that appears on the product page. The app does not mention it. The free-shipping badge hides more people, machines, documents, and decisions than most films have characters.

This chapter is about the system that made that cart possible.

1.1.1 The World Behind the Cart

A $5 mug, delivered to your door, for free. It sounds trivial, almost boring. It should not be.

How did a ceramic cup get from a factory in Asia or Europe or Latin America to your doorstep without anyone you know touching it?

Who chose which ship it would ride on?

Who decided that it would leave from the port of Hai Phong instead of Da Nang, or from Ningbo instead of Shanghai?

Who booked the truck that picked it up from the factory? Who reserved container space on a vessel run by Maersk or MSC or CMA CGM?

Who made sure customs in the exporting country allowed it to leave, and customs in your country allowed it to enter, and that neither side demanded extra taxes or special safety tests?

How did the cost of all of that, strung over thousands of miles, shrink down to a sliver of that $5 price tag?

There is an entire, mostly invisible industry built to answer those questions every single day.

An industry of people whose job is to move your mug from "click" to "cup."

They work with ships the size of skyscrapers laid on their sides, with ports that look like cities made of metal boxes, with databases full of product codes and trade rules. They line up trucks, trains, airplanes, warehouses, cranes, and couriers until your one small order quietly appears at your front door.

If the internet moves data packets, this system moves boxes. Instead of routers and switches, it uses ports and freight terminals. Instead of IP addresses, it has container numbers and warehouse locations.

Most of this is choreographed by a group of companies and professionals that rarely appear in headlines: freight forwarders, brokers, logistics managers, port operators, and carriers.

This chapter will introduce them through the story of Alex's mug.

1.1.2 Chapter Promise

In the pages that follow, you will trace that $5 coffee mug from a factory floor to a kitchen cabinet.

You will meet the people and companies that touch it along the way: the factory export manager in Vietnam or China, the freight forwarder who organizes the journey, the truck drivers, the port workers, the customs broker, the warehouse team, and the last-mile courier.

You will see how many steps have to go right. How a wrong code on one customs form or a missed connection at a port can turn a cheap mug into an expensive headache.

By the end of the chapter, you will understand why this "hidden" world matters—whether you are a curious reader, a small business owner trying to import products, an early-career professional thinking about logistics, or simply someone who wonders why shipments get delayed and prices go up.

Every ordinary object around you, from that mug on your desk to the phone in your hand, has a secret, globe-spanning adventure story. Freight forwarding and logistics are the storytellers and stage managers of that journey.

1.2 A Day in the Life of a Shipment: Following the $5 Mug

Now let us step away from the shopping app and follow the mug you just bought.

We will give it a starting point: a ceramics factory near Ho Chi Minh City in Vietnam. We will give it a destination: Alex's apartment in North America. Everything in between is the journey this chapter explains.

1.2.1 Birth of the Mug: More International Than It Looks

On the outskirts of Ho Chi Minh City, an industrial zone sits where rice fields used to be. In one of its low concrete buildings, a factory turns wet clay into coffee mugs.

Inside, the air is hot and dusty. Workers in light blue uniforms walk between spinning molds and gas fired kilns. Conveyor belts carry rows of unfinished mugs that look pale and fragile, like eggs without shells.

The clay came from a mine a few hundred kilometers away. Some of the glaze ingredients arrived in drums from South Korea. The cardboard boxes that will hold the mugs were made in a plant near the port, using paper pulp imported from Indonesia.

On the label, the mug will be "Made in Vietnam." In practice, it is already the product of several countries.

In a glass walled office above the factory floor, Linh, the export manager, scrolls through her inbox. A retailer in Canada wants 3,000 mugs. An online seller in Germany has ordered 1,200. A wholesaler in the United States wants 10,000 with a different glaze color.

Her job sounds simple and is not: move those mugs from this factory to customers on other continents without breaking them, losing them, or getting them stuck in paperwork.

To a twelve year old, you could explain it this way. The mug is a character in a video game. Level 1 is the factory. The final level is your kitchen shelf. Between them lie ports, ships, warehouses, and customs checkpoints. At each level, the mug meets different helpers and obstacles: a truck driver, a freight forwarder, a customs officer.

The factory does not load mugs on a ship that sails directly to your house. That would be like asking a village bus to turn into an international airline overnight. There are always middle steps and middle people.

Even before shipping starts, the five dollar mug is already the end point of several stacked supply chains: clay, glaze, packaging, labor, and machinery. Its global journey has started long before you click "Buy."

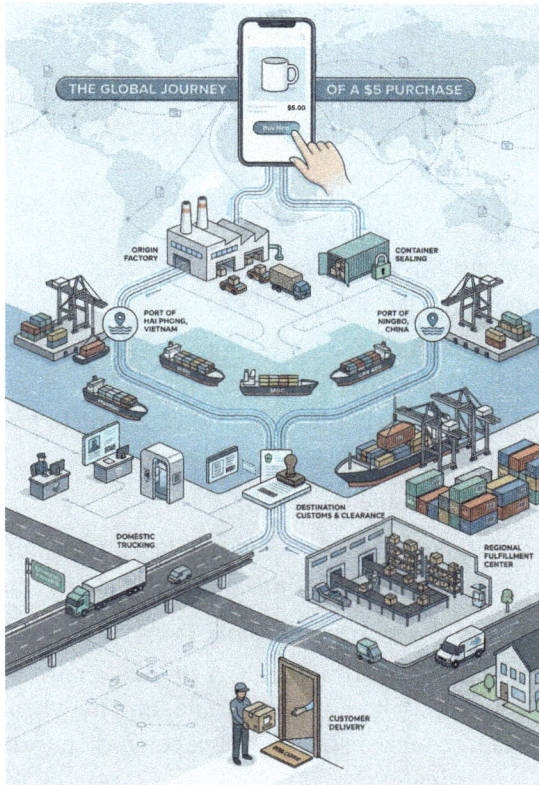

Figure 1: Global Supply Chain Journey

1.2.2 Meet the Freight Forwarder

Linh understands how to manufacture mugs and how to satisfy foreign customers. What she does not want to do is become an expert in container shipping, customs codes, port schedules, and insurance.

So she works with a freight forwarder.

The freight forwarder is the mug's travel agent. Instead of booking flights and hotels for people, they book trucks, containers, and vessels for cargo. They do not usually own the ships or the ports. Instead, they coordinate among many different players.

1.2.2.1 Why the Factory Needs Help

Imagine the factory tried to do everything itself.

Every time a buyer placed an order, Linh's team would have to:

- Find a trucking company willing to pick up pallets at the factory and deliver them to the right terminal.
- Compare schedules and prices across several shipping lines.
- Reserve space on a vessel that actually has room when the mugs will be ready.
- Prepare customs documentation for export and make sure all the product codes and values are correct.
- Arrange for a customs broker and a trucking company at the destination, in a time zone half a day away.

The factory could do this for a few shipments a year. But as orders grow, the complexity explodes. Ports have their own rules. Carriers change schedules. Customs rules are updated. A supplier might start selling to new countries with different requirements.

Specialization solves this problem.

Factories focus on designing and producing products. Freight forwarders focus on stitching together the journeys that move those products across borders.

1.2.2.2 What a Freight Forwarder Actually Does

From Linh's point of view, the forwarder is a single point of contact. She tells them what she is shipping, where it needs to go, and by when. They turn that into booked trucks, space on a vessel, export paperwork, customs coordination, and final delivery at destination.

Chapter 2 will unpack their role in detail. For now, you only need to see the forwarder as the company that connects Linh's factory to the rest of the journey without her having to learn global logistics from scratch.

1.2.3 Step 1: Export Haul – Factory to Forwarder's Warehouse

Once the mugs are packed in cartons and stacked on pallets, they are ready to leave the factory.

1.2.3.1 The First Truck Ride

A trucking company contracted by the forwarder sends a small truck to the factory gate. Workers load pallets of mugs onto the truck's bed or into its container. The driver signs for the cargo and pulls onto the highway toward the city.

This short trip from the factory to the forwarder's warehouse or consolidation center is called the **export haul**.

On its own, Linh's shipment is not enough to fill a 40-foot container. Her order is one of many small and mid-sized loads the forwarder is moving that week. The warehouse is where those pieces get combined.

1.2.3.2 Small Shipment, Big World: Consolidation

At the forwarder's warehouse near Ho Chi Minh City, dozens of trucks arrive every day with textiles, electronics, furniture, and food.

Inside, workers scan barcodes, check packing lists, and sort pallets by destination. One part of the floor handles cargo for North America, another for Europe, another for Australia.

Linh's pallets join other products going to similar places. Together they fill a single container. This process, where many small shipments are combined into a larger one, is called **consolidation**.

Think of it as ride sharing for freight. Instead of one shipper paying for an entire container, many shippers share the same space and divide the cost.

Consolidation is a key reason a $5 mug can be delivered with "free" shipping. The real cost per mug shrinks because it is spread across thousands of units and many customers.

1.2.4 Step 2: Customs and Paperwork – Getting Permission to Move

Before the mugs can leave Vietnam, the shipment needs something like a passport.

Every country controls what enters and leaves its borders. Customs authorities want to know:

- What is being shipped.
- How much it is worth.
- Where it came from.
- Where it is going.

They use this information to apply taxes and duties, enforce safety and health rules, and track trade statistics.

For Alex's mug, the key document is the **commercial invoice**. It lists the buyer and seller, the number of units, the unit price, the total value, and a description of the goods.

Alongside the invoice is a packing list that spells out how many cartons and pallets are in the shipment, and how they are arranged. For many products there will also be certificates that prove things like origin, safety testing, or compliance with particular regulations.

Each product is assigned an **HS code**, a number from the Harmonized System used by customs agencies worldwide. It determines which duty rate applies and whether special rules are triggered.

If the code is wrong, or the value is suspiciously low, customs can delay the goods, impose extra charges, or even seize the shipment.

This is why freight forwarders either work closely with customs brokers or have customs specialists on their team. For routine shipments, digital systems help pre-fill much of the data. For unusual goods or new trade lanes, humans step in.

Once the export declaration is accepted, the shipment is cleared to leave the country. Only then can the container move toward the port.

1.2.5 Step 3: Origin Handling – The Port as an Airport for Ships

After consolidation and export clearance, the container holding Linh's mugs is sealed with a metal bolt. The number stamped on the seal is recorded in the forwarder's system and on the shipping documents.

A truck hauls the sealed container to the port.

From above, the container terminal looks like a forest of colored boxes. Containers sit in stacks five, six, sometimes ten high. Rubber-tired gantry cranes roll between the rows, lifting boxes on and off trucks and rail wagons. Near the water, giant ship-to-shore cranes tower over enormous vessels, lifting containers on and off decks.

A seaport functions a lot like an airport for ships.

There is a check-in process, where carriers submit manifests of what will arrive and depart. Security checks, customs surveillance, and scanners monitor cargo flows. Ships have assigned berths similar to gates. Each vessel has a schedule and a narrow time window to load and unload thousands of containers.

Long before the container reached the port, the freight forwarder booked space with an ocean carrier—the shipping line that operates the vessel.

For Linh's mugs, the forwarder chooses a sailing from Cat Lai Terminal near Ho Chi Minh City to the port of Long Beach in California, with a stop in Busan, South Korea. The booking includes:

- The vessel name.
- Departure date and time.
- Expected arrival date.
- The container number.
- The seal number.

To the carrier, the forwarder is a customer filling part of the ship's "seats." To Linh, the forwarder is the guide who turns a stack of cartons into a container on a specific ship.

Origin handling is the moment where your mug is packed into a steel box, assigned to a particular vessel, and checked into this giant airport for ships.

1.2.6 Step 4: Ocean Freight: The Longest Leg

Once the container is on board, it disappears into a steel landscape.

A large container ship can carry more than 20,000 containers. Think of a floating skyscraper turned on its side, nearly 400 meters long, with boxes stacked nine or ten high on deck and more in the holds below.

Inside one of those boxes sit thousands of mugs in the dark, separated from seawater by only a few millimeters of steel and paint.

The ship leaves the berth with the help of tugboats and heads into open water. From Vietnam to the west coast of North America, a common route crosses the South China Sea, passes through the Strait of Malacca, then crosses the Indian Ocean and turns south around the Cape of Good Hope into the Atlantic before heading toward the Americas. On other trade lanes, a ship might cross the Pacific, pass through the Panama Canal, and enter the Caribbean and then the Atlantic on the way to the east coast of North America.

Depending on the exact ports and route, your mug is likely to travel somewhere between about 12,000 and 20,000 kilometers by sea.

Ships do not normally sail point to point between every origin and destination. Instead, carriers rely on hub ports such as Singapore, Busan, Rotterdam, or Dubai as connection points.

The container with Linh's mugs might be unloaded in Busan and stacked in the yard with thousands of others. It waits there until another vessel arrives that is bound for the west coast of North America.

This transfer from one vessel to another is called **transshipment**. In passenger terms, the container is changing planes. The container yard is the layover area.

If the first ship is delayed by weather, mechanical problems, or congestion at a previous port, the container can miss its connection and sit until the next sailing. The result is the maritime version of an unexpected overnight stay, except the stranded traveler is a steel box full of ceramic.

Ocean freight is the mug's long distance flight across the world's oceans, usually with at least one layover in a major hub.

1.2.7 Step 5: Import Customs and the Border Guard on Arrival

Two or three weeks after leaving Asia, the vessel reaches the Port of Long Beach. Giant cranes reach into the stacks of containers and lift each one onto trucks or rail cars.

Linh's mugs travel only a few hundred meters at first, moved to a container yard inside the terminal. There they wait again.

Before the container can leave the port, the goods inside must be cleared by the customs authorities of the destination country. The people who navigate this step are **customs brokers**.

Working on behalf of the importer, the broker:

- Files an import declaration that lists each product and its code.
- Uses the correct value for the goods, based on the commercial invoice.
- Calculates duties and taxes.
- Checks for any extra rules, such as safety standards for products that touch food, or special markings required on consumer goods.

If values or codes look wrong, customs may order a physical inspection. The container is moved to an inspection area. Port workers break the seal, open the doors, and sometimes unpack many cartons. Officials count and compare.

While the container waits, costs pile up: storage fees for extra days in the yard, inspection fees, and charges from the carrier if the container is not returned in time.

These extra costs can easily climb into thousands of dollars, even on low-value goods.

Import customs is the second border checkpoint. If the information is not right, your mug can get stuck, inspected, or hit with charges long before it ever sees a delivery truck.

> **When Customs Systems Look Ahead** On some trade lanes, carriers and forwarders must send data days before a vessel arrives. Systems automatically score containers for risk and decide which ones to inspect. Good data is the cheapest way to stay out of the inspection line.

1.2.8 Step 6: Destination Handling and Last-Mile Delivery

1.2.8.1 From Port to Warehouse: The Import Haul

Once customs releases the container, it can finally leave the port. A trucking company hauls it to a distribution center inland. In North America, large ports are connected to vast logistics zones filled with warehouses, rail yards, and truck depots.

At a warehouse in the Inland Empire east of Los Angeles, Sara watches her screen. She is a logistics manager for the online retailer that sold Alex the mug.

Her software shows containers as colored blocks. Some are still at sea, some are in yards, some have arrived at warehouses. She balances what is coming in with what customers are ordering. If a shipment of mugs is delayed, she might shift advertisements to another product or limit how many units a single customer can buy.

1.2.8.2 Deconsolidation: Breaking the Box

At the warehouse, workers open the container's heavy doors. Inside are pallets from many exporters. Some hold mugs, others hold completely different goods.

They unload and sort the pallets. This process is called **deconsolidation**. It is the reverse of what happened at origin.

Linh's mugs are now separated from the knives, electronics, toys, and clothing they travelled with. They move deeper into the warehouse, where shelves and automated systems store and track them.

1.2.8.3 The Last Mile: Warehouse to Alex's Door

Once the mugs are in the retailer's system, the part you see begins.

Alex's order is just one line in a long stream of data. A picker in the warehouse receives an instruction on a handheld device, walks to the right shelf, and places a mug into a bin or tote. Conveyors or robots move that bin to a packing station.

There, someone packs the mug in a smaller box with padding, prints a label with Alex's address, and hands the parcel to a parcel carrier—another truck, another route, another sequence of scans.

Within a day or two, a van stops outside Alex's building. The driver drops the box on the porch or at the lobby desk, scans it as delivered, and moves on.

For Alex, the story ends when the new mug meets the espresso machine. For everyone in freight, this is just one more tiny success inside a vast, continuous flow.

1.2.9 Zoom Out: How Many Things Had to Go Right?

Pause for a moment and look back at the journey.

For one $5 mug to land on Alex's counter, all of this had to go mostly right:

- Clay mined, kilns fired, boxes made, factory shifts scheduled.
- Purchase orders issued, production slots allocated, quality checks passed.
- Pallets loaded on time, trucks available, no accidents on the road.
- Room in a consolidation warehouse, a container available, no last-minute booking cancellations.

- Export documentation filled out correctly, HS codes chosen accurately, customs systems satisfied.
- A vessel leaving on schedule, space reserved, the container loaded and stowed safely.
- Weather and mechanical issues mild enough that delays do not cause missed transshipments.
- Import customs systems satisfied again, no random inspections or major errors.
- Sufficient trucks, chassis, and drivers to evacuate containers from the port.
- Warehouse space ready, deconsolidation staff available, software functioning.
- Parcel networks operating, vans fueled and staffed, no storm or strike shutting things down.

If you pictured each step as a coin flip, with only success or failure, the chance of everything working would look awful. In practice, the people running these systems add buffers, backup plans, and contracts that share risk so the odds are far better than a simple coin toss.

But the point remains: "free shipping" is anything but simple.

1.3 When Things Go Wrong: The High Stakes of "Small" Mistakes

So far we have followed a mug that mostly had a good trip. To see why logistics matters, it helps to look at the journeys that go wrong.

1.3.1 The $5 Mug That Got Stuck and Cost $150

Imagine a similar shipment handled by a less careful exporter.

The factory wants to save money on duties, so someone suggests declaring a lower value for customs and using a vague product description. On the commercial invoice, each mug is listed at $0.40 instead of $1.50. The description reads "decorative ceramic ornaments" instead of drinking vessels.

On paper, the shipment now looks cheaper and perhaps eligible for a lower duty rate.

The container arrives at the port of Rotterdam. The customs system automatically compares this declaration to others. It notices that most shipments with similar descriptions and weights have a higher declared value. This one stands out as suspicious.

Customs flags it.

The container is pulled aside. Inspection is ordered.

Port workers move it to a special area. The seal is cut. Officials open cartons and see row after row of functional mugs, not ornaments. They suspect under-valuation and misclassification, both serious offenses in customs law.

What follows is a small disaster for the importer:

- Two weeks of delay while documents are reviewed and corrected.
- Storage fees charged by the port terminal for each extra day.
- Inspection fees.
- Demurrage and detention charges from the carrier because the container is not returned on time.
- Higher customs duties calculated on the corrected higher value, plus potential fines.

By the time the container leaves the port, the importer has paid an extra $1,500 on a load that might only have been worth $7,000 or $8,000.

In global shipping, a small paperwork error on a low-value product can trigger costs larger than the goods themselves.

1.3.2 Incoterms: Who Pays When the Ship Is Late?

Behind every journey is an agreement that decides who bears that kind of pain. Those agreements use a standard set of three-letter codes called **Incoterms**.

Incoterms (International Commercial Terms) are standard trade rules created by the International Chamber of Commerce. They define who is responsible for transport, insurance, export and import clearance, and risk at each stage of a shipment.

Think about a group project in school. One student promises to research, another writes the slides, another does the presentation, and you agree who works until which point. If someone fails their part, everyone feels it.

Incoterms are that agreement for trade.

If Linh sells the mugs under **FOB**, Free On Board, at the port of Ho Chi Minh City, her responsibility ends when the mugs are loaded on the ship. From that moment, the buyer owns the risk and pays for the ocean freight, insurance, and everything at the destination.

If she sells under **DAP**, Delivered At Place, buyer's warehouse, then her side must handle almost everything: export haul, export clearance, ocean freight, import clearance, destination haul, right to the buyer's door. The buyer pays upon arrival but does not manage the logistics.

Now imagine the vessel is delayed three weeks because of congestion at a transshipment port. Or a storm damages containers on deck. Whether the buyer or the seller pays for delays, extra storage, or insurance claims depends heavily on the chosen Incoterm.

Incoterms quietly decide who pays, who worries, and who takes the hit when something goes wrong on your mug's ocean adventure.

1.3.3 Why "Boring" Logistics Details Made Global Headlines

For most people, logistics only becomes visible when it breaks.

In March 2021, the container ship *Ever Given* ran aground in the Suez Canal and blocked one of the world's most important waterways for six days. Satellite images showed hundreds of vessels waiting at both ends of the canal. Analysts estimated that each day of blockage held up roughly nine to ten billion dollars of trade.

For many consumers, it was a meme and a headline. For people inside supply chains, it was a vivid reminder that one stuck ship can ripple through inventories, factory schedules, freight rates, and retail shelves on multiple continents. The *Ever Given* showed, in a single dramatic moment, how much of daily life quietly depends on corridors most people never think about.

1.3.4 Rolled at Busan: Saving a Seasonal Launch

Container ships do not just arrive late. Sometimes a container misses its connection entirely.

In 2019, a European home goods retailer planned a summer campaign built around outdoor furniture. The centerpiece was a new line of compact balcony sets produced at a factory near Ho Chi Minh City. The marketing team had already booked advertising and photo shoots. Stores expected displays to go live in late May.

The forwarder designed a route: truck from the factory to Cat Lai Terminal, feeder vessel to Busan, then a mainline vessel from Busan to Rotterdam, and finally rail and truck into central European distribution centers.

Everything went smoothly at first. The container left Vietnam on time and arrived in Busan for transshipment. Then a series of small events collided.

- Heavy fog had delayed several inbound vessels earlier in the week.
- A crane breakdown slowed one of the terminal's main berths.
- Yard space was tight, so containers were being shuffled constantly.

By the time the balcony set container was moved into position, the mainline vessel it was supposed to connect to had already finished loading. The captain was not going to wait. Departure windows are tight, and port fees mount quickly when a ship overstays.

The container was "rolled" to the next sailing, meaning it would wait for a later vessel.

The forwarder's tracking system flagged the missed connection. Within a few hours the operations team had options on the screen.

- Do nothing and accept the roll. That meant the container would arrive in Rotterdam nearly two weeks later, threatening the launch.
- Move the container to a different mainline service leaving sooner, but at a higher rate.
- Split the shipment, flying a small urgent batch of sets to Europe while letting the rest follow by sea on the later vessel.

The retailer's logistics manager and the forwarder's key account manager joined a quick call with the merchandising and finance teams.

Together they chose the split approach.

- The forwarder arranged for the terminal to pull a few pallets of balcony sets out of the container and route them via air freight from Incheon to Frankfurt, then by truck to the retailer's largest distribution center.
- The rest of the container stayed in Busan and boarded the next available vessel to Rotterdam at the original ocean rate.
- The marketing department quietly adjusted the scale of the early store displays so that the limited air freight stock would be enough to cover the first weeks. Full roll out waited until the sea freight arrived.

On paper, the air freight was expensive. Spread across all the units in the launch, however, the added cost per set was modest. More importantly, the retailer kept its promotion dates, avoided empty shelves in flagship stores, and maintained momentum that would have been much harder to regain later.

From the outside, customers saw nothing unusual. They walked into stores in late May and saw balcony sets on display. Inside the retailer's systems, the shipment history showed a container that missed its connection in Busan, a quick series of decisions, and a forwarder that treated a "rolled" box as a problem to solve instead of a shrug.

This is what forwarders mean when they talk about managing exceptions. In global shipping, delays and missed connections happen. The difference is in how quickly someone notices, who has the authority to choose a Plan B, and whether the business understands its own trade offs between cost, timing, and reputation.

1.4 What You Will Learn in This Book

By following the mug and its cousins through the global system, this book will give you a set of mental models for how trade really works.

You will learn:

- How freight forwarders, carriers, customs brokers, and other players fit together to move a single shipment.
- How concepts like Incoterms, consolidation, and customs clearance shape cost, risk, and timing.
- How the "physical internet" of ports, warehouses, rail hubs, and parcel networks sits behind every scroll in your shopping app.
- Why disruptions such as blocked canals, port congestion, or sudden tariff changes show up as empty shelves, delayed parcels, or price spikes.
- What questions to ask and what pitfalls to avoid if you ever have to move products across borders yourself.

Chapter 2 zooms in on one of the central characters in this story: the freight forwarder. You have seen them here in action around a single mug. Next, you will see how their business works, what they are and what they are not, and why their decisions matter so much when the system is under stress.

Field Guide: The 5 Dollar Mug

Key concepts

- A small, low priced item can pass through many hands, modes, and borders before it reaches a doorstep.
- Freight forwarders, customs brokers, carriers, and ports each play distinct roles in that journey.
- Consolidation and deconsolidation explain how cheap items can share containers and still support "free" shipping.
- Incoterms quietly decide who pays and who carries the risk when things go wrong.
- Ports, canals, and major hubs act as chokepoints whose failures ripple through global trade.

Common mistakes

- Treating "free shipping" as if logistics were costless instead of recognizing that cost is buried in unit price and volume.

- Assuming that the seller or platform will always absorb delays and extra costs, without understanding where responsibilities actually lie.
- Focusing only on the last mile and ignoring how upstream events at factories, ports, or canals shape delivery times.

Warning signs

- Quotes or offers that show a very low ocean rate but are vague about "local charges" and who pays them.
- Sales or marketing plans built on tight calendars with no buffer for port congestion or missed transshipments.
- A lack of clarity inside your own business about which Incoterms you use and what they mean in practice.

Practical shortcuts

- When you see a shipping offer that looks unusually cheap, ask yourself, "Where is this cost really hiding?" and think through origin, ocean, and destination legs.
- For any important shipment, draw a simple timeline from factory to customer and mark who is responsible at each step; use that map to spot weak points.
- When you first hear a disruption story in the news, such as a blocked canal or a congested port, pause and ask which of your products or suppliers might be on routes that depend on that node.

If You Only Remember Three Things

1. A cheap, simple product like a mug usually crosses thousands of kilometers and several companies, modes, and borders before it reaches a kitchen cabinet.
2. Freight forwarders, carriers, customs brokers, and ports each own specific parts of that journey, and unclear roles or Incoterms turn small errors into expensive delays.
3. Any quote, promotion, or business plan that ignores how the underlying logistics network works is a bet that everything will go right without your help.

Chapter 2: What Freight Forwarders Actually Do

2.1 A Single Shipment, a World of Moving Parts

The email that changed everything was only three lines long.

> Hi, we love your products. Can you supply 500 sets of your eco kitchen kit for our Berlin stores, delivered DAP Berlin? Best, Purchasing, GrünHaus Retail GmbH

Two people sat in a small office outside Columbus, Ohio, staring at the screen.

Their company, Leaf & Ladle, sold reusable kitchen tools made from bamboo and recycled plastic. Until now, all their customers had been in the United States. They shipped via parcel carriers and the occasional pallet by truck to a warehouse in Chicago.

Now a German retailer wanted a bulk order. Five hundred full kits. Paid in euros. Delivered to a distribution center they had never heard of, in a city they had never visited.

The excitement lasted about fifteen minutes. Then reality walked in.

They grabbed a yellow legal pad and started making a list.

- Get the pallets from our warehouse to... where, exactly?
- Figure out what "DAP Berlin" actually means.
- Decide between ocean, air, or some mix.
- Understand export rules from the U.S. and import rules into Germany.
- Buy insurance.
- Track the shipment.

Within a day, the owner's browser history looked like a crash course in global trade:

- "bill of lading meaning"
- "HS code plastic kitchenware"
- "what is FCL vs LCL"
- "Incoterms explained"
- "freight carrier New York to Hamburg"

Every answer seemed to open three more questions.

The next morning, she called the packaging supplier who made their boxes. He sold to customers all over the world; if anyone local knew how to ship abroad, it would be him.

"We just got our first international order," she said. "They want delivery DAP Berlin. The internet is yelling acronyms at me. What do I actually do?"

He laughed, not unkindly.

"You talk to a freight forwarder. They'll organize everything. Seriously. You focus on packing the product. Let them handle the maze."

A new term joined the scribbled list: **freight forwarder**.

Leaf & Ladle did not need someone to drive a truck or captain a ship. They needed someone who knew how to put all the pieces together—someone who could turn that three-line email into a working plan.

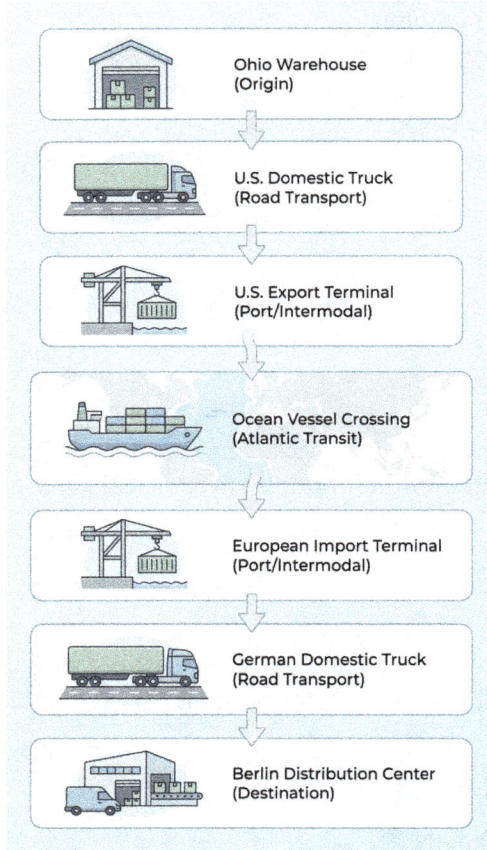

Figure 2: Leaf & Ladle's Door-to-Door Journey

2.2 What a Freight Forwarder Is (and Is Not)

2.2.1 The Orchestrator, Not the Vehicle

By now you have met the freight forwarder in two stories: around the $5 mug in Chapter 1, and in Leaf & Ladle's panicked phone call.

We can now sharpen that picture.

A **freight forwarder** is a company that:

- Designs a shipment plan from origin to destination.
- Buys capacity from carriers (trucking companies, shipping lines, airlines, rail operators).

- Bundles transport, documentation, and customs coordination into one managed service.
- Monitors the journey and intervenes when things go wrong.

Forwarders usually do **not**:

- Own large fleets of ocean vessels or aircraft.
- Take long-term commercial title to the goods.
- Replace the importer or exporter in legal responsibility for the trade itself.

They are orchestrators. They choose routes, book space, prepare or check paperwork, and line up hand-offs so that a shipment can move smoothly across borders and modes.

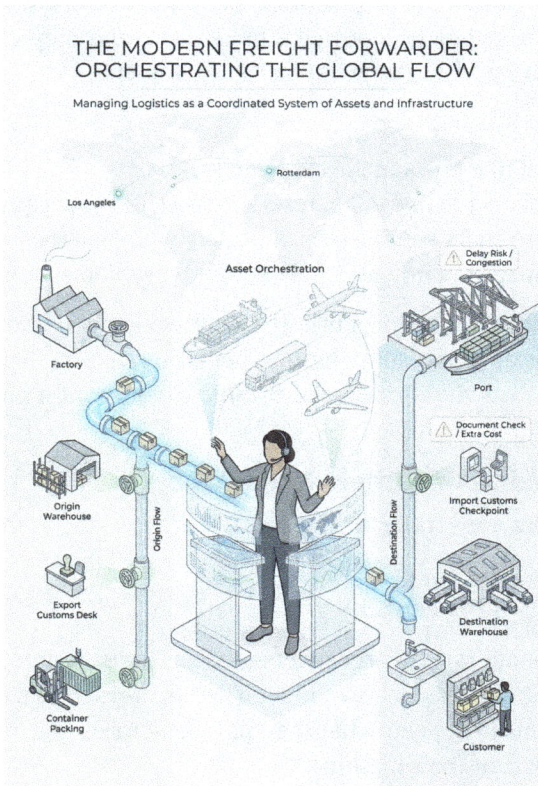

Figure 3: Freight Forwarding Process Flow

If the global supply chain is a set of interconnected levels in a video game, the forwarder is the player who knows the map, not the one who builds the roads or owns the vehicles.

2.2.2 What a Freight Forwarder Is Not

Because "freight company" is used loosely, it helps to draw clear lines.

A freight forwarder is **not**:

- **A carrier in the traditional sense.** Carriers own or operate the physical vehicles and issue their own transport documents when you book with them directly. An ocean carrier runs the ship; a forwarder books space on that ship.
- **A pure freight broker.** Brokers, especially in trucking, match loads to available trucks and earn a margin on the spread. They rarely handle warehousing, consolidation, or customs paperwork from end to end.
- **A customs authority or law firm.** Forwarders work with customs rules every day, but they do not make those rules and they cannot guarantee outcomes if information is wrong or incomplete.

You can picture it this way:

- Carriers are like bus and airline operators.
- Freight brokers are like ticket resellers who find you a seat at short notice.
- Freight forwarders are like tour managers who plan the entire trip, handle tickets, manage documents, and deal with problems along the route.

Chapter 1 introduced these roles briefly. Here we focus on how the forwarder sits in the middle of them, and why that position matters. Appendix B at the back of the book lists these roles side by side if you want a quick comparison while you read.

2.2.3 How Freight Forwarders Make Money

Freight forwarders are service businesses. Their revenue comes mainly from three sources.

1. Buying and reselling capacity

Forwarders negotiate rates with carriers—ocean lines, airlines, trucking companies, rail operators—based on volume. They then resell that capacity to shippers. The difference between what they pay the carrier and what they charge the customer is part of their margin.

This is why volume matters. A forwarder who moves hundreds of containers a month can often negotiate better rates than a small exporter ever could on their own.

2. Service and handling fees

They charge for documentation, customs filing coordination, consolidation and deconsolidation, warehousing, and other handling services. Some fees are itemized; others are included in bundled quotes.

3. Value-added services

Many forwarders offer extras:

- Cargo insurance.
- Supply-chain visibility platforms and dashboards.
- Consulting on Incoterms, routing options, and cost modeling.
- Specialized handling (for example, dangerous goods, cold chain, oversized cargo).

These services can be highly profitable if they save the shipper time, money, or risk.

You can think of a forwarder's P&L in simple terms: they buy transport and services at wholesale, add expertise and coordination, then sell a complete solution at retail. Their real product is not a truck or a ship—it is reduced complexity and a higher chance that everything arrives as promised.

2.3 Inside the Freight Forwarding Workflow

From the outside, working with a forwarder can feel like magic. You send a few documents and some measurements; a few weeks or months later, your customer sends a thank-you email and a payment.

Inside the forwarder, that "magic" is a repeatable process.

Most international shipments follow a recognizable seven-step workflow:

1. Quote request.
2. Booking and planning.
3. Export pickup.
4. Origin handling and export customs.
5. International transport.
6. Destination handling and import customs.
7. Final delivery.

We will walk through these steps using Leaf & Ladle's first shipment to Berlin as our running example.

2.3.1 Step 1 – Quote Request: Turning "Can You Ship This?" Into Options

After talking to their packaging supplier, Leaf & Ladle emails a recommended forwarder.

"We need to ship 500 eco kitchen kits to a retailer in Berlin, delivered DAP. Can you help?"

From the shipper's point of view, that feels like a reasonable question. From the forwarder's point of view, it is missing almost everything needed to design a shipment.

A good forwarder responds with a short, structured list of questions:

- What exactly are you shipping? (Product description and HS code if known.)
- How many cartons or pallets, and what are the dimensions and weight?
- Where will the goods be picked up? (Full address.)
- Where should they be delivered? (Full address, including any appointment requirements.)
- What Incoterms are agreed with the buyer? (In this case, DAP Berlin.)
- When will the goods be ready, and when must they arrive?
- Are there any special requirements? (For example, temperature control, hazardous materials, or strict labeling rules.)

In the background, the forwarder also checks whether there are any obvious red flags:

- Are there export controls on this type of product?
- Are there special certifications needed in the destination country?
- Does the shipment size make more sense as LCL (a shared container) or FCL (a full container)?

Once they have basic data, the forwarder can turn "Can you ship this?" into actual options—usually a small menu balancing speed and cost.

In recent years, many small shippers have first seen those options presented on a web dashboard rather than in a long email thread. Digital forwarders and online marketplaces, including well known platforms such as Flexport and Freightos, show door to door quotes in an "Expedia style" interface, and many traditional forwarders now offer similar portals. The screens may look modern, but they are still built on the same questions and trade offs you have just seen.

2.3.2 Step 2 – Booking and Planning: Locking in Space and Timings

With the shipment defined, the forwarder proposes one or more routes.

For Leaf & Ladle, the menu might look like this:

- **Ocean + truck, standard:** Pickup in Ohio, LCL consolidation in New York, ocean to Hamburg, truck to Berlin DC. Transit time 25–30 days door to door.

- **Ocean + truck, faster vessel:** Similar, but using a premium service and a port with better rail access. Transit time 20–24 days, higher cost.
- **Air + truck, urgent:** Truck to Chicago or New York airport, air freight to Berlin, truck to DC. Transit time 4–6 days, much higher cost.

Each option is a combination of mode, route, and service level. The forwarder also spells out assumptions:

- Cut-off dates for delivering goods to the consolidation warehouse or airport.
- Validity period of the quote (rates for ocean and especially air change frequently).
- Included and excluded charges (for example, customs duties and taxes are usually excluded).

Once Leaf & Ladle chooses an option—say, standard ocean via New York—the forwarder starts booking capacity:

- Truck pickup from the Ohio warehouse.
- Space in a consolidation warehouse or container.
- A spot with an ocean carrier on a specific vessel and sailing.
- A destination trucking slot from Hamburg to Berlin.

Planning is about aligning these bookings with realistic timings. If the vessel departure is on the 10th and the terminal cut-off is the 8th, the forwarder might plan:

- Pickup at Leaf & Ladle on the 6th.
- Cargo at the forwarder's warehouse by the 7th.
- Container gated in at the terminal on the 8th.

In parallel, a documentation team prepares a simple but strict checklist: which export filings are needed from the U.S. side, and what import data the German broker will require.

2.3.3 Step 3 – Export Pickup: The First Physical Move

Export pickup is where the plan meets reality.

A local carrier, contracted by the forwarder, collects the goods from the shipper and brings them to either:

- A forwarder's warehouse or consolidation center, or
- Directly to the port or airport if the cargo already fills a container or air unit.

The forwarder:

- Chooses the trucking partner and sends precise pickup instructions.
- Confirms that goods are packed, labeled, and ready.
- Adjusts the plan quickly if quantities or weights differ from what was quoted.

Even at this early stage, small surprises matter. If Leaf & Ladle's pallets weigh more than declared, the forwarder may need to re-rate the shipment or adjust how much cargo can go into a given container or on a given flight.

2.3.4 Step 4 – Origin Handling and Export Customs

Once the cargo reaches the forwarder's facility or the export terminal, origin handling begins.

At the origin warehouse, staff:

- Count pieces and compare them to the packing list.
- Check packaging and labels.
- Consolidate small shipments into shared containers or air pallets when needed.

In parallel, the documentation team prepares export filings using the same core data that will later feed import clearance. Well-run forwarders try to collect clean data once and reuse it, rather than retyping variations at every border.

As you saw in Chapter 1, customs is effectively passport control for cargo. Forwarders and customs brokers work together so that the shipment's "identity"—product codes, values, and documents—matches from export to import.

> **One Data Set, Many Borders** The same core data about a shipment (what it is, how much it weighs, how much it is worth) feeds:
> • Export declarations • Carrier manifests • Security filings • Import declarations Getting that data right once is cheaper than correcting it three times.

Once export clearance is granted and the container or pallets are accepted at the terminal, the shipment waits for its main leg: the international move.

2.3.5 Step 5 – International Transport: The Long Middle

Now comes the part most people picture when they think of global shipping: the ship or the plane.

For ocean freight, the container sits on a vessel for 10–30 days, depending on route. For air freight, the cargo might move airport-to-airport in under 24 hours.

The forwarder does not steer the ship or fly the aircraft. Instead, they:

- Track schedules and actual positions.

- Watch for port omissions, weather diversions, or strikes.
- Prepare downstream legs so that rail, truck, and warehouses are ready when cargo arrives.

When something breaks the plan, the forwarder becomes a problem-solver: rerouting via a different port, splitting a shipment, or upgrading a portion from ocean to air for urgent stock.

2.3.6 Step 6 – Destination Handling and Import Customs

At the destination port or airport, the shipment enters a mirror image of origin handling.

The forwarder or their local partner:

- Moves the container or pallets from the terminal to a warehouse if deconsolidation is needed.
- Pays or arranges payment for local handling charges.
- Coordinates with a customs broker for import clearance.

Import customs is where duties and taxes are assessed, so data quality matters even more. In many countries, customs systems use risk scoring. Declared values far below typical levels, or vague product descriptions, can trigger inspections and delays.

Because the forwarder has already collected and checked the shipment's identity upstream, they can usually respond quickly to any queries.

2.3.7 Step 7 – Final Delivery: Closing the Loop

Once customs has released the cargo and terminal charges are cleared, the forwarder arranges final delivery.

A local carrier delivers the shipment to a distribution center, factory, retail store, or sometimes a large end customer. The forwarder:

- Books the truck and shares delivery requirements.
- Manages appointments and access rules at destination sites.
- Sends proof of delivery and final documents to the shipper.

For Leaf & Ladle, this looks like a truck collecting four pallets in Hamburg and delivering them to a distribution center outside Berlin. The receiver signs a delivery note; the forwarder closes the file and invoices Leaf & Ladle.

Most of the complexity has stayed outside the Ohio office. The founders see status updates and, at the end, a single summary of costs instead of a pile of disjointed invoices.

2.4 Why Freight Forwarders Matter

2.4.1 Flattening Complexity for Smaller Businesses

Global shipping is full of friction: different rules, languages, time zones, and cut-off times. Large multinationals build in-house logistics teams to handle it. Smaller companies usually cannot.

Freight forwarders give them, in effect, a rented logistics department.

A good forwarder:

- Turns eight or ten counterparties into one point of contact.
- Consolidates many charges into one understandable invoice.
- Translates trade-offs: cost versus speed, ocean versus air, direct versus transshipment.

The Toronto coffee roaster, the Ohio kitchenware brand, or a small cosmetics label in Lagos all benefit from the same thing: expertise they do not have to hire full-time.

2.4.2 Risk Management and Problem-Solving

In calm years, forwarders quietly execute plans. In volatile years, they are crisis managers.

Ports back up. Canals restrict transits. Strikes halt rail lines. Customs systems crash.

When that happens, a forwarder's value shows up in three verbs:

- **Detect:** Track shipments and spot problems early.
- **Decide:** Propose realistic alternatives with costs and trade-offs.
- **Communicate:** Keep shippers and receivers informed, with clear expectations.

During the Suez Canal blockage and later port congestions, forwarders rerouted containers via alternative ports, shifted urgent fractions to air, and explained to non-specialists what "rolled cargo" and "blank sailings" meant for their inventory.

2.4.3 When to Call a Freight Forwarder Sooner

Many companies only call a forwarder when something has already gone wrong. A better rule of thumb is simpler:

- If your shipment crosses a border **and** matters to your cash flow or customer promises, talk to a forwarder early.
- If you are changing products, countries, or volumes, get advice before you quote delivery dates or "free shipping" offers.

The earlier a forwarder sees the full picture, the more options they have to design a route that fits your risk and budget, rather than firefighting a crisis that was avoidable.

2.5 Chapter Takeaways

By now you should be able to:

- Describe what a freight forwarder actually does day to day.
- Distinguish forwarders from carriers and freight brokers without repeating the basics from Chapter 1.
- Trace the standard seven-step forwarding workflow from quote to final delivery.
- Explain, in plain language, how forwarders make money and why volume matters to them.
- See why forwarders are especially important for small and mid-sized businesses without their own logistics departments.

In Chapter 3, you will zoom out from individual shipments and companies to the larger network they move through: the "physical internet" of ports, warehouses, hubs, and modes of transport that sits behind every tracking update on your screen.

Field Guide: What Freight Forwarders Actually Do

Key concepts

- Freight forwarders orchestrate door to door movements across multiple modes and borders without usually owning the vehicles.
- The seven step forwarding workflow runs from quote to booking, pickup, origin handling, main carriage, destination handling, and final delivery.
- Forwarders buy capacity from carriers at wholesale, add coordination and risk management, and sell complete solutions at retail.
- Good forwarders flatten complexity for small and mid sized shippers by becoming a single point of contact.
- Forwarders add most value when they are involved early, before promises are made to customers.

Common mistakes

- Calling a forwarder only after a shipment is already delayed or a customs problem has appeared.
- Treating forwarders as interchangeable "shipping companies" rather than as partners with different strengths, networks, and specializations.

- Giving forwarders incomplete data about cargo, deadlines, Incoterms, or documentation and then being surprised by misquotes or delays.
- Assuming that a forwarder automatically handles customs, insurance, or inland trucking without explicitly agreeing roles.
- Chasing the absolute lowest forwarding fee while ignoring service quality, communication, and problem solving ability.

Warning signs

- Frequent last minute booking requests for urgent international shipments that "must arrive" by a fixed date.
- Internal confusion about which forwarder owns which lanes, or who to call for which region or product.
- A pattern of rolled containers, missed cutoffs, or repeated surprise charges with no clear joint review between shipper and forwarder.
- Quotes that arrive slowly, with minimal explanation of route, transit time, or assumptions.

Practical shortcuts

- For any new lane or major order, send your forwarder a short, structured brief covering product, volumes, Incoterm, timing, and special require- ments; refer back to the seven step workflow to make sure nothing is missing.
- Keep a simple scorecard for your main forwarders, tracking on time per- formance, responsiveness, clarity of quotes, and how they handle prob- lems, not just price.
- As a default rule, talk to a forwarder early whenever you commit to deliver across a border in a way that would hurt if it went wrong; it is easier to design a good plan than to rescue a bad one.

If You Only Remember Three Things

1. A freight forwarder is not a general term for any shipping company; it is a specific role that orchestrates multi step, cross border movements between many carriers.
2. Forwarders earn their keep by buying capacity, managing paperwork and risk, and turning a messy chain of steps into a single plan and invoice.
3. You get the most value from a forwarder when you involve them before you promise prices and delivery dates, not after something has already failed.

Chapter 3: The Physical Internet Behind Every Click

3.1 The $20 T-Shirt That Traveled 20,000 km

On a Tuesday night, a student in Toronto clicks "Buy now" on a black T-shirt that costs $20. The online store promises free 3–5 day shipping. A tracking number appears. The student shrugs, closes the laptop, and goes back to studying.

On their side of the screen, that is all that happens: one click, one charge on a card, one package that will show up soon.

On the logistics side, that T-shirt has already lived a much longer and more complicated life.

The cotton may have been grown in Gujarat, India, on a farm that sells to a regional gin. From there, bales traveled by truck to a spinning mill near Coimbatore, where the cotton became yarn. That yarn may have been shipped to a knitting factory in Ho Chi Minh City, turned into fabric, then cut and sewn into T-shirts in a garment plant in Bình Dương province, Vietnam.

Cartons of finished shirts were loaded onto a truck and hauled to Cat Lai Terminal near Ho Chi Minh City. A freight forwarder booked them on a container vessel to the Port of Los Angeles, a journey of about 13,000 kilometers across the Pacific. In Los Angeles, the container joined a train headed inland, then was stripped at a warehouse. Some cartons continued by rail toward Chicago, others by truck toward Vancouver and Toronto.

The shirt for our student was picked in a suburban warehouse outside Toronto, packed by an automated machine, labeled, and passed to a delivery van on an evening route. By the time the doorbell rings three days after the order, the shirt has moved by truck, ship, train, and van. It has crossed at least three national borders and traveled something like 12,000–20,000 kilometers.

The student never sees the cotton fields, the cranes, the customs inspections, the freight invoices, or the people who touched that shirt along the way. They see a clean tracking page with messages like "Departed facility" and "Out for delivery."

Behind each of those updates sits a decision. Someone chose ocean instead of air, rail instead of long-haul trucks, one port instead of another. Each choice balanced speed, cost, risk, and the infrastructure available on the route.

If you have ever tried to organize a school field trip for 200 kids, you already know the feeling in miniature. You have to book buses, check train times, budget for snacks, plan bathroom breaks, collect permission slips, and hope the weather cooperates. Now swap children for containers, buses for ships and trucks, and school districts for dozens of countries with different rules. Stretch the trip across oceans and months instead of a single day. That is the world of logistics.

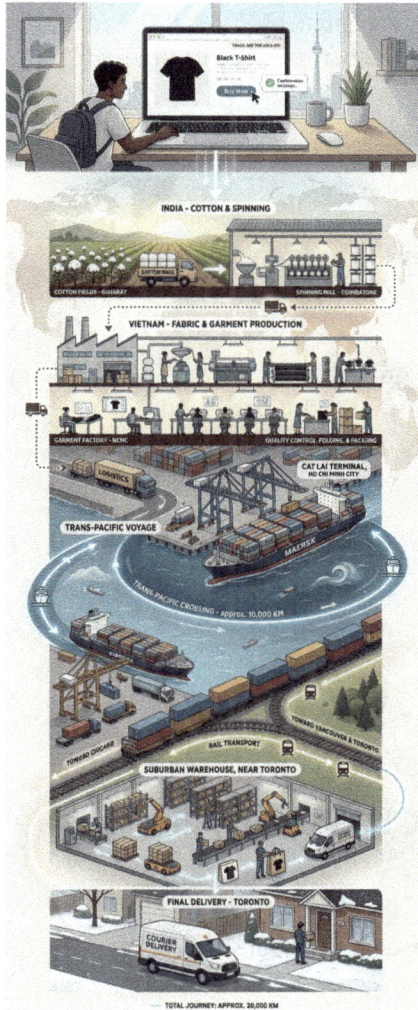

Figure 4: Global Supply Chain Journey

3.1.1 Link Back to Freight Forwarding

In the previous chapter, we focused on freight forwarders, the companies that orchestrate multimodal journeys for cargo. They do not usually own ships or planes. Instead, they organize shipments, prepare documentation, clear customs, consolidate cargo, and make sure freight keeps moving.

Freight forwarding is only one piece of the story. It sits inside a wider field called **logistics**. In this chapter, we zoom out another level. We will define logistics and logistics management, look at the main modes of transport, and see how businesses choose between ocean, air, road, rail, and inland waterways.

3.1.2 Section Takeaway

That 20 dollar T-shirt on your back sits on top of a complex web of decisions about how goods are moved and stored. Understanding that web, and the "physical internet" it creates, is what this chapter is about.

3.1.3 How This Chapter Fits the Book

Chapters 1 and 2 followed individual shipments and the freight forwarders who manage them. This chapter zooms out one more level.

Here, you will build a mental map of global trade as a network:

- **Nodes:** ports, rail yards, airports, warehouses, and fulfillment centers.
- **Links:** the main transport modes that connect those nodes.
- **Flows:** the movement of goods, data, and money across that network.
- **Bottlenecks:** the few critical points where delays and disruptions ripple outward.

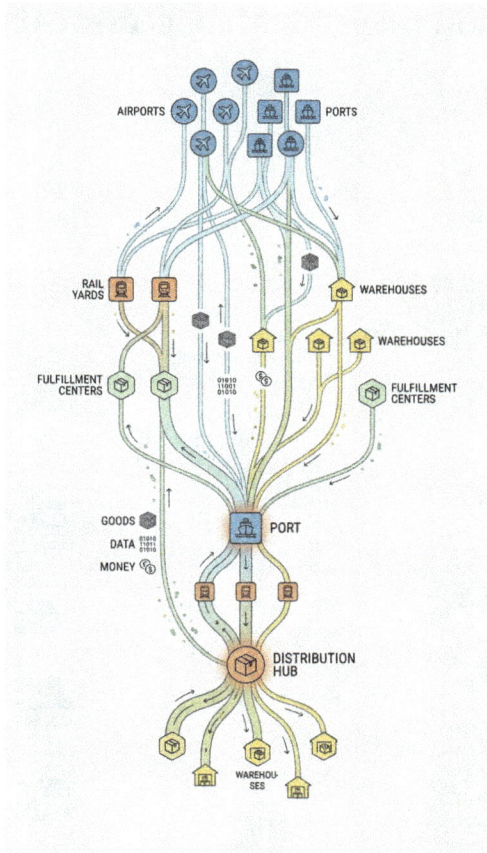

Figure 5: Global trade as a Network

By the end of the chapter you should be able to look at any tracking update such as "Arrived at hub," "Held at customs," or "Departed facility" and have a clear picture of the physical world behind those words.

3.2 Logistics and Logistics Management 101

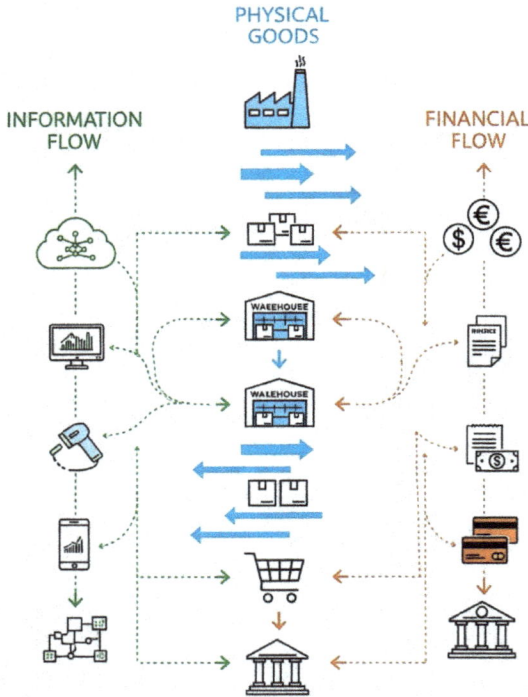

Figure 6: Three Flows of Logistics

3.2.1 What Is "Logistics" Really?

Logistics is the planning, movement, and storage of goods from where they are made or sourced to where they are used or consumed. It also includes the flow of information and money that supports that movement.

You can think of logistics as three connected flows.

First, the physical flow of goods. Raw materials move to factories. Parts move to assembly plants. Finished products move to warehouses, stores, and finally to you. Coffee beans travel from farms in Minas Gerais, Brazil, to export warehouses in Santos, then to roasters in Hamburg or Seattle, then to cafes and grocery shelves.

Second, the flow of information. Orders, forecasts, inventory levels, tracking events, and customs filings all move alongside physical goods. When information is late or wrong, physical goods tend to pile up in the wrong place.

Third, the flow of money. Invoices, freight charges, duties, and insurance premiums move in the opposite direction to goods. A shipment may travel thousands of kilometers, but it is the flow of money that keeps the system running.

When all three flows line up—goods, information, and money—logistics feels invisible. When any one of them fails, everyone suddenly notices.

3.2.2 What Is Logistics Management?

Logistics management is the discipline of designing and running those flows.

At a basic level, it answers questions like:

- Where should we place warehouses and distribution centers?
- How often should we ship, and in what quantities?
- Which carriers and forwarders should we work with?
- How much inventory should sit where in the network?
- What is our plan B if a port, factory, or route goes down?

In a small company, logistics management might be one person whose job title is something else—operations manager, founder, "the person who deals with shipping." In larger companies, it becomes an entire department using software, data science, and contracts to tune the system.

3.2.3 Logistics vs Supply Chain Management vs Freight Forwarding

These terms are often used loosely, but they point to different levels of zoom.

- **Logistics** is about moving and storing things: trucks, ships, warehouses, pallets, cartons.
- **Supply chain management** adds sourcing, production, and relationships with suppliers and customers. It cares about what to make, where, and when, not just how to move it.
- **Freight forwarding** is a specialized service inside logistics focused on international transport and border crossings.

If you picture a hierarchy:

- Supply chain management is the full movie.
- Logistics is a major set of scenes where goods move and wait.

- Freight forwarding is a key supporting character in the international scenes.

3.2.4 Classic Logistics Trade-offs: Speed, Cost, Risk

Almost every logistics decision balances three forces:

- **Speed:** how quickly goods move.
- **Cost:** how much it costs to move and store them.
- **Risk:** how often things go wrong, and how bad it is when they do.

Ship everything by air and you get speed, but at a high cost and with exposure to shocks in fuel prices and air capacity. Ship everything by slow ocean routes and you save money, but you need more inventory and have more risk if a port or canal is disrupted.

You can picture these trade-offs as a triangle. You can optimize for two corners, but rarely for all three at once.

3.2.5 Logistics as a Competitive Advantage

For many companies, logistics used to be a back-office cost center. Today it is often a front-line competitive weapon.

- Retailers compete on delivery speed and reliability.
- Manufacturers compete on how little inventory they can hold without running out.
- E-commerce brands compete on how broad a market they can serve profitably.

Behind all of that is logistics design: where warehouses are placed, which ports are used, how often containers sail, which carriers and forwarders get the business.

The best-run companies treat logistics as a core capability, not an afterthought. They know that clever marketing and product design are not enough if goods cannot reach customers on time and at a viable cost.

3.2.6 Transition to Modes of Transport

To understand logistics decisions, you need to understand the building blocks they work with: the main modes of transport. Each mode (ocean, air, road, rail, and inland waterways) has its own pattern of cost, speed, capacity, environmental impact, and reliability. Modern logistics is largely the art of combining them.

3.2.7 Section Takeaway

Logistics is the practical side of supply chains: moving and storing goods while keeping information and money flows aligned. Freight forwarders operate inside this bigger field. To see how they work, you need a clear picture of the transport "toolbox" they reach for.

3.3 Modes of Transport: Ocean, Air, Road, Rail, and Inland Waterways

3.3.1 Overview: The Transportation Toolbox

If logistics is the choreography, transport modes are the dance moves.

The main ones in global trade are:

- **Ocean freight** – slow, cheap, enormous capacity.
- **Air freight** – fast, expensive, limited capacity.
- **Road transport (trucks and vans)** – flexible, medium cost and speed.
- **Rail freight** – efficient over land, high capacity, medium speed.
- **Inland waterways (rivers and canals)** – very low cost, slow, great for heavy bulk.

No single mode is best at everything. The right choice depends on the cargo, the distance, the infrastructure, and the promises made to customers.

3.3.2 Ocean Freight

Ocean freight carries the bulk of world trade by volume. Containers full of manufactured goods, tankers full of liquid cargoes, and bulk carriers full of grain and ore all move on regular sea lanes.

Costs per ton-kilometer are the lowest of any major mode. A single large container ship can carry more than 20,000 containers. That scale spreads fuel, crew, and capital costs over a huge amount of cargo.

The trade-off is speed and exposure to certain risks:

- Typical Asia–North America or Asia–Europe voyages take two to five weeks port-to-port.
- Weather, port congestion, and canal bottlenecks can delay ships and disrupt schedules.
- Ships must call at ports, so inland legs by truck, rail, or barge are still needed.

From an environmental perspective, modern container ships are relatively efficient per ton-kilometer, though absolute emissions are still large because volumes are huge.

Ocean freight is like a slow, heavy conveyor belt between continents—unmatched for cost and capacity, but not built for last-minute rushes.

One example is the steady stream of container ships that move consumer electronics, clothing, and household goods from factories in southern China and Vietnam to ports such as Los Angeles, Rotterdam, and Hamburg. The rates and schedules on those Asia to North America and Asia to Europe lanes quietly influence the prices and availability of products on store shelves worldwide.

3.3.3 Air Freight

Air freight moves a small share of global trade by weight, but a large share by value.[1]

Think of:

- Pharmaceuticals and medical devices.
- High-value electronics and components.
- Fashion and fast-moving consumer goods near launch dates.
- Emergency shipments to keep factories running or hospitals supplied.

Costs per kilogram are many times higher than ocean or rail. The reward is speed: intercontinental shipments that would take weeks by sea can move in 24–72 hours airport-to-airport.

Most small e-commerce exporters meet air freight through parcel carriers and express integrators rather than by booking pallets directly. From the shipper's point of view, it feels like printing a label and choosing between "express" and "economy." Behind the scenes, those parcels move through dedicated air networks and scheduled passenger flights that allocate belly space to cargo. Capacity is limited and tightly managed, which is why cut off times, dimensional weight rules, and security screening matter so much.

Pharmaceutical and medical shippers typically use specialized "cool chain" services with temperature controlled facilities, tighter handling procedures, and additional documentation. For a box of clinical trial medicine or vaccines, the choice is rarely between ocean and air. It is between different air routings, ser-

---

[1]

Indicative value shares and emissions profiles by mode draw on UNCTAD transport reviews, IEA transport sector reports, and European Environment Agency modal comparison briefs.

vice levels, and temperature bands, all built on top of strict regulatory requirements.

Air freight is highly sensitive to:

- Aircraft and airport capacity.
- Fuel prices.
- Security rules and screening requirements.

Its environmental footprint per ton-kilometer is the highest of the main modes, which is one reason companies try to reserve it for truly time-critical or high-value cargo.

Air is the express lane of the physical internet—used sparingly for packets that really need it.

For example, when a new smartphone launches, manufacturers often fly the first batches from assembly plants in East Asia to Europe and North America by air so that retailers can stock launch day displays. Once demand stabilizes, replenishment volume shifts to slower but cheaper ocean services.

3.3.4 Road Transport

Road transport with trucks, trailers, and vans is the most flexible mode.

Trucks can:

- Go door to door without terminals.
- Serve locations that railways, rivers, or airports do not reach well.
- Handle a wide variety of cargoes with different trailer types.

Costs per kilometer and per ton-kilometer sit in the middle of the pack. Speed is moderate; over short and medium distances, trucks often beat rail or barge because they avoid extra handling.

Road freight is sensitive to:

- Fuel prices.
- Driver availability and regulations on hours of service.
- Traffic, road quality, and border controls.

Environmental performance varies with vehicle type and load factor. A nearly empty truck is both expensive and wasteful; a fully loaded, modern truck is far more efficient.

Road is the "last mile" workhorse of logistics and an important connector between all other modes.

In Europe, for instance, fresh produce picked in southern Spain often travels by refrigerated truck to supermarket distribution centers in Germany, the Netherlands, and Scandinavia. Those trucks link farms to regional hubs that ships, trains, and barges cannot reach directly.

3.3.5 Rail Freight

Rail freight shines on long inland corridors where infrastructure is good.

Key features:

- **High capacity:** long trains can carry the equivalent of dozens or even hundreds of trucks.
- **Energy efficiency:** steel wheels on steel rails create low rolling resistance.
- **Predictable routes:** rail lines concentrate flows along known paths.

Speed is medium. On short distances, trucks can be faster door to door. Over hundreds or thousands of kilometers, well run rail corridors match or beat trucks, especially if passenger traffic does not clog the line.

Rail has significantly better environmental performance per ton kilometer than road in most cases. Reliability depends on network quality, maintenance, and labor relations; strikes or infrastructure failures can have large impacts.

Rail is like a conveyor belt laid across the land. Once cargo is on it, movement is steady and efficient—but you need terminals at each end and track in between.

A real world example is the intermodal rail corridor between the ports of Los Angeles and Long Beach and inland hubs near Chicago. On busy years, those ports together handle close to 17 to 20 million TEU of containers, much of which flows inland on double-stack container trains that each carry the equivalent of hundreds of truckloads.[2] Trucks then handle the shorter final legs to warehouses and stores.

3.3.6 Inland Waterways

Inland waterways use rivers and canals to move goods by barge or small vessels inside a country or region.

Examples include:

- The Mississippi River system in the United States.
- The Rhine and Danube in Europe.
- The Yangtze in China.

---

[2] Approximate TEU ranges and inland rail shares are drawn from Port of Los Angeles and Port of Long Beach annual statistics and fact sheets in the early 2020s.

Costs per ton are extremely low, often rivaling or beating ocean freight. Barges can be coupled into long trains pushed by a single tugboat. The trade-off is speed and dependency on water conditions:

- Low water levels in dry seasons can restrict loads.
- Floods, ice, or lock closures can halt traffic.

From an environmental perspective, barges are among the most energy-efficient transport options. For heavy, non-urgent goods, they are hard to beat.

Inland waterways are like moving sidewalks for bulk cargo—slow but smooth and gentle on fuel.

On the United States Gulf Coast, petrochemical plants along the lower Mississippi River ship large volumes of chemicals, fuels, and plastic feedstocks by barge between refineries, storage terminals, and export docks near New Orleans and Houston. Using barges instead of trucks keeps heavy cargo off congested highways and makes those low value per kilogram products economical to move.

3.3.7 Comparing Modes

Viewed side by side, the profiles look like this in broad terms:

- **Ocean:** very low cost, slow speed, very high capacity, good environmental performance per ton-kilometer, but dependent on ports and canals.
- **Air:** highest cost, fastest speed, limited capacity, worst environmental footprint per ton-kilometer, relatively reliable but vulnerable to capacity crunches.
- **Road:** moderate cost, flexible and fairly fast, medium capacity, moderate environmental impact, reliability affected by traffic and regulations.
- **Rail:** low to moderate cost, medium speed, high capacity, strong environmental performance, reliability tied to network quality and labor stability.
- **Inland waterways:** very low cost, slow speed, high capacity, very strong environmental performance, reliability tied to water levels and infrastructure.

No mode is "best" across all five attributes. Logistics management is about choosing and combining them, given specific products and promises.

3.3.8 Multimodal and Intermodal Transport

Most international shipments do not use a single mode from start to finish. They combine several.

Intermodal transport means goods stay in the same container or unit while moving by multiple modes. For example, a 40-foot container might go by truck from a factory to a port, by ship across an ocean, then by rail inland, then by truck again to a warehouse. The goods are not unpacked along the way; the container is lifted from truck to ship to train and back to truck.

Multimodal transport usually refers to the use of multiple modes under one contract and one responsible party. A freight forwarder or logistics provider might sell a service from a factory gate in Vietnam to a warehouse in Spain. That door-to-door movement uses trucks, ships, and trains, but the customer sees one contract, one price, and one liability chain.

You can think of a shipping container as a world-traveling suitcase. A factory fills it with product and seals the doors. A truck hauls it to the port. Cranes load it onto a vessel bound for another continent. At the destination, the same sealed box rides a train and then another truck to a warehouse. Only there does someone cut the seal and unload the cartons inside.

The journey is like taking a suitcase on a trip. You roll it from your house to a car, then onto an airport trolley, into the plane, into a taxi, and finally into a hotel. You do not unpack and repack at every change of vehicle. The container is the suitcase of global trade.

3.3.9 How Inland Transport Connects to Sea Ports and Inland Ports

To see logistics clearly, it helps to think in networks, not isolated trips.

Seaports are like major train stations or airports in a big city. Inland rail yards, river ports, and regional warehouses are smaller stations. Road, rail, and barges connect them in all directions.

Take grain from an Iowa farm to a bakery in Egypt. A truck hauls harvested corn or wheat from the field to a local grain elevator. From there, it goes by barge down the Mississippi River to export terminals near New Orleans. There it is loaded onto a bulk carrier that crosses the Atlantic and the Mediterranean. At an Egyptian port, the grain is discharged, then moves by rail or truck to inland mills and, ultimately, by truck again to bakeries.

International and domestic legs blend into one continuous system. Freight forwarders map that system and arrange each link. In the classic seven-step forwarding process, they book export haulage, manage export customs, oversee origin handling at the warehouse, book the ocean or air leg, handle import customs, coordinate destination handling, and arrange import haulage.

3.3.10 Transition to Mode Selection

Now that we have met the main modes and seen how they connect, the next challenge is practical: how do companies decide which mode, or mix of modes, to use for a given product and route?

3.3.11 Section Takeaway

Each mode of transport has its own pattern of cost, speed, capacity, environmental impact, and reliability. Modern logistics stitches these modes together, often through intermodal containers and multimodal contracts, so that global and local movements form a single flow.

3.4 Choosing the Right Mode of Transport in Your Supply Chain

3.4.1 A Simple Decision Framework: 5 Big Questions

There is no magic formula, but a few questions guide most mode decisions. A useful checklist fits into five words: **Value, Urgency, Volume, Distance, Infrastructure.**

Value of the product. High-value items, like electronics or jewelry, can absorb higher freight costs and are often more sensitive to damage or theft. Low-value bulk goods, like grain, sand, or scrap metal, cannot support expensive modes. They almost always move by ocean, rail, or barge.

Urgency. How quickly must the goods arrive? Are you meeting a product launch date, preventing a factory shutdown, or shipping perishable food with a short shelf life? Or are you replenishing stock with plenty of buffer?

Volume and weight. A few cartons can be shipped almost any way. Hundreds of tons of cargo cannot go by air even if you wanted to. Bulky but light items, such as plastic furniture, fill up space before they hit weight limits. Dense metals hit weight limits first.

Distance. Short domestic moves lean toward road. Very long overland corridors may favor rail. International routes across oceans must use sea or air for the main leg.

Infrastructure availability. Are there nearby seaports, airports, rail lines, or navigable rivers? Some landlocked regions have strong rail links. Others rely on trucks over mountain roads. Regulations, customs efficiency, and security conditions also influence what is realistic.

Choosing a mode is a bit like choosing how to get to a friend's house. If they live two streets away, you walk or bike. If they live across town and you have time, you take the bus. If you are late and need to cross the city quickly, you might pay for a taxi. The logic is the same in logistics, only the distances, values, and stakes are larger.

3.4.2 Example 1: High-Value Electronics vs Bulk Grain

Consider smartphones traveling from factories in southern China to retailers in Europe.

A single phone is small, valuable, and time-sensitive around launch dates. For the very first batches of a new model, manufacturers often book air freight to fill distribution centers in Europe and North America in time for the marketing push. If air freight costs six dollars per kilogram and a phone represents 500 dollars per kilogram of value, freight is just over one percent of the value. Missing launch day could cost far more in lost sales and buzz.

Once demand stabilizes, companies may shift part of the volume to ocean to cut costs. They maintain a base inventory in regional warehouses, topped up by slower sea shipments, and reserve air for urgent replenishment of hot markets.

Now compare that with bulk grain moving from the U.S. Midwest to North Africa. Wheat is low value per kilogram and moves in huge quantities. Air freight might cost four dollars per kilogram on such a route. Wheat selling for 0.30 dollars per kilogram would effectively be wiped out by freight. Even if you could physically fit the volume on aircraft, which you cannot at scale, the economics would be absurd.

Instead, farmers and grain traders use a chain of truck or rail to river terminals, barges down the Mississippi, then large ocean bulk carriers to ports in Morocco, Egypt, or elsewhere. On the destination side, they use rail and road again.

The contrast makes the logic clear: value, urgency, and volume pull electronics toward air (at least at first) and keep grain firmly in the ocean and inland waterway world.

3.4.3 Example 2: Fast Fashion Retail vs Industrial Machinery

Now imagine two different businesses:

- A fast fashion retailer launching new designs every few weeks.
- A manufacturer shipping heavy industrial machinery worth hundreds of thousands of dollars per unit.

The retailer cares intensely about calendar dates and trends. If a shipment of jackets arrives a month late, they may need to discount heavily or miss the season entirely. They might:

- Use ocean for base volumes to keep costs manageable.

- Reserve air freight capacity for replenishing sizes and colors that sell out fastest.
- Place warehouses close to major cities to shorten last-mile deliveries.

The machinery manufacturer faces a different problem. Each unit is expensive and may be made to order. Shipping a single machine by air could cost tens of thousands of dollars, but if a late delivery would delay the opening of a factory, that might still be cheaper than paying penalties or losing a contract.

They might:

- Ship standard components by ocean to hold in regional stock.
- Move critical replacement parts or urgent machines by air.
- Use specialized road and sometimes barge transport for oversized pieces.

Both companies juggle the same five factors — value, urgency, volume, distance, and infrastructure — but they balance them in very different ways.

3.4.4 How Incoterms and Contracts Shape Mode Decisions

Mode decisions do not live in a vacuum. Contracts and Incoterms quietly shape who chooses what.

If a seller agrees to **CIF** or **DAP** terms, they are responsible for arranging international transport. They, or their forwarder, decide whether to use slow ocean or faster but more expensive options. The buyer mainly sees the final price and the promised delivery time.

If the sale is under **FOB** or **EXW**, the buyer takes control earlier. Their logistics team or forwarder chooses modes and routes. A buyer with strong logistics capabilities might prefer this, because they can leverage their own volumes and network.

In other words:

- Incoterms decide who holds the steering wheel for logistics.
- That party then chooses modes based on their own cost structure, risk appetite, and capabilities.

Understanding this link helps explain why two otherwise similar shipments might move very differently: one buyer might insist on air for reliability; another might happily wait for ocean to save money.

3.4.5 Risk, Disruptions, and Mode Flexibility

Real-world logistics does not happen in a static environment. Ports clog. Rivers run low. Canals limit transits. Fuel prices swing.

Smart logistics strategies build in backups. Companies may:

- Qualify multiple carriers and routes.
- Hold extra inventory of critical items.
- Pre-plan alternative routings with their freight forwarders.
- Use a mix of modes so they are not entirely dependent on any single corridor.

The logic is similar to having more than one way to reach school. If the main bridge is closed, you can take a bus and then a train instead of your usual bike route. It might take longer, but at least you arrive.

In recent years, several events have tested this flexibility:

- Severe congestion at the LA/Long Beach port complex left dozens of ships waiting offshore for days or weeks.
- Low water levels on the Rhine forced barge operators to cut loads drastically or stop sailing, pushing cargo onto rail and road and hitting industrial output.
- Drought-related transit caps at the Panama Canal created queues and delays, forcing some vessels to reroute via the Suez Canal or even around the Cape of Good Hope.

These are not rare exceptions. They are reminders that mode and route choices sit inside a living system shaped by labor, infrastructure, and climate. Building flexibility into that system is no longer optional.

3.4.6 Everyday Business Decisions Tied to Mode of Transport

The shipping options you see at checkout screens are not just marketing choices. They are expressions of underlying mode and network decisions.

- "Free standard shipping in 5–7 business days" typically means the seller will use ground services. Internally, that might involve ocean from overseas factories to a home-country distribution center, then trucks to regional hubs, then parcel vans.
- "Express 1–2 day shipping" relies on either domestic air segments, very fast and dense ground networks, or warehouses placed close to major markets. The cost is much higher per order, which is why many companies charge extra for it or bake it into premium product pricing.

Bulk discounts for large orders reflect economies of scale in modes. Filling an entire truckload or container is usually cheaper per unit than shipping many small parcels. If a retailer orders a full container of shoes by ocean, its freight cost per pair is lower than if it ordered the same shoes one carton at a time by air.

A small online store that wants to offer free two-day shipping to every customer soon learns these realities. Serving dense urban areas from a single warehouse might work, but reaching distant rural customers in two days might require expensive express services. The business must decide whether to raise product prices, open additional warehouses, limit the offer to certain regions, or accept lower margins.

Freight forwarders provide the hard numbers behind these decisions. They quote mode costs, realistic transit times, and the impact of customs processes. Without these logistics inputs, marketing promises can turn into expensive mistakes.

3.4.7 Section Takeaway

Choosing the right mode of transport is about matching the characteristics of your product and your promises to customers with the realities of distance, infrastructure, cost, and risk. Value, urgency, volume, distance, and infrastructure frame the decision. Contracts, Incoterms, and expectations set the rules. Freight forwarders help companies play within those rules, balancing speed, cost, and reliability.

3.5 Bringing the Mental Models Together

By now you have three overlapping pictures in your head:

- The **story view** from Chapters 1 and 2: a single mug, or a Leaf & Ladle shipment, moving step by step.
- The **role view** from Chapter 2: freight forwarders, carriers, brokers, and customs brokers doing different jobs.
- The **network view** from this chapter: nodes, links, modes, and trade-offs between speed, cost, and risk.

Taken together, they form the "physical internet" behind every scrolling product page and tracking update.

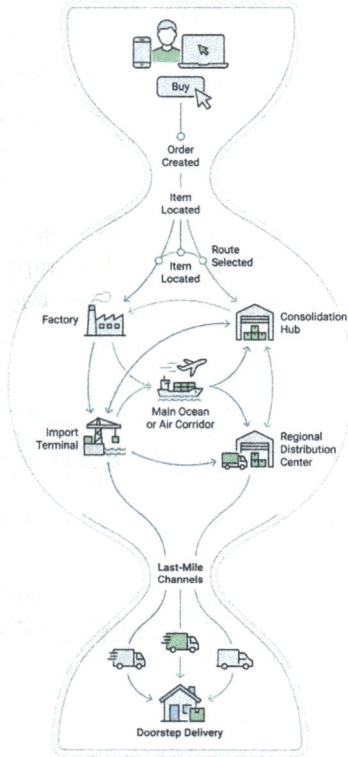

Figure 7: From Click to Logistics

When you hear about a port strike, a canal drought, a sudden spike in air freight prices, or a new regional warehouse opening, you can now ask sharper questions:

- Which nodes are affected? Which links are stressed or broken?
- Which modes become more or less attractive as a result?
- Which companies are exposed because of where their stock sits and how they move it?

In the chapters that follow, we will apply these mental models to real disruptions and strategic choices—from pricing and contracts to inventory placement, cold chains, careers, and crisis response.

Field Guide: Modes, Networks, and Choices

Key concepts

- Logistics consists of flows between nodes (factories, ports, warehouses, terminals) connected by links (road, rail, air, sea, inland waterways).
- Each mode has a characteristic profile of cost, speed, capacity, environmental impact, and reliability.
- Most real supply chains are multimodal; the container or pallet travels by several modes before reaching a customer.
- Value, urgency, volume, distance, and infrastructure are the five main filters for mode selection.
- Contracts and Incoterms decide who actually chooses modes and routes in practice.

Common mistakes

- Choosing a mode based only on headline price or only on speed, without considering risk and infrastructure constraints.
- Using air freight by default for urgent shipments that could be handled by faster ocean services or better inventory planning.
- Treating inland moves as secondary, leading to cheap ocean contracts that are undone by expensive or unreliable inland legs.
- Ignoring environmental and regulatory trends that may make some modes more costly or constrained in the future.
- Relying on a single "favorite" port or route long after congestion or water level issues make it fragile.

Warning signs

- Frequent recourse to emergency air shipments to avoid stock outs.
- Warehouses and stores that swing between overstock and empty shelves despite stable demand.
- A lane design that uses only one port, one carrier, and one inland corridor for critical flows.
- Marketing promises (for example "two day delivery everywhere") that do not match the physical network design.
- Teams that cannot quickly explain why a given route uses a particular mode mix.

Practical shortcuts

- For any major product and lane, sketch the network: origin node, intermediate hubs, destination, and mode on each link; ask where a different mode might reduce risk or cost.
- When considering air freight, ask whether a combination of better forecasting, slightly higher inventory, or faster ocean services could achieve the same business goal more cheaply.

- Use a simple decision lens of value, urgency, volume, distance, and infrastructure whenever you debate mode options; if you cannot justify a choice on at least three of those five, revisit it.
- Periodically review your most important routes for hidden chokepoints and lack of alternatives, not just for rate levels.

If You Only Remember Three Things

1. Every shipment moves through a network of nodes and links, not a single line on a map, and each node and link brings its own risks and constraints.
2. Mode choices are business choices: value, urgency, volume, distance, and infrastructure decide whether a box belongs on a vessel, a train, a truck, or a plane.
3. Robust supply chains are built on options; if you rely on one port, one mode, or one corridor for a critical flow, you are accepting more risk than you think.

Chapter 4: The Hardware of Global Trade

Containers, Ships, Ports, and Inland Infrastructure

4.1 Inside a Construction Site: Where Steel Meets Global Trade

A construction site at 6 a.m. is already alive with machines and workers. Cranes swing I-beams into place. Forklifts shuttle pallets of concrete blocks. An excavator claws at the earth while a cement mixer rumbles in the background.

None of it would be there without the hardware of global logistics working in the background:

- The steel beams probably crossed an ocean on a bulk carrier, fed by iron ore and coal that each had their own journeys.
- The excavator and forklift arrived on roll-on/roll-off (Ro-Ro) vessels or were shipped as project cargo on heavy-lift ships.
- The diesel that powers them came on tankers and moved through pipelines and terminals.
- The specialized electronics inside the cranes likely crossed on container ships.

Every piece depended on ports, cranes, container yards, highways, and rail lines to reach this site.

Four ship types, one container standard, and a vast amount of concrete and steel make up the invisible infrastructure behind every construction project.

The goal of this chapter is to turn that physical infrastructure into clear mental pictures. You will see how containers, vessels, ports, and inland links fit together, and why freight forwarders have to understand the hardware, not just the paperwork.

4.2 Containers: The Basic Unit of Global Trade

Containers are the modular bricks of modern logistics. They are standardized metal boxes that can be lifted, stacked, and secured in the same way on ships, trucks, and trains.

The most common sizes are:

- 20-foot containers: 1 TEU (twenty-foot equivalent unit)
- 40-foot containers: 2 TEU
- Width: usually 8 feet
- Height: 8'6" (standard) or 9'6" (high cube)

The industry measures capacity in TEU. A ship, a terminal, or even a trade lane is described in terms of how many TEU it can handle. Containers are not only boxes; they are capacity units in a global system.

When something breaks in that system—a canal blockage, a prolonged port closure, or a sharp swing in demand—the first practical problem often sounds very simple:

> Is there a container of the right type, at the right depot, on the day of the cargo cut-off?

During the pandemic, containers were stuck in North American and European import ports while factories in Asia waited for empties. Exporters who needed 40-foot high-cube reefers could not swap to standard dry boxes. Forwarders spent months repositioning empties over long distances just to assemble the right equipment for each booking.

You will see those disruptions again in Chapter 12. For now, treat every headline about "congestion" or "shortages" as a series of very concrete questions at depot level.

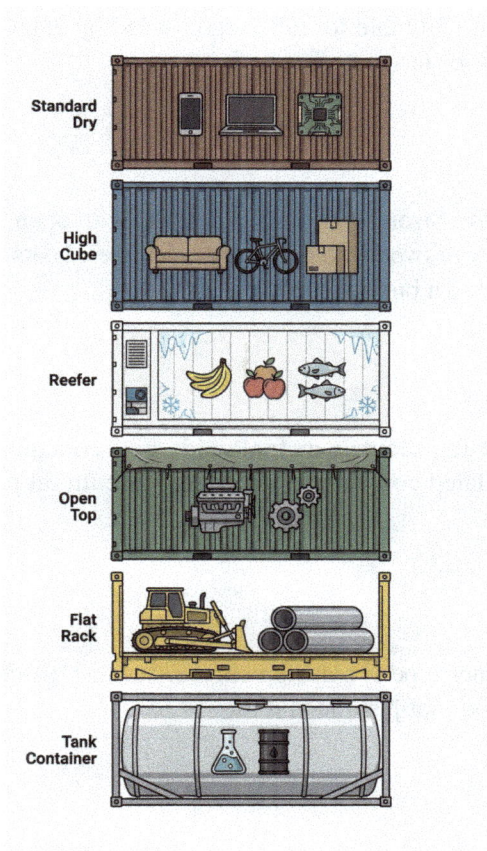

Figure 8: Container Types and Their Uses

4.2.1 Core Container Types

Standard dry containers The basic workhorse. Steel walls, weatherproof, lockable doors. Used for electronics, clothing, furniture, packaged food, machinery, and most dry manufactured goods.

High cube (HC) containers Similar footprint to standard dry, but taller (usually 9'6"). Useful for lighter but bulkier cargo, tall machinery, or goods that need more vertical space for packaging.

Refrigerated containers (reefers) Insulated containers with built-in cooling units. They plug into ship, terminal, or truck power. Used for meat, dairy, fruit, frozen foods, pharmaceuticals, and temperature-sensitive chemicals.

Open-top containers Standard footprint, but with a removable tarpaulin instead of a fixed roof. Suitable for tall cargo loaded by crane from above, such as machinery, pipes, or large components.

Flat-rack containers Strong base and end walls, with open sides and often no roof. Used for heavy or oversized machinery, vehicles, boats, or steel structures that can be lashed down but not enclosed.

Special equipment Tank containers for liquids, bulk containers for dry granules and powders, ventilated containers for certain agricultural products, and other specialized designs.

Takeaway: Container type is a design choice. It must match the cargo profile and handling method, not just the volume.

4.3 Ships: Different Vehicles on the Ocean

Think of the ocean as a giant highway. On land you do not move gasoline in cardboard boxes or sand in milk tankers. You use different vehicles for different cargo. The same logic applies at sea, at a much larger scale.

TYPES OF SHIPS: A VISUAL COMPARISON

CONTAINER SHIP

CARGO: Standardized intermodal containers (TEUs).
FEATURES: Cellular holds, deck cell guides, high stacking capacity, gantry cranes in ports.
FUNCTION: Efficient transport of manufactured goods globally.

TANKER

LIQUID CARGO

CARGO: Liquid bulk (crude oil, refined products, chemicals, LNG/LPG).
FEATURES: Multiple separate tanks, double hull, complex piping and pumping systems.
FUNCTION: Safe transport of hazardous and non-hazardous liquids.

BULK CARRIER

CARGO: Unpackaged dry bulk (grains, coal, iron ore, bauxite).
FEATURES: Large open holds, hatch covers, reinforced hull, onboard cranes/conveyors.
FUNCTION: Efficient transport of raw materials in massive quantities.

RoRo VESSEL (Roll-on/Roll-off)

CARGO: Wheeled cargo (cars, trucks, trailers, heavy machinery).
FEATURES: Multi-level decks with internal ramps, large stern/side ramps, drive-through capacity.
FUNCTION: Fast loading/unloading of vehicles.

Figure 9: Types of Ships

- Container ships are the truck and rail system of the ocean.
- Tankers are pipelines at sea.
- Bulk carriers are giant open-top railcars for raw materials.
- Ro-Ro and heavy-lift ships handle vehicles and oversized equipment.

Forwarders have to match cargo to ship type, route, and port, not just "book a boat."

4.3.1 Container Ships – Workhorses for Standardized Boxes

Container ships carry standardized containers stacked on deck and in holds. Their design is optimized for:

- Fast loading and unloading by gantry cranes.
- High stack heights of containers.
- Efficient port calls along regular service loops.

They range in size from small feeders serving regional routes to ultra-large container vessels (ULCVs) carrying 20,000 TEU or more on the biggest East–West trades.[3]

Container ship operations interlock tightly with ports and hinterland networks:

- Schedules are built around weekly or biweekly loops calling at several ports.
- Stowage plans dictate where each container sits on board, balancing weight, destination, and stability.
- Terminals plan crane gangs and yard flows to turn ships quickly.

For the $5 coffee mug and the $20 T-shirt in earlier chapters, container ships are the main ocean leg.

4.3.2 What Container Ships Actually Carry

Open a container ship and you will find much more than consumer goods.

Inside those boxes sit:

- Machinery and machine parts.
- Food and beverages.
- Chemicals and plastics.
- Furniture and building materials.
- Pharmaceuticals and medical equipment.

In effect, container ships move the manufactured world. Their very existence depends on the container standard you saw earlier: ISO dimensions, corner castings, and lashing systems that let one box fit everywhere.

4.3.3 Tankers – Pipelines at Sea

Tankers carry liquids in bulk: crude oil, refined petroleum products, chemicals, liquefied natural gas (LNG), and liquefied petroleum gas (LPG).

Key features:

- Cargo holds are divided into tanks, often with coatings or materials suited to specific products.
- Pump systems load and discharge via hoses and arms connected to shore terminals.
- Safety systems manage flammable or toxic cargoes.

---

[3]

Typical size classes and capacities are based on data summarized in UNCTAD's *Review of Maritime Transport* and industry fleet statistics from Alphaliner and Drewry.

Tankers are less visible to consumers than container ships, but they quietly underpin energy systems and chemical supply chains. When tanker markets tighten, fuel prices and many freight rates feel the impact.

4.3.4 Bulk Carriers – Moving Raw Materials in Loose Form

Bulk carriers (or bulkers) move unpackaged dry cargo such as:

- Iron ore and coal.
- Grain and soybeans.
- Fertilizers.
- Cement, bauxite, and other minerals.

They have large cargo holds accessed through wide hatches on deck. Loading and unloading use grabs, conveyor belts, and specialized terminal equipment.

Bulk terminals are built for volume and weight:

- Elevators and conveyors link silos or stockpiles to ship holds.
- Large land areas store stockpiles.
- Heavy rail and barge links connect mines, farms, and factories to the port.

Bulk carriers are optimized for huge volumes of low unit-value raw materials. Their logistics and terminals are completely different from container operations.

4.3.5 Specialized Ships: Ro-Ro, Heavy-Lift, Multipurpose, and Others

Beyond box ships, tankers, and bulkers there is a cast of specialized vessels:

- **Ro-Ro (roll-on/roll-off):** Floating parking garages. Vehicles and wheeled equipment drive on and off via ramps. Used for cars, trucks, buses, and heavy machinery.
- **Heavy-lift and project cargo ships:** With powerful cranes and reinforced decks, they carry oversized items such as wind turbine blades, transformers, and offshore modules.
- **Multipurpose (MPP) ships:** Flexible vessels that can carry a mix of containers, breakbulk cargo (steel coils, timber, paper), and project pieces. Often serve smaller ports without large cranes.
- **Reefer ships:** Dedicated refrigerated vessels for high-volume perishable trades like bananas or fish.
- **Livestock carriers:** Ships configured to move live animals with ventilation and welfare systems.

These vessels often have less frequent sailings and fewer operators. Their value lies in solving problems that standard container or bulk systems cannot.

4.3.6 Ship Type, Freight Rates, and Forwarder Choices

Each ship type has its own rate logic:

- **Container shipping:** space sold in container units, with frequent schedules and structured surcharges.
- **Bulk carriers:** rates often quoted per ton per voyage, closely tied to commodity cycles.
- **Tankers:** charter markets influenced by energy demand and geopolitics, feeding into fuel prices.
- **Specialized vessels:** fewer sailings and limited competition, with pricing driven by project specifics.

Forwarders look at total cost, not just the ocean leg:

- Ocean freight.
- Port charges, handling, and storage.
- Inland transport.
- Insurance and customs fees.
- Costs of special handling or equipment.

Sometimes a more expensive ship choice reduces total cost by simplifying inland moves or avoiding congestion risks.

Takeaway: Ship type determines not only what you can move but how the cost behaves. Forwarders have to match cargo and route to the right vessel family and rate structure.

4.4 Ports and Terminals: Sea-to-Land Interfaces

Ports and terminals are where ocean hardware meets land hardware. They are the interfaces between ships on one side and trucks, trains, and barges on the other.

4.4.1 Port Layouts, Berths, and Cranes

A typical large port complex includes:

- Multiple terminals, often specialized by cargo type.
- Berths where ships moor to load and discharge.
- Access channels dredged to required depth.
- Turning basins and anchorage areas.
- Container yards, bulk stockpiles, tank farms.

Figure 10: Terminal Movements

At container terminals:

- Ship-to-shore cranes lift containers on and off ships.
- Yard cranes and equipment (RTGs, RMGs, reach stackers) move boxes within the yard.
- Truck gates and rail sidings connect the yard to inland transport.

At bulk and tanker terminals:

- Conveyor systems, loaders, unloading arms, and pipelines replace container cranes.
- Large storage areas and tank farms handle massive volumes of single commodities.

Port capacity is a function of berth length, depth, crane productivity, yard space, and gate throughput. Weakness in any one of these can cause congestion.

Takeaway: Ports are engineered systems with specific limits. Each design choice, from berth length to crane reach, constrains what ships can call and how quickly cargo can be handled.

4.4.2 Yards and Hinterland Links

Inside the terminal, the yard is the buffer between ship schedules and land transport schedules. Yards store containers or bulk cargo while it waits for its next move.

Outside the fences, hinterland links carry cargo inland:

- Highways for trucks.
- Rail corridors for intermodal trains and bulk flows.
- River and canal systems for barges.
- Inland ports or dry ports that extend the seaport inland.

Examples include inland container hubs where boxes can clear customs away from congested coastal terminals and be sorted toward final destinations.

Takeaway: Terminals and yards bridge time and mode. Hinterland links then extend the port's reach into the wider economy.

4.4.3 Disruptions at the Port Interface

Ports are not isolated points. They are choke points. When something fails at the interface, effects ripple deep inland.

Examples:

- A partial shutdown at a major container terminal can cut ship calls to a fraction of normal. Containers pile up in yards, ships anchor offshore, and carriers begin omitting the port. Factories that rely on that port suddenly cannot ship, even if their production is fine.
- A labor strike, health-related absenteeism among crane operators, or a shortage of truck drivers can create chain reactions and long dwell times.
- Inland rail or barge capacity can lag behind surging import volumes, turning the port into a storage area rather than a transit point.

For forwarders, practical questions include:

- Can cargo be routed via an alternate port with stronger rail or barge options?
- If river barges are disrupted by low water, is there enough trucking capacity to absorb the volume?

- How will yard congestion affect cut-off times and the risk that a container misses its intended vessel?

You will see these dynamics play out in specific case studies in Chapter 12.

Takeaway: Port and terminal constraints are often the real source of "shipping" problems. Understanding layout and hinterland capacity is key to designing robust routes.

4.5 Inland Infrastructure: Roads, Rail, and Rivers

Once cargo leaves the seaport, inland infrastructure determines how predictably and cheaply it can reach the final customer.

4.5.1 Highways

Highways link ports to cities, industrial zones, and distribution centers. Congested or poorly maintained roads increase lead times, add uncertainty, and raise trucking costs.

4.5.2 Rail Corridors

Rail is the backbone for long-distance inland moves of containers and bulk cargo:

- Intermodal trains move containers between ports and inland terminals.
- Heavy-haul rail carries ore, coal, and grain from mines and farms to export ports and domestic plants.

Rail capacity, reliability, and access rights can have as much impact on supply chains as ocean capacity.

4.5.3 River Systems and Barges

Navigable rivers allow cargo to move by barge between ports and inland regions. This is often cost-effective for large volumes and heavy cargo.

However, river systems are sensitive to:

- Water levels and seasonal changes.
- Lock and dam maintenance.
- Weather events and flooding.

Drought events can reduce draft, forcing barges to sail partly loaded or suspending services entirely. As seen on major rivers in recent years, this can create shortages for factories and push freight onto rail and road, spiking prices there too.

4.5.4 Intermodal and Inland Hubs

Intermodal hubs and dry ports provide:

- Rail terminals for containers.
- Warehousing and distribution centers.
- Customs clearance inland.
- Consolidation and deconsolidation services.

Forwarders use these nodes to design routings such as:

- Port A → barge → inland hub → truck to final consignee.
- Port B → rail → inland hub near customer clusters.

Takeaway: Inland infrastructure is not secondary. It is often where climate, geography, and public investment decisions first show up in logistics performance.

4.6 How Forwarders Match Cargo to Hardware

For every shipment, a forwarder is implicitly answering a sequence of hardware questions:

1. **Cargo profile**
   - Liquid or solid.
   - Packaged or loose.
   - Hazardous or non-hazardous.
   - Volume and weight.
2. **Route and infrastructure**
   - Which origins and destinations are available.
   - Which ports can handle the cargo and the right ship types.
   - Which inland modes exist along the corridor.
3. **Time, cost, and risk**
   - Transit time requirements.
   - Budget and value of the goods.
   - Seasonality, congestion, and political or climate risks.

Examples:

- A small e-commerce shipment: LCL in a standard dry container on a container ship, using well-connected ports and inland hubs.
- A large grain export: bulk carrier via grain terminals, with heavy rail to port and possibly river barges inland.
- Wind turbines: heavy-lift or multipurpose ship with suitable cranes and deck strength, plus specialized inland transport.

- Hazardous liquids: dedicated chemical tanker or tank containers on a container ship, depending on volume and route.

The forwarder is not just finding "a ship." They are matching container type, vessel type, port, and inland infrastructure into a coherent, risk-aware plan.

Takeaway: Hardware choices are central to freight forwarding. The right combination of container, ship, port, and inland mode is a design decision, not a detail.

4.7 Transition and Chapter Wrap-Up

The hardware of global trade, from containers and vessels to ports and inland infrastructure, operates as a tightly linked system.

You have seen that:

- Containers are standardized capacity units, with multiple specialized variants.
- Different ship types act like different vehicle families on the ocean highway.
- Ports and terminals are sea-to-land interfaces with specific physical limits.
- Inland infrastructure determines whether port throughput translates into reliable door-to-door flows.
- Forwarders operate in this hardware landscape, matching cargo to the right physical path.

In quiet years, you might not notice any of this. Whether your goods sailed on a 6,000-TEU ship or a 20,000-TEU ship, whether they went via Port A or Port B, may seem irrelevant.

In stressful years with blocked canals, rivers limited by drought, and terminals running at partial capacity, all those details suddenly matter. The choice of container type, vessel size, port, and inland route can determine whether cargo moves with a delay or does not move at all.

A forwarder who understands the hardware can:

- Spot when a disruption in one river, port, or canal will affect distant routes.
- Propose realistic alternatives that fit cargo type, infrastructure limits, and timing.
- Explain why a slightly more expensive equipment or route choice reduces larger hidden risks.

With that physical lens in place, the next step is to understand how the economics sit on top of this hardware. The next chapter will look at shipping costs and freight rates: how space on these ships is priced, how port and inland charges stack up, and how all of it flows into the final landed cost of goods.

Field Guide: Hardware of Global Trade

Key concepts

- Containers are standardized "boxes" that allow cargo to move seamlessly between ships, trucks, and trains, with specialized variants such as reefers and flat racks.
- Different ship types (container, tanker, bulk, Ro Ro, heavy lift) exist because different cargoes and trades have different physical needs.
- Ports and terminals are interfaces between sea and land, with design limits on depth, berth length, crane reach, yard space, and gate capacity.
- Inland infrastructure (roads, rail, rivers, inland ports) determines whether port capacity actually translates into reliable door to door service.
- Forwarders create hardware "matches," aligning cargo type and route with appropriate containers, vessels, ports, and inland modes.

Common mistakes

- Treating all ports and terminals as interchangeable, ignoring draft limits, yard capacity, and hinterland links.
- Booking equipment based only on availability or rate without checking whether the container or ship type truly fits the cargo.
- Ignoring inland constraints (for example bridge heights, road weight limits, low river levels) until a shipment is already en route.
- Assuming that a bigger ship or busier port is always better, even when it increases transshipment or congestion risks.
- Leaving decisions about special cargo (oversize, hazmat, temperature controlled) to last minute improvisation.

Warning signs

- Frequent requests from carriers or terminals to switch ports or equipment types at short notice.
- Oversized or heavy cargo that "just fits" on paper but repeatedly runs into loading, clearance, or permit problems.
- Routes that require multiple transshipments through already congested hubs.
- Inland delivery points accessible only via weak infrastructure, such as narrow mountain roads or seasonal rivers, with no backup plan.

- A bill of lading that uses vague port descriptions without clarity on which terminal and inland connections are actually in play.

Practical shortcuts

- For any new lane or major project cargo, hold a simple "hardware check" meeting: confirm container type, ship type, port choice, and inland mode explicitly.
- Ask your forwarder which ports and terminals they prefer for certain cargoes and why; use their answers to refine your own port and route shortlists.
- When routing critical shipments, favor combinations that reduce the number of handoffs and transshipments, even if pure ocean rates are slightly higher.
- On special cargo, involve forwarders, carriers, and port partners early enough to secure the right equipment, permits, and time windows instead of relying on leftover capacity.

If You Only Remember Three Things

1. Containers, ships, ports, and inland infrastructure form one physical system, and each piece has hard limits that you must respect in any plan.
2. Different cargoes need different hardware; a one size fits all attitude toward ports, vessels, and containers is a reliable way to create risk.
3. Forwarders who understand hardware can often see disruptions and alternatives earlier, because they watch where metal, concrete, and water levels will allow boxes to move.

Chapter 5: Ports, Congestion, and the Hidden Gateways of Global Trade

5.1 The Day Your Order Got Stuck at Sea

The shoes first appeared on the app as a blue dot in the Pacific.

A reader in Chicago had ordered limited edition sneakers from a Korean brand. The brand promised delivery in 14 days. For the first week everything looked fine. The app showed updates as the parcel moved from factory to warehouse to export terminal. The status changed to "Loaded on vessel." The blue dot slid across the ocean.

Then the message changed.

"Arrived at port - delayed."

One day. Two days. Five days. The dot did not move. Social media filled with complaints about "ridiculous shipping costs" and "slow boats." People blamed the brand, blamed the carrier, blamed "the supply chain."

Out on the West Coast, the real story sat on the water.

Dozens of container ships waited in a line off the coast of California. Some had sailed from China, others from Vietnam, South Korea, and Japan. Each one carried thousands of containers. One of those boxes held the sneakers.

The engines worked. The ocean crossing had gone exactly as planned. What failed was the next part. The port did not have a free berth, enough cranes, enough yard space, or enough truckers to move boxes out. Until a slot opened on the dock, the ship carrying the sneakers was simply one more steel island, burning fuel and waiting.

That waiting changed everything.

The brand that had budgeted for a 14 day transit would now wait 24 days. Demurrage and storage charges at the congested port would eat into profit. The freight forwarder handling the shipment would spend the next month warning other customers, rerouting cargo, and quietly dropping that port from future routings where possible.

From the apartment in Chicago, all that was invisible. The app still said only "Arrived at port - delayed."

Inside the brand's logistics office in Seoul, it looked very different.

Dana, the logistics manager, had the forwarder's email open on one screen and a spreadsheet of upcoming launches on the other.

> "We are at day 6 beyond free time," the email read. "Terminal storage plus demurrage now total about 1,200 dollars per container and will keep climbing until we can get trucks in. Recommend we either divert later volumes through Oakland and Vancouver or pull back on West Coast promotions until the queue clears."

On a video call, the forwarder pulled up satellite images of ships anchored off the port and a table of gate appointment slots that were already full for the next several days. They explained that the vessel had arrived on time. The failure was not at sea. It was on the dock and in the yards.

Dana could see the costs in real time. Each extra day at the terminal added more storage fees and made detention charges on the empty containers more likely if trucks could not return them on schedule. Marketing wanted to keep pushing "14 day delivery" on the website. Finance wanted to know why freight and port bills were suddenly running thousands of dollars higher per shipment.

The brand and the forwarder made three decisions that afternoon.

- First, they stopped promising fixed delivery dates for new orders into the congested region, switching to a range and a clear explanation of port delays on the checkout page.
- Second, they rebalanced routes for the next wave of containers, sending some through smaller, less congested ports and accepting longer inland legs to reach the same distribution centers.
- Third, they asked the forwarder to negotiate slightly longer free time for demurrage and detention on future contracts, trading a modest increase in ocean rate for protection against runaway terminal charges.

For customers, the only visible change was that the delivery estimate on the app became "2 to 4 weeks" instead of "14 days." For the brand, the lesson was sharper: a port they had barely thought about when designing their launch calendar had just dictated their costs, timelines, and customer promises.

What sat between that vague tracking status and the real problem was the black box of the modern seaport.

Ports are rarely on tourist maps. They sit behind fences at the edge of cities, with their own roads, rules, and languages. Even in logistics, people talk casually about "shipping to Rotterdam" or "coming through LA" without really knowing what happens once a ship crosses the harbor wall.

This chapter opens the gates.

Ports are where a freight forwarder's plan either holds together or comes apart. They decide whether a "35 day transit time" is realistic or fantasy. Port fees, storage charges, demurrage and detention all start here. So do most of the delays that show up later as higher freight rates.

You will see three kinds of ports that work together like train stations on a long journey: big sea ports on the coast, inland ports far from the ocean, and river ports along interior waterways. Then we will walk a single container through a port, step by step, and see how congestion in one place can raise costs everywhere.

Once you understand ports, that "Arrived at port - delayed" message will never feel simple again.

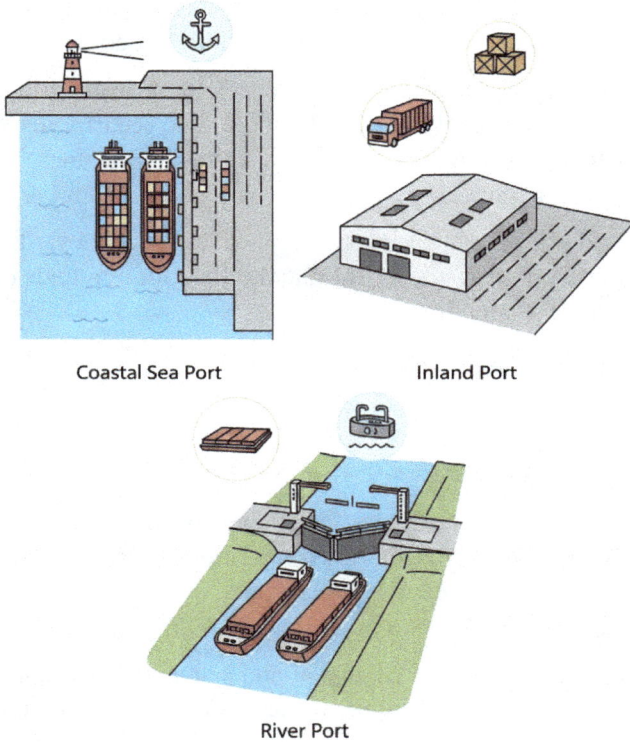

Figure 11: Three Types of Ports: Sea, Inland, River

5.2 Ports 101: What Is a Port, Really?

A port is not just a pier where a ship ties up.

In practical terms, a port is three things at once:

- It is where cargo moves between ship and land transport such as trucks, trains, or barges.
- It is a controlled border crossing for goods, with customs officers, security checks, and inspections.
- It is an industrial city dedicated to logistics, packed with cranes, terminals, warehouses, repair shops, fuel tanks, offices, and software systems.

Think of a port as three big systems working together.

First, picture a giant train station. The platforms are like berths for ships. Different platforms handle different kinds of "trains": container ships, oil tankers, bulk carriers full of coal or wheat, and car carriers loaded with vehicles.

Next, add something like an airport border checkpoint. Instead of passports and visas, you have customs declarations, HS codes, and security inspections. You will not see people queuing with suitcases. Instead, containers wait for x ray scans and document checks.

Around that, add a huge logistics park. Warehouses, trucking yards, refrigerated storage, maintenance garages, rail links, and offices for hundreds of companies. All of this together is a modern port.

In the freight forwarding journey from earlier chapters, the steps looked roughly like this:

Export haul → export customs → origin handling → main transport → destination handling → import customs → import haul

Ports sit in the middle of that chain. Origin port handling and destination port handling are where documents turn into crane moves, inspections, and invoices. Many of the extra costs inside a shipment, such as storage fees, demurrage, or "terminal handling charges," start here.

Not every port looks the same. Shanghai and a small river terminal in Illinois both count as ports, but the equipment they use and the role they play in the network are very different.

5.3 Types of Shipping Ports: Sea Ports, Inland Ports, River Ports

5.3.1 Sea Ports: The Ocean Gateways

Sea ports sit on coasts and handle ocean going vessels. They are the classic image: container cranes against the skyline, tank farms, bulk terminals, and long lines of ships offshore in busy times.

Major examples include:

- Shanghai and Ningbo in China, each handling on the order of 30 to 45 million TEU a year on recent figures, making them among the busiest container ports in the world.
- Rotterdam and Antwerp in Europe, with throughputs in the low to mid tens of millions of TEU and large volumes of bulk and tanker cargo on top.

- Los Angeles, Long Beach, and New York - New Jersey in North America, where each complex typically handles several million TEU per year and together they anchor transpacific and transatlantic flows.

Sea ports can specialize:

- Container terminals for standardized box cargo.
- Bulk terminals for grain, coal, ore.
- Tanker terminals for oil, gas, chemicals.
- Ro Ro and vehicle terminals for cars and equipment.

For the cargo owner, the sea port is often just a name in the routing. For forwarders, it is a bundle of very specific constraints: draft limits, berth availability, crane productivity, gate congestion, and customs processes.

5.3.2 Inland Ports: Dry Ports and Logistics Hubs Away from the Coast

Inland ports, sometimes called dry ports, take some seaport functions and move them inland along rail or barge corridors.

They typically offer:

- Rail terminals where containers arrive from sea ports on intermodal trains.
- Customs clearance and inspection facilities.
- Storage yards for containers and trailers.
- Warehousing and distribution centers.

Examples include:

- Inland hubs around Chicago that receive containers from West Coast ports.
- Duisburg in Germany, which acts as a major inland node for North European sea ports.
- Dry ports in landlocked countries that serve as gateways to neighboring sea ports.

Inland ports reduce pressure on congested sea terminals and bring port functions closer to factories and consumers. For forwarders, they create new routing options and chances to clear customs away from coastal bottlenecks.

5.3.3 River Ports: The Waterway Connectors

River ports sit along navigable waterways such as the Mississippi, the Rhine, the Danube, or the Yangtze.

They handle:

- Barges carrying bulk commodities like grain, coal, or aggregates.
- Barges or small container vessels feeding cargo to and from sea ports.
- Local and regional distribution along the river system.

In many regions, river ports are the cheapest way to move heavy goods over long distances. Their limits are tied to water levels, lock capacity, and seasonal conditions.

5.3.4 How Sea Ports, Inland Ports, and River Ports Work Together

Think of these three port types as stations on different parts of the same network.

- Sea ports connect oceans to major land corridors.
- Inland ports extend those corridors deep into countries and continents.
- River ports tie river basins to sea ports and inland hubs.

A container of machinery might move by truck from a factory to an inland port, then by train to a sea port, by ship to another continent, and finally by barge up a river to a regional river port. At each transfer point, local port logistics decide whether that path is smooth or painful.

Understanding the roles of sea, inland, and river ports makes it easier to see why one "port problem" in the news can hit businesses far from the coast.

5.4 Port Logistics: How Port Logistics Works Day to Day

Port logistics is about what happens inside the fences: how ships, trucks, trains, cranes, yards, warehouses, and software work together to move cargo on and off the water.

5.4.1 What Is "Port Logistics"?

Port logistics covers:

- Berth scheduling and ship arrivals.
- Loading and unloading containers, bulk, or liquid cargo.
- Yard storage and equipment moves.
- Customs inspections and security checks.
- Gate operations for trucks and intermodal transfers for rail and barge.

In a well run port, these pieces line up so that ships spend as little time alongside as possible and containers or bulk cargo do not sit around longer than necessary.

In a stressed port, small problems compound:

- A crane breakdown slows a ship.
- That delay pushes another ship into an anchor queue.

- Full yards force more container reshuffles.
- Truck turn times increase, so fewer containers leave each day.

What the public sees as "port congestion" is often the result of many small slowdowns inside the port logistics system.

5.4.2 Key Players in Port Logistics

Several players share responsibility for port logistics:

- **Port authority:** Manages the harbor, berths, and long term development. Sets rules and collects certain fees.
- **Terminal operators:** Run specific terminals inside the port, such as a container terminal or a bulk grain terminal. They control cranes, yards, gates, and much of the day to day operation.
- **Shipping lines:** Own or operate vessels. They book berth windows, coordinate arrival times, and provide stowage plans.
- **Customs and other government agencies:** Oversee border control, safety, and compliance with trade and health rules.
- **Trucking and rail companies:** Move cargo in and out of the port.
- **Freight forwarders and logistics service providers:** Coordinate shipments that pass through the port and connect all these players on behalf of shippers and consignees.

No single actor "controls" everything. Port performance depends on collaboration and information sharing among all these parties.

5.4.3 A Container's Journey Through a Port

To make port logistics concrete, follow one of the containers holding our Chicago sneakers into and out of a sea port.

Arrival at the terminal gate A container ship approaches the harbor, guided by pilots and tugs. Once the port authority assigns a berth, the ship is tied up at the quay. The terminal receives the ship's manifest and discharge plan.

Discharge from the ship Ship to shore cranes lift containers from the vessel, one by one, according to the stowage plan. Each move is logged in the terminal operating system, which tracks where each box is headed: yard stack, direct truck transfer, or rail.

Yard storage Most containers spend some time in the yard. Yard cranes stack them in blocks, organized roughly by destination, carrier, or mode. The terminal balances several goals at once: use space efficiently, keep stacks accessible, and respect customs holds and hazardous cargo rules.

Customs and inspections If customs selects a container for inspection, it is moved to a designated inspection area. It may pass through x ray scanners or be opened and unpacked. This can add hours or days, depending on staffing and how many containers are under review.

Gate out by truck or rail When a container is cleared and the consignee or forwarder has arranged pickup, the terminal schedules a truck appointment or a rail slot. The container is retrieved from the stack, loaded onto a chassis or rail wagon, and leaves the facility.

Each of these steps has its own time, cost, and potential failure points. When many containers move smoothly, the port feels invisible. When too many get stuck at any one step, congestion becomes visible on tracking screens and in headlines.

5.4.4 Where Delays and Extra Costs Appear

Ports are complex systems, and many things can go wrong. Here are some common issues that cause delays and extra costs:

Documentation errors If the shipping documents, such as the bill of lading or commercial invoice, have mistakes, customs clearance can be delayed. Correcting documents or providing missing information takes time.

Customs holds Containers may be selected for inspection by customs or other authorities. This can happen randomly or because of specific risk factors. Inspections take time, and any issues found can lead to additional charges.

Congestion Just like traffic jams on roads, ports can experience congestion. If too many ships arrive at once or if there are not enough cranes or workers, delays occur. Containers can get stuck in the yard, and truck or rail pickups may be delayed.

Equipment availability Delays can happen if the necessary equipment, like cranes or trucks, is not available when needed. This can be due to mechanical issues, scheduling conflicts, or unexpected demand.

Weather conditions Bad weather can delay ship arrivals or departures, crane operations, and transportation to and from the port.

Labor issues Strikes, labor shortages, or other workforce related issues can slow down operations at the port.

Security checks Enhanced security measures or random checks can add time to the cargo handling process.

Storage and demurrage fees If a container stays in the port or terminal yard longer than the allowed free time, storage fees apply. Demurrage fees are charged by the shipping line if a container is not picked up in time. In calmer periods at major container ports, free time may be as short as 3 to 5 days, with combined demurrage and detention charges commonly starting around 75 to 150 United States dollars per container per day and rising on a stepped scale after the first week.[4] In severe congestion, some ports and lines have applied higher levels and shorter free time, which is why understanding these terms in advance matters so much.

Modern ports also depend on digital systems as much as on cranes.

A terminal operating system tracks every container move inside the facility. It knows which slot each box occupies, which crane will handle it, and in what sequence. It connects to the shipping lines' stowage systems and to customs databases, so the yard plan respects legal holds and hazardous cargo rules.

Port community systems go a step further. They connect the wider port ecosystem: port authority, terminals, customs, shipping lines, trucking firms, rail operators, and freight forwarders. One shared platform allows these parties to exchange arrival notices, clearance messages, appointment bookings, and status updates without mountains of paper or endless email threads.

Tracking tools then expose useful slices of this information to shippers. Ships broadcast their positions through AIS, the Automatic Identification System. Trucks carry GPS units. Terminals send electronic data messages when a container is discharged, cleared, or gate out. A modern forwarder combines these feeds so clients can see where their cargo is and what is holding it up.

You can think of the port's IT layer as a giant multiplayer game server. Each participant logs in as a different "player," but they all share one underlying world. Container 123456 is either under hold or it is not. It is in stack B3, row 7, tier 4, or it has left the terminal. The shared system keeps everyone on the same version of reality.

Without that shared reality, coordinating thousands of boxes a day would be impossible.

---

[4]

These ranges are based on typical tariff sheets published by major container lines and terminals in North America and Europe in the early 2020s; actual free time and fee levels vary by carrier, port, and contract.

5.5 How Forwarders and Shippers Can Work with Ports More Smartly

5.5.1 Choosing Ports and Terminals Wisely

Not all ports and terminals are the same. Some are known for efficiency, while others have regular congestion issues. When planning shipments, it helps to ask:

- Which sea ports and inland ports will you use for this route, and why these ones?
- Are there regular congestion issues at those ports or on the connecting rail and barge routes?
- How much free time is included for demurrage and detention on containers?
- Is there an inland port or depot option that could reduce storage costs or provide more predictable pickup?

Port and terminal selection is not only about geography. It is about reliability, hinterland connections, and the true cost of using that gateway.

5.5.2 Planning for Congestion and Disruption

Congestion and delays are sometimes unavoidable. Good planning can reduce their impact:

- **Build buffer time.** Do not treat a carrier's quoted "transit time" as the full door to door lead time. That number often covers only port to port on the water. Add days at origin and destination for handling, customs, and potential delays. Add extra for known bottlenecks and peak seasons.
- **Use alternate ports and routings.** Forwarders may suggest using a slightly less convenient but more reliable port, especially during peak seasons.
- **Stage inventory.** For critical products, holding stock closer to customers can reduce dependence on a single congested port.

Here is where forwarders earn their reputation. During the congestion waves of 2020 and 2021, some small importers in Europe survived only because their forwarders shifted part of their volumes through smaller North European sea ports combined with inland ports, rather than leaving everything in the queue at one big gateway. Delivery took a few days longer than in normal times, but goods kept flowing while competitors faced empty shelves.

Ports are also governed by Incoterms and contracts. Choosing who is responsible for which port and which charges matters. A small importer might choose terms where the seller remains responsible for origin port risks, while the buyer handles destination port issues, or vice versa. Changing where cost and risk transfer can place port congestion in the hands of the party best equipped to manage it.

The most valuable action, however, is often simple communication. Good forwarders monitor port conditions and warn clients ahead of known congestion periods, such as pre Christmas peaks or planned dockworker strikes. They urge shippers to move cargo earlier, build more safety stock, and accept slightly longer but more reliable routes.

5.6 Congestion, Capacity, and the Ripple Effect on Ocean Freight

5.6.1 What Is Port Congestion?

Port congestion happens when more ships and containers want to use a port's facilities than the port can handle in its normal time.

The symptoms are visible from many angles. Ships wait at anchor outside the harbor. Stacks of containers pile high in the yard. Truck lines trail onto public roads. Local news carries drone images of dozens of vessels off Los Angeles and Long Beach, like a parking lot on the ocean.

Congestion has many causes. Demand spikes, such as peak retail seasons, send more cargo than usual to the same gateways. Limited numbers of berths or cranes slow down operations. Labor shortages, strikes, or health restrictions reduce working hours. Customs slowdowns, scanner failures, or a lack of trucks and chassis can all add friction.

A simple way to picture it is a highway toll plaza with not enough booths. Even if the road beyond is wide open, cars pile up in front of the toll gates. The sea beyond the port might be empty, but if the berths and cranes are overloaded, ships still have to wait.

5.6.2 How Capacity Limits Slow Port Logistics

Port capacity comes from several elements working together.

Berth capacity limits how many ships can load or discharge at one time. If all berths are occupied, arriving ships have no option but to anchor and wait.

Crane capacity limits how fast containers can move on and off each ship. A typical large ship to shore crane might handle 25 to 35 container moves per hour in good conditions. Breakdowns, high winds, or yard congestion can drop that rate.

Yard capacity caps how many containers the terminal can store and still operate efficiently. Once stacks are too high and space is tight, simple tasks take longer. Cranes must reshuffle more boxes to reach the one they need. That extra handling reduces the number of moves per hour.

Labor and equipment shortages compound these limits. Too few crane operators, not enough internal trucks, or a shortage of chassis for outbound trucks can bring operations down a notch. When rail schedules cannot absorb the volume pouring off ships, containers hang around longer, filling precious yard slots.

During peak seasons this becomes painfully visible. Before major holidays, retailers around the world race to stock shelves. Ports like LA and Long Beach, already busy, might see containers arriving 20 percent faster than the normal rate. Yards overflow. Truck turn times climb from one hour to five. Some carriers choose to skip a congested port entirely and unload at an alternate port rather than risk days of delay.

Capacity is not just about physical space. It is about how many coordinated moves the system can complete in a given time. Once that limit is reached, every extra box makes things worse.

5.6.3 Ripple Effects Through Inland Ports, River Ports, and Supply Chains

Delays at a sea port do not stay at the coast.

If import containers cannot leave the terminal in time, trains and barges that connect to inland and river ports run late or half empty. Inland ports receive cargo later than planned, which disrupts their own schedules for unloading, customs, and distribution.

Exporters feel the pinch in the other direction. Empty containers may be plentiful inside the sea port yet scarce 500 kilometers inland, because repositioning moves are late or canceled. Factories wait for boxes. They fill storage yards with finished goods while they watch their vessel cut off dates slip.

A congestion wave at the Port of Los Angeles has hit the United States interior more than once. When ships back up offshore, fewer trains depart on time for Chicago and other Midwestern hubs. Importers there wait extra days or weeks for parts and products. Assembly lines slow or stop. Some firms switch to expensive air freight for critical components just to keep production going.

Globally, delays change the rhythm of ship rotations. A vessel that spends four extra days waiting in one port reaches the next port four days late. That port may then face a clump of arrivals in a short window, which causes its own backlog. Containers end up piled in regions that do not need them, while exporters somewhere else search desperately for available boxes.

The network behaves a bit like a power grid with a damaged hub. One overloaded node sends instability across the system.

Case Study: Yantian 2021 - When One Terminal Coughs, Supply Chains Catch a Cold In late May 2021, a COVID 19 outbreak among workers at Yantian International Container Terminal in Shenzhen led authorities to impose strict health controls and temporarily halt most export container intake. At one point, the main terminal was operating at only about 30 percent of normal capacity, more than 40 ships were waiting at anchor, and an estimated 23,000 plus containers were backlogged on the ground (Source: Reuters, 3 June 2021). Carriers began skipping Yantian or diverting ships to alternate South China ports. For forwarders and shippers, that meant missed cut off times, last minute trucking scrambles, and increased risk of containers being "rolled" to later sailings. Downstream importers in Europe and North America saw delayed stock and paid higher spot rates as capacity tightened. The lesson was simple: a disruption at a single terminal, in a single city, can send shock waves through inventories, freight rates, and delivery promises on the other side of the world.

Case Study: New York–New Jersey 2021 - When the Backup Moves East During 2021, as shippers tried to avoid long queues off California, more Asia to United States cargo flowed to East Coast gateways. The Port of New York and New Jersey handled record container volumes that year, with double digit growth compared with pre pandemic levels and several months above 800,000 TEU of throughput.[5] At times, ships waited at anchor in the approaches to the harbor, yard densities ran high, and rail and truck dwell times increased. Importers who had shifted routings to "escape" West Coast congestion discovered that no port is immune when volumes surge and inland capacity is constrained. Some faced the same demurrage, storage, and appointment problems they had hoped to

---

[5] Approximate throughput ranges and growth rates are based on Port of New York and New Jersey 2021 statistics and trade press coverage of East Coast congestion.

leave behind, just on a different coast. The practical lesson was that diversions can buy time, but only if inland gateways and networks have room to absorb the extra volume. Forwarders and shippers that treated East Coast ports as part of an integrated network, not a magic escape hatch, coped better than those who simply redirected boxes and hoped for the best.

5.6.4 Impact on Ocean Freight Rates and Total Shipping Costs

Port congestion does not only cause delays. It also changes prices.

When ships spend more time waiting and fewer complete round trips in a given period, effective capacity shrinks. If demand stays high, carriers can charge more per container. Spot rates climb. Contract rates follow at the next negotiation cycle.

Other cost elements also rise:

- Terminals may introduce congestion surcharges.
- Truckers charge more to cover long waiting times at gates.
- Storage, demurrage, and detention fees climb as containers sit longer in yards or on chassis.

For shippers, the headline "freight rate" can double or triple in a year of severe congestion. The true cost impact is often even larger once all surcharges and delay driven charges are added.

5.6.5 How Freight Forwarders Respond to Port Congestion

Freight forwarders have limited control over port capacity, but they can change how their customers are exposed to it.

Common responses include:

- Rerouting some volumes through alternate ports or inland ports.
- Encouraging earlier shipping before known peak periods.
- Recommending different Incoterms so that the party with better logistics capabilities controls critical ports.
- Breaking up shipments to split risk: not everything on one sailing, at one port, at one time.

In practice, a forwarder might move some of a retailer's containers from a very congested West Coast port to a smaller Gulf or East Coast port, then use rail to reach the same inland markets. Transit times change, but the risk of indefinite delay at one clogged gateway is reduced.

5.7 Practical Tips for Shippers and Beginners: Making Ports Work for You

Ports can feel distant if you run a small business or are new to logistics, but decisions about ports shape your costs and lead times more than you might expect.

Useful questions to ask your freight forwarder include:

- Which sea ports and inland ports do you plan to use for this route, and why these ones?
- What congestion or capacity issues have you seen recently at those ports?
- How much free time is included for demurrage and detention?
- Is there an inland port or depot option that could reduce storage costs or provide more predictable pickup?
- How much buffer time should we plan around the port in our lead times?

Documentation is your best defense against port surprises. Accurate commercial invoices, packing lists, HS codes, and any required certificates reduce the chance of customs holds. Knowing your Incoterms and who is responsible for which charges at which port avoids painful disputes later.

A small importer of specialty foods offers a simple example. In its first year, the firm paid almost as much in demurrage and storage as in base ocean freight. Containers of olive oil and canned goods sat at a Mediterranean sea port while customs argued over labeling rules. After a harsh lesson, the company started working with a forwarder who pre checked every document with a customs broker, then routed containers through a nearby inland port where inspections were easier to schedule and storage was cheaper. Within a year, unpredictable port costs had almost disappeared, even though the ocean rate itself had not changed much.

5.7.1 Case Study: Peak Season Warehouse Meltdown

Ports are not the only places where congestion hurts. Distribution centers can melt down too.

During one November peak season, a large ecommerce brand in Europe ran a single mega warehouse outside Berlin. The site handled both imports from Asia and domestic returns. All inventory for Germany and neighboring countries flowed through this building.

Marketing had promised "two day delivery for almost everything" in the run up to Black Friday. Orders poured in faster than any previous year. At the same time:

- Several containers arrived late from a congested port, but the goods were still promised for sale.
- A new warehouse management system had recently gone live and staff were still learning its quirks.
- A seasonal labor shortage meant fewer trained pickers per shift than planned.

Inside the DC, pallets of inbound stock piled up along aisles. Some never made it to proper racks or bin locations in the system. Pickers could see boxes of hot selling items sitting on the floor, but the system showed them as "not yet received" and refused to release them to orders.

Outbound, carriers began missing their collection windows because trailers could not be loaded on time. Parcels that did leave the building did so hours behind schedule. Customer service dashboards lit up with "where is my order?" messages.

From the outside, it looked like a simple delivery delay. From the inside, it was a warehouse traffic jam: too many inbound containers, not enough clear processes for triage, and a system that insisted on full receiving before it would let stock be picked.

The operations team and their forwarder jointly implemented a rescue plan.

- They created a temporary "fast lane" for the top 50 products driving most of the sales. Containers with those SKUs were prioritized at the port and trucked directly to a separate cross dock area at the DC.
- Instead of a full system receiving process, they used a simplified scan in procedure for those fast lane items, accepting a small increase in inventory reconciliation work later in exchange for bare shelves today.
- Non urgent containers, such as slow moving items and some returns, were diverted to a satellite warehouse 50 kilometers away to free floor space.
- Together with parcel carriers, they added extra late evening pickup slots for a limited period so that orders picked after normal cutoff could still move.

The fix did not make the peak season smooth. Staff still worked long hours and some orders arrived late. But the fast lane kept the core of the promotion alive and prevented a backlog that might otherwise have taken weeks to clear.

In the following year, the company invested in:

- Better peak season forecasting and earlier port bookings.
- A second, smaller DC to split the load.

- Clear playbooks for triaging inbound containers and creating temporary cross docks when volumes spike.

The lesson is similar to port congestion. When volume surges hit a warehouse that is already running near its limits, you either create controlled overflow paths or you get chaos in the aisles. Forwarders and warehouse operators who plan those paths together cope far better with peak season demand.

5.8 Chapter Wrap Up: Seeing the Hidden Port Network

Those sneakers stuck offshore did not suffer from a slow ocean crossing. They were trapped by a congested port.

Behind that vague tracking message stood a network of sea ports, inland ports, and river ports, each with its own cranes, rules, software, and constraints. A delay at one big sea gateway sent ripples through rail yards in the interior, truck schedules on nearby highways, and the balance of containers halfway across the world.

Ports are more than parking spots for ships. They are working border zones and industrial logistics hubs where sea routes plug into inland roads, railways, and rivers. In this chapter you have seen them in three main roles:

- Sea ports, the coastal gateways for ocean going vessels.
- Inland ports, or dry ports, which pull port functions into the interior along rail and road corridors.
- River ports, which anchor the "liquid highways" of inland waterways.

Inside these ports, port logistics directs the flow: berths, cranes, yards, warehouses, customs zones, gates, and the software that ties it all together. Efficiency or congestion at this level shapes everything else: reliable arrival times, freight rates, and all the "mystery charges" that can appear on your invoice.

Freight forwarders live in this world every day. They choose routes through the port network, anticipate bottlenecks, adjust Incoterms and buffer times, and reroute shipments when congestion spikes. They cannot control the weather or the global economy, but they can help clients avoid the worst queues and the sharpest costs.

With this chapter, ports and port logistics should feel less like a black box. You have seen the structure of the network and traced a container's path inside it. The next step is to look more closely at how different transport modes, from ocean to rail to truck, connect through these ports and create complete, end to end freight solutions.

Once you see ports clearly, the rest of the journey from factory to final customer starts to make a lot more sense.

Field Guide: Ports, Congestion, and Hidden Gateways

Key concepts

- Sea ports, inland ports, and river ports are interconnected gateways that move containers between ocean and inland networks.
- Terminals have physical and operational limits on berths, cranes, yard space, and gate throughput; when one limit is reached, congestion spreads.
- Port congestion creates both time delays and extra charges, including surcharges, storage, demurrage, and detention.
- Inland links (rail, road, barge) determine whether a port is truly efficient for your specific origins and destinations.
- Forwarders and shippers can reduce exposure by choosing ports, routes, and Incoterms with port risk in mind.

Common mistakes

- Selecting ports purely on ocean rate tables without considering inland costs, congestion history, or hinterland connectivity.
- Assuming that "port to port" transit times in carrier schedules equal real door to door times.
- Ignoring free time limits and failing to plan for quick pickup and return of containers.
- Treating all terminals inside a port as identical, even when they differ in performance and inland connections.
- Failing to coordinate warehouse and carrier readiness for peak season arrivals, leading to yard pileups.

Warning signs

- Carrier advisories about congestion, restricted gate hours, or reduced free time at ports you rely on.
- Rising demurrage and detention costs on your invoices, especially during predictable peak seasons.
- Increasing truck turn times at specific terminals, or regular complaints from drayage carriers about access.
- Containers repeatedly missing planned vessels or rail connections due to terminal backlogs.
- Warehouses that receive more containers than they can process during key weeks, spilling stock into aisles.

Practical shortcuts

- Ask your forwarder for a simple "port profile" on the gateways you use: congestion trends, typical free time, preferred terminals, and inland options.
- For important lanes, simulate "what if the main port is blocked?" and identify realistic alternates, including smaller ports combined with inland rail.
- Track demurrage and detention separately from base freight in your reports; spikes there are early indicators that port or inland processes need attention.
- Before peak seasons, align port bookings, DC staffing plans, and carrier pickup capacity so that inbound containers move quickly off the terminal and into controlled storage.

If You Only Remember Three Things

1. Ports are not just dots on a map; they are complex, capacity limited systems whose performance shapes your real transit times and hidden charges.
2. Demurrage, detention, storage, and inland delays usually reflect process and planning gaps, not bad luck, and they can be reduced with better coordination.
3. Choosing and managing ports is a strategic decision; the right combination of sea gateway and inland links often matters more than a slightly lower ocean rate.

Chapter 6: What Shipping Really Costs

6.1 The USD 4,000 Surprise on a "Cheap" Shipment

Alex still remembers the email subject line.

"Great news! Ocean freight only USD 1,800."

If you remember Alex from Chapter 1, he started as a curious online shopper clicking "buy" on a single mug. Now he is on the other side of the equation, running a growing home décor brand and importing full containers himself. That shift turns abstract shipping costs into very real line items.

He had just placed his first big order of handmade acacia wood furniture from a small factory outside Ho Chi Minh City. Coffee tables, bookshelves, a few dining sets. Enough to fill a 20 foot container. For his brand in Austin, this was a serious leap.

The quote looked comforting.

Ocean freight: 1 x 20 foot container HCMC to Houston: USD 1,800.

A few other lines followed: documentation fee, origin handling, "local charges destination TBD."

He glanced at them, but his eyes went straight back to the bold number.

"Okay," he thought, "same idea as a plane ticket. The price to get from A to B. That must be everything."

Eight weeks later the ship arrived. That is when the invoices started to land.

First came Terminal Handling Charges (THC) at Houston: USD 310.

Then a documentation and delivery order fee from the shipping line: USD 85.

His customs broker charged USD 175 for the import declaration, plus USD 65 in government filing fees.

Unfortunately, customs did not go smoothly. The shipment was selected for an x ray exam, which meant extra handling at the terminal and a fee of USD 250 for the exam itself.

By the time the container was finally cleared, the free storage period at the port had ended. Three extra days of storage: USD 210.

The trucker he hired to deliver the container to his small warehouse ran into trouble. The warehouse did not have a dock and was not ready for a live unload. The driver waited two extra hours, billed him waiting time, then took the half empty container back to the yard. That meant an extra trip to return it to the port and two days of container detention fees from the shipping line.

By the time he added it all up, Alex had paid just over USD 5,000 in total logistics costs.

The original "ocean freight" was still USD 1,800. That part had been real.

Shipping costs are like an iceberg in cold water. The part you see is the line everyone stares at: "ocean freight." The heavy part below the surface is every-thing else: surcharges, handling at both ends, documentation, customs, storage, and time based penalties when something, anything, goes a little bit wrong.

This chapter is about that hidden part.

You will see the main pieces of the iceberg. You will learn how freight rates are built, how to stack rough estimates yourself, and how to read a freight quote so you do not repeat Alex's mistake.

Before you can avoid surprises like his, you need to understand what you are actually paying for when you move goods around the world.

A low ocean freight number does not mean a low total shipping cost. The total sits in the invisible layers around it.

Ocean Freight

1,800

● **Surcharges**   ●1,200
● **Handling**
● **Documentation**   ●1,800
● **Customs**   ●3,45
● **Storage**   ●3,200
● **Penalies**

1,200

3,200

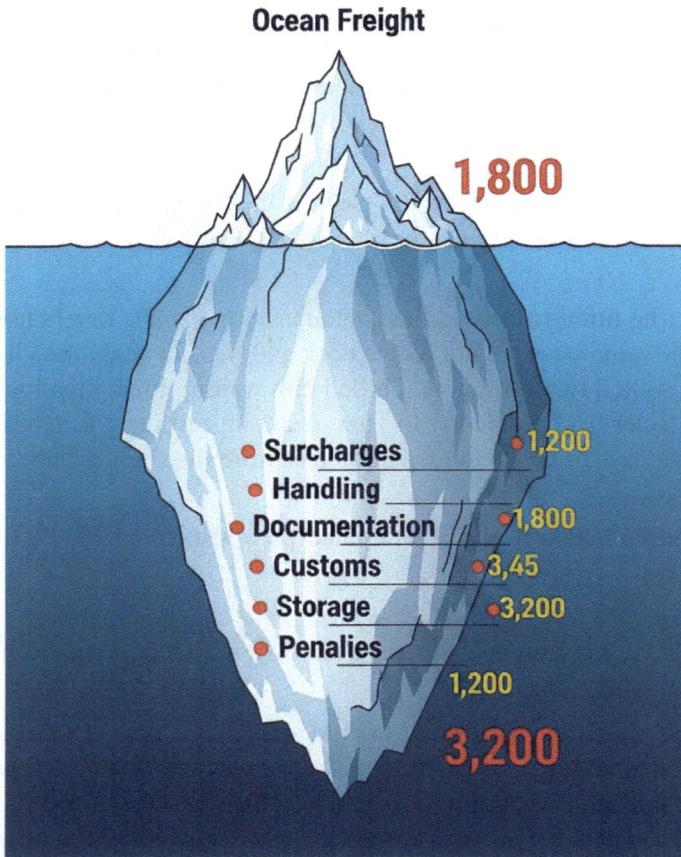

Figure 12: Shipping Cost Iceberg

6.2 Why Shipping Prices Feel Like a Mystery (and Should Not)

Put two cardboard boxes side by side on a floor.

Same size. Same weight. One goes from Shanghai to Los Angeles by sea. The other goes by express air courier. The ocean move might cost a few hundred dollars. The air courier might run USD 2,000 or more.

In another case, sending a small parcel to a nearby town by express can cost more per kilogram than sending a whole pallet by sea halfway around the world.

If shipping prices feel random, you are not alone. Most people only ever see one number on a website or in an email. They never see all the pieces that number covers, and the pieces it quietly leaves out.

A simple way to think about it for a twelve year old is to compare shipping to a trip.

You have a basic bus ticket from one city to another. That is the base transport price.

Then add luggage fees if your bags are big or heavy.

Then add airport or station taxes and fuel surcharges, costs you cannot escape because the operator must pay them.

Finally you pay for taxis to and from the station, because you still have to get from your house to the bus and then from the bus stop to where you are really going.

If you only look at the bus ticket price when planning the trip, you will be badly wrong about what the trip will cost.

Shipping is the same. There is not one "shipping cost." There is a stack of costs:

- Transport by sea, air, road, or rail.
- Handling at each end.
- Paperwork and compliance.
- Insurance.
- Government duties and taxes.
- Sometimes, penalties or extras.

Prices rise and fall based on demand, capacity, fuel, and risk, but the structure of the cost stack is not mysterious. Once you see that structure, quotes stop feeling like magic and start looking like math.

6.3 The Building Blocks of Shipping Costs

From a freight forwarder's point of view, there are three big buckets of cost in any international shipment:

1. Transport itself.
2. Handling and services at origin and destination.
3. Risk and compliance costs.

Each bucket has several layers.

6.3.1 Transport: Ocean, Air, Road, Rail

Transport is the movement of goods:

- Ocean freight for containers or bulk.
- Air freight for urgent or high value cargo.
- Road transport for local and regional moves.
- Rail for long inland corridors.

Each mode follows its own logic:

- Ocean is cheap per unit, slow, and tied to port infrastructure.
- Air is fast and expensive, with strict limits on volume and weight.
- Road is flexible but sensitive to fuel, rules, and driver availability.
- Rail is efficient over distance where good networks exist.

The price you see as "freight" is usually the cost of one main leg, such as port to port at sea or airport to airport in the air. It is rarely the full journey.

6.3.2 Handling at Origin and Destination

Even a simple shipment has a surprising number of hands on it:

- Truckers and warehouse workers at origin.
- Terminal operators and port staff.
- Customs brokers and inspectors.
- Truckers, rail operators, and warehouse staff at destination.

Handling costs include:

- Terminal Handling Charges (THC) at ports and container depots.
- Warehouse loading and unloading fees.
- Container stuffing and stripping for LCL cargo.
- Local document handling by forwarders and agents.

These are often listed as "local charges" on quotes and invoices. They can easily equal or exceed the base ocean freight on short routes or for complicated shipments.

6.3.3 Paperwork, Compliance, Duties, and Taxes

Documentation and compliance costs may not move boxes physically, but they determine whether boxes are allowed to move.

Typical items include:

- Export documentation and filing fees.
- Bills of lading and airway bills.
- Certificates of origin and other trade documents.
- Customs broker fees at destination.
- Import duties and taxes based on HS codes and product values.

Ignoring these does not make them go away. It simply pushes them into the "surprise" column when customs sends a bill or a shipment is held at the border.

6.3.4 Risk Costs: Insurance, Delays, and Mistakes

Risk introduces two kinds of cost:

- The cost of protection, such as cargo insurance.
- The cost of problems, such as storage, demurrage, and detention when something goes wrong.

You do not need to insure every shipment, but you should at least understand what the carrier's standard liability covers. As Chapter 1 showed, carrier liability limits can be far below your cargo value.

Delay related costs are trickier. They do not appear on a quote. They show up as:

- Storage fees when goods linger at terminals.
- Demurrage and detention when containers are not picked up or returned on time.
- Expediting costs when you have to switch to faster modes to catch up on schedule.

All of these building blocks will appear in the stories and numbers that follow. The rest of the chapter is about turning this list into a usable mental calculator.

6.4 Weight, Volume, and the Strange World of Chargeable Weight

Before we talk about prices, we need to talk about how carriers measure what they are pricing.

If you ship heavy metal blocks, the limiting factor is weight. If you ship inflated beach balls, the limiting factor is volume. Pricing must reflect both.

Freight systems therefore use:

- **Actual weight**, the weight on a scale.
- **Volumetric weight**, a calculated weight based on how much space a shipment takes up.

For air freight, volumetric weight is often calculated using a factor such as 1 cubic meter equals 167 kilograms of chargeable weight. If your shipment is 1 cubic meter but weighs only 50 kilograms, the carrier will charge you for 167 kilograms, because the box takes up space that could have held something heavier.

For LCL ocean freight, a common rule of thumb is to charge by W/M, meaning per weight or measure, whichever is higher. One cubic meter is treated as if it weighs one metric ton. If a shipment weighs 2 tons but only occupies 1 cubic meter, the carrier charges for 2 tons. If it weighs 500 kilograms but occupies 3 cubic meters, they charge for 3 cubic meters.

The key idea is **chargeable weight**. This is the number that pricing applies to. For air, it is the higher of actual and volumetric weight. For LCL sea freight, it is the higher of weight or volume using the W/M rule. For FCL, the limiting factor is usually the physical limit of the container and road regulations, but over weight containers can attract extra charges or even be refused.

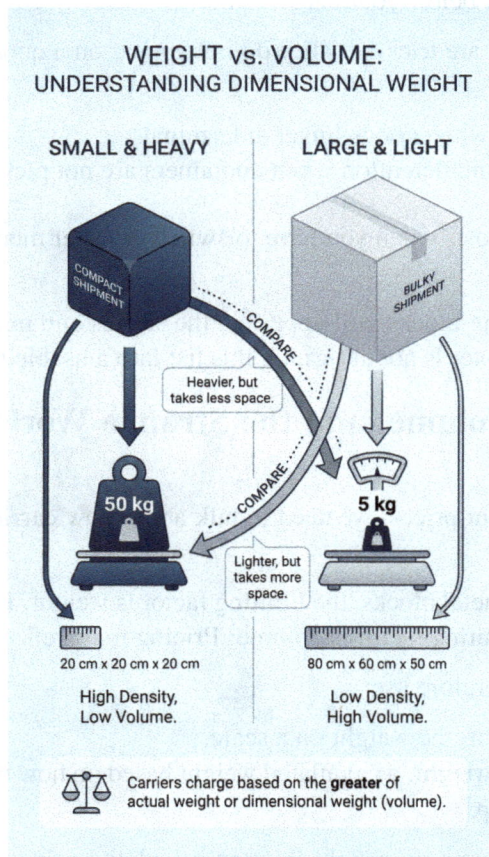

WEIGHT vs. VOLUME:
UNDERSTANDING DIMENSIONAL WEIGHT

SMALL & HEAVY   LARGE & LIGHT

COMPACT SHIPMENT

BULKY SHIPMENT

COMPARE

Heavier, but takes less space.

50 kg   5 kg

COMPARE

Lighter, but takes more space.

20 cm x 20 cm x 20 cm   80 cm x 60 cm x 50 cm

High Density,   Low Density,
Low Volume.   High Volume.

Carriers charge based on the **greater** of actual weight or dimensional weight (volume).

Figure 13: Weight vs Volume

As a shipper, you can use chargeable weight to design more efficient shipments:

- Combine small, light items into fewer larger boxes to reduce wasteful volumetric charges.
- Avoid packing extremely dense goods into one container that will exceed road weight limits.
- For air, adjust packaging where reasonable to reduce volume without risking damage.

Once you know your shipment's dimensions and weight, you can calculate a chargeable weight and start to estimate cost.

6.5 Ocean Freight Pricing: FCL, LCL, and Surcharges

Ocean freight is where many people first meet serious international shipping costs, so it is worth breaking down.

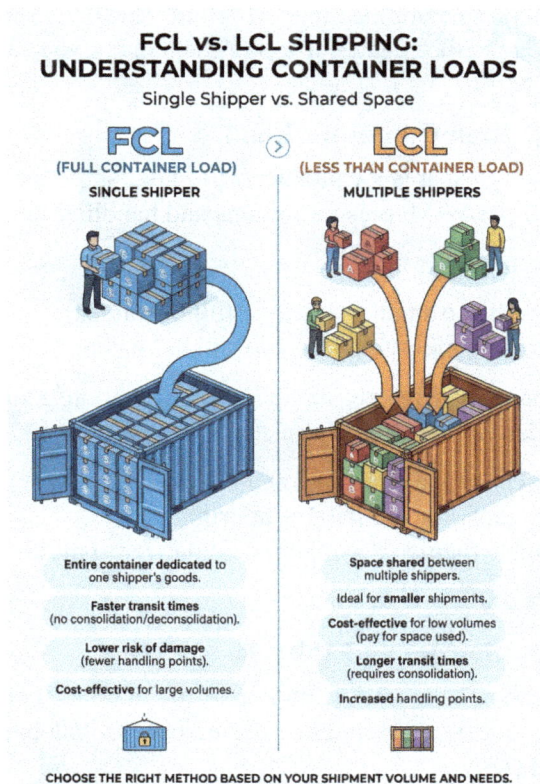

FCL vs. LCL SHIPPING:
UNDERSTANDING CONTAINER LOADS
Single Shipper vs. Shared Space

FCL — (FULL CONTAINER LOAD) — SINGLE SHIPPER

LCL — (LESS THAN CONTAINER LOAD) — MULTIPLE SHIPPERS

Entire container dedicated to one shipper's goods.

Faster transit times (no consolidation/deconsolidation).

Lower risk of damage (fewer handling points).

Cost-effective for large volumes.

Space shared between multiple shippers.

Ideal for **smaller** shipments.

Cost-effective for low volumes (pay for space used).

Longer transit times (requires consolidation).

Increased handling points.

CHOOSE THE RIGHT METHOD BASED ON YOUR SHIPMENT VOLUME AND NEEDS.

Figure 14: FCL vs LCL

6.5.1 FCL: Full Container Load

When you book a full container load (FCL), you are paying for the use of an entire container for a trip between two ports, regardless of how full you pack it.

The base price depends on:

- Trade lane (for example, Asia to North America West Coast).
- Container size (20 foot, 40 foot, 40 foot high cube).
- Carrier and transit time.
- Current market conditions and season.

On top of the base rate come surcharges:

- Bunker Adjustment Factor (BAF) for fuel.
- Peak Season Surcharge (PSS) in busy periods.
- Low sulphur or environmental surcharges on certain routes.
- Security surcharges and canal surcharges where relevant.

Most shippers see these combined into an "all in" rate or as separate lines on a rate sheet. The total is the ocean portion of the iceberg you saw at the start of the chapter.

6.5.2 LCL: Less than Container Load

With LCL, your cargo shares a container with other shippers' cargo. You pay per cubic meter or per W/M, plus minimums and handling fees.

LCL is useful when:

- Your volume is too small to justify a full container.
- You want to ship more frequently in smaller batches.

It tends to be more expensive per cubic meter than filling a full container, because the forwarder or consolidator must:

- Receive and handle many small shipments.
- Consolidate them into containers at origin.
- De-consolidate them at destination and deliver to multiple consignees.

The trade off is flexibility versus unit cost.

6.5.3 Typical Surcharges and Why They Exist

People often talk about "the rate" from Port A to Port B as though it is a single number. In reality, most ocean freight rates are built from a base rate plus a set of surcharges and fees.

The base ocean freight rate is the simple price to move a container from one port to another. For an FCL shipment, that might be USD 2,200 for a 40 foot high cube from Shanghai to Los Angeles, port to port. For LCL, the base could be a price per cubic meter.

On top of that, shipping lines and forwarders add surcharges.

- The Bunker Adjustment Factor (BAF) is a fuel surcharge. Ship fuel, called bunker fuel, is one of a carrier's largest expenses. When fuel prices climb sharply, the BAF rises. When they fall, the BAF can drop. It works much like a taxi fare that adds a fuel surcharge when gasoline costs spike.
- Terminal Handling Charges (THC) are fees that terminal operators charge for lifting containers on and off ships, moving them through the yard, and handling documentation. These exist at both origin and destination and are often paid through the forwarder or the shipping line.
- A Peak Season Surcharge (PSS) appears when demand for space climbs, often before major retail seasons such as the months before Christmas or Chinese New Year. Carriers raise rates when space is tight and they put that increase into a specific surcharge line.
- On certain routes, carriers also add low sulphur or environmental surcharges to recover the cost of using cleaner fuel in regulated emission control areas, and security surcharges to cover extra screening or compliance work.
- There can also be route specific extras, such as a Panama Canal surcharge when a vessel must pay higher tolls to transit the canal, or a war risk surcharge for voyages near conflict zones.

These items can be included in an "all in" rate or shown separately. The number you first hear, such as "USD 2,000 from Qingdao to Long Beach," might be just the base rate, or it might already include BAF and PSS. You should always ask: what exactly is included in this rate, and which surcharges are separate?

To see why these numbers swing over time, it helps to look at the bigger forces that drive them.

6.6 How Forwarders Build a Quote

You do not need a perfect forecast before you ask for quotes. You just need a reasonable ballpark so you can design your prices and margins and know whether a supplier in one country is truly cheaper than another once logistics are included.

Here is a practical method you can use for planning and sanity checks.

First, define the basics of your shipment. Note the origin city and country and the destination city and country. Decide which Incoterm you are working with, such as FOB Shanghai or CIF Hamburg, because that tells you which parts you will be paying. Choose your mode: sea FCL, sea LCL, or air. Measure or obtain the dimensions and weights of your cartons or pallets, then calculate total volume and, if using air or LCL, the chargeable weight.

Second, estimate the main transport cost. For FCL ocean containers on major Asia to North America or Asia to Europe routes in relatively calm markets, a 20 foot container might run anywhere from USD 1,500 to USD 3,000, and a 40 foot from USD 2,000 to USD 5,000.[6] This has swung wildly in recent years, but you can use recent invoices, public rate indices, or indicative quotes from digital platforms as reference.

For LCL ocean, you will see pricing per cubic meter or per W/M. On popular lanes like Shenzhen to Los Angeles, you might find USD 80 to USD 150 per cubic meter as a rough range, depending on market conditions and service quality.[7]

For air, rates often range from USD 3 to USD 8 per kilogram of chargeable weight on common routes, but they can go higher in peak seasons or on unusual corridors.

Third, add origin and destination handling. For an FCL shipment where you are responsible for both ends, a simple rule of thumb might be USD 300 to USD 600 at origin and USD 300 to USD 800 at destination for basic port handling and documentation. If your factory is far from the port, inland trucking can easily add hundreds more. For LCL, there are usually per shipment minimums and per cubic meter handling charges on each side.

Fourth, add documentation and customs fees. Expect to pay for a bill of lading or airway bill, export documentation, and customs broker services. Individual documents might be USD 50 to USD 150 each. Brokers on basic entries might charge USD 75 to USD 200 per shipment, plus small government filing fees.

Fifth, estimate duties and taxes. This part depends on your product and destination country. Use your HS code and look up the customs duty rate in that country's tariff schedule or with an online calculator. Multiply that percentage by the customs value of your goods, usually the invoice value plus some or all of the freight. Then add import VAT or sales tax if applicable.

---

[6]

These broad rate bands reflect pre-pandemic and mid-cycle conditions reported in industry benchmarks such as the Freightos Baltic Index and Drewry indices, averaged over several years.

[7]

Illustrative LCL price ranges draw on forwarder quotes and market commentary for common Asia–North America lanes in the late 2010s and early 2020s.

Sixth, add insurance if you want full protection. Cargo insurance often costs between 0.3 and 0.8 percent of the cargo value for standard coverage, sometimes with a minimum premium.

Finally, add a buffer for surprises. A contingency of 10 to 20 percent on the freight, handling, and documentation portion helps cover smaller unplanned items: minor storage, rate fluctuations between planning and shipment, small port fees, or modest inspection charges.

Here is a compact example.

You are importing USD 20,000 of home décor in one 20 foot container from Ningbo to Los Angeles on FOB NINGBO terms. You pay from the port of loading onward.

You look up recent rates and decide that USD 2,000 is a plausible ocean freight estimate. At destination, you expect USD 600 in terminal handling and local charges and USD 400 to truck the container from the port to your warehouse. Documentation, including the bill of lading and customs broker fee, might total USD 250.

Your product carries a 5 percent customs duty rate. On USD 20,000 of goods, that is USD 1,000 in duty. You buy cargo insurance at 0.5 percent of cargo value, so USD 100.

Add these:

- USD 2,000 ocean freight
- USD 600 destination handling
- USD 400 delivery trucking
- USD 250 documentation and broker
- USD 1,000 duty
- USD 100 insurance

Subtotal: USD 4,350.

Then add a 10 percent buffer on the freight, handling, trucking, and documentation portion. Ten percent of USD 3,250 is USD 325. That brings you to about USD 4,675 as a working estimate of total landed logistics cost, not counting any local sales tax.

When the real quotes come in, you can compare them to this mental picture. If one quote is wildly below your estimate, you will know to look closely at what is missing. If one is higher, you can see exactly which component seems out of line.

To sharpen that picture still further, it helps to look more closely at how ocean rates are influenced by capacity, demand, and external shocks. Chapter 12 will revisit those dynamics in detail.

6.7 Reading a Real Freight Quote Without Getting Burned

Quote formats vary, but most contain the same core ingredients. When you receive one, read it with three questions in mind:

1. What exactly is included in this price?
2. What is explicitly excluded?
3. Where could extra charges appear if things do not go perfectly?

Look for:

- The route and mode: origin and destination ports or airports, carrier, and estimated transit time.
- The container size or chargeable weight used for pricing.
- A breakdown of base rate and surcharges, or an "all in" rate with a note about which surcharges it includes.
- Local origin and destination charges, especially THC, documentation, and delivery.
- Payment terms, validity dates, and any conditions about volume or frequency.

If a quote looks dramatically cheaper than others, it is often because:

- Some surcharges are excluded and will be added later.
- Local charges at one or both ends are not included.
- The quote assumes a longer free time than you will actually receive.

Good forwarders are transparent about what is and is not included. You should be wary of any quote that cannot be explained line by line.

Appendix C shows simplified examples of commercial invoices, packing lists, bills of lading, and arrival notices. You can use those samples alongside this section to see where the charges and references discussed here typically appear in real paperwork.

6.8 Designing Shipments to Control Total Cost

Designing shipments is one of the few levers shippers control directly. Small changes can have large effects on cost and risk.

Options include:

- Choosing FCL instead of LCL when your volume justifies it, to reduce per unit cost.
- Shipping earlier and by ocean instead of paying for emergency air freight.
- Using inland ports or rail where possible instead of long all truck routes.
- Adjusting packaging to fit more product per cubic meter without damaging goods.

The right answer depends on your product, your customers, and your cash flow. Chapter 11 will return to this design mindset and show how to build simple end to end plans with cost in mind.

6.9 Quick Recap: From "Cheap Freight" to Total Landed Cost

By now you have seen why Alex's USD 1,800 ocean rate turned into a USD 5,000 logistics bill.

- Freight quotes usually show only a slice of the real cost.
- Ocean, air, road, and rail each have distinct price patterns.
- Handling, documentation, customs, and risk costs can rival or exceed the base freight.
- Chargeable weight and volume determine how pricing applies to your shipment.
- Surcharges and local charges matter as much as the base rate.

Total landed cost is what matters for your business. It includes the price you pay the supplier, all logistics costs, and duties and taxes, divided by the number of units you can sell.

In later chapters, especially Chapter 11, you will use this lens to make better decisions about suppliers, Incoterms, and shipping plans. For now, the important step is to stop seeing "shipping cost" as a single number and start seeing it as a stack of understandable, manageable parts.

6.10 Worked Cost Examples

This section gives you two compact cost breakdowns you can adapt to your own products.

6.10.1 LCL Ocean Shipment: Small Furniture Order from Shenzhen to Rotterdam

Assume you are importing 5 cubic meters (CBM) of flat packed furniture from Shenzhen to Rotterdam, under FOB SHENZHEN terms. Your supplier delivers the goods to the export terminal and clears export customs. You pay from there onward.

Example cost stack:

- LCL ocean freight: USD 120 per CBM x 5 CBM = USD 600
- Origin LCL handling and documentation: USD 40 per CBM x 5 CBM = USD 200
- Destination LCL handling (unpacking, documentation): USD 50 per CBM x 5 CBM = USD 250
- Destination port and warehouse fees (small fixed items): about USD 150
- Truck delivery from Rotterdam depot to your warehouse in Belgium: USD 280
- Customs broker fee and small government charges: USD 180
- Import duties at 4 percent on goods valued at USD 8,000: USD 320
- Cargo insurance at 0.5 percent on USD 8,000: USD 40

Estimated total logistics cost: USD 600 + 200 + 250 + 150 + 280 + 180 + 320 + 40 = **USD 2,020**

If you import 160 units in this shipment, logistics adds roughly USD 12.60 per unit. That number helps you judge whether a retail price covers not just purchase cost but also shipping and duty.

6.10.2 Air Shipment: Urgent Spare Parts from Frankfurt to Chicago

Now assume you must ship 300 kilograms of urgent machine spare parts from Frankfurt to Chicago under FCA FRANKFURT terms. Your supplier hands the goods to your forwarder at an airport warehouse. You pay from that point onward.

Example cost stack:

- Chargeable weight: 300 kilograms (dimensions are compact, so volumetric weight is lower than actual weight).
- Air freight base rate: USD 5.50 per kilogram x 300 kg = USD 1,650
- Air fuel and security surcharges: USD 1.20 per kilogram x 300 kg = USD 360
- Origin airport handling and documentation: USD 220
- Destination airport handling and delivery order: USD 260
- Trucking from Chicago airport to your factory in Indiana: USD 320
- Customs broker fee and government processing charges: USD 180
- Import duties at 2.5 percent on goods valued at USD 25,000: USD 625
- Cargo insurance at 0.4 percent on USD 25,000: USD 100

Estimated total logistics cost: USD 1,650 + 360 + 220 + 260 + 320 + 180 + 625 + 100 = **USD 3,715**

For a shipment of high value, urgent parts, the air cost is justified if it avoids a production line stoppage worth far more than USD 3,715 per day.

These numbers are illustrative, not quotes. The point is how each component fits into the total and how quickly you can turn a few assumptions into a working landed cost estimate.

Field Guide: What Shipping Really Costs

Key concepts

- Shipping cost is a stack that includes main carriage, origin and destination handling, documentation, duties, taxes, insurance, and sometimes penalties.
- Chargeable weight and volume, not just actual weight, drive many air and LCL rates.
- Surcharges such as BAF, peak season surcharges, and equipment imbalance fees can materially change total cost.
- Total landed cost per unit is the right metric for pricing and sourcing decisions.
- Quotes must be read for what they exclude as much as for what they include.

Common mistakes

- Comparing only the base ocean or air rate and ignoring local charges and surcharges.
- Underestimating or omitting duties and taxes when evaluating supplier offers.
- Failing to budget for demurrage, detention, or storage risk when free time is tight.
- Using outdated or incomplete product data (dimensions, weights, HS codes) in cost models.
- Treating one unusually low quote as the "new normal" instead of asking what is missing.

Warning signs

- Quotes using phrases such as "local charges as per tariff" without clear estimates.
- Invoices where "destination charges" are a large, unexplained lump sum.

- Regular surprises from port bills or carrier invoices that were not antici-
pated.
- A business that cannot state, even roughly, its average logistics cost per
unit for key products.

Practical shortcuts

- For any significant shipment, build a quick cost stack like the examples
in section 6.10 using simple assumptions; treat that as your sanity check.
- When evaluating quotes, mark each line as "sea," "origin," "destination,"
"duty/tax," or "risk/buffer" to see which bucket you might be underestimating.
- Add a small percentage contingency (for example 10 to 20 percent on
freight and handling) when planning, then adjust over time as you learn
how often and where costs overrun.

If You Only Remember Three Things

1. Ocean or air rates are only one part of the bill; handling, duties, taxes,
and risk costs can easily match or exceed the base freight.
2. Total landed cost per unit, not the headline freight rate, is the number that
should drive pricing, sourcing, and Incoterm choices.
3. A simple, repeatable cost stack for your main products and lanes is more
useful than a perfect model you never use; rough estimates, updated often,
beat guesswork.

Chapter 7: The Rules of the Game - Incoterms, HS Codes, and Export Declarations

7.1 When a "Simple" Shipment Goes Sideways

The email from Paris looked like a dream.

A boutique on Rue de Turenne wanted to order 2,000 hand poured soy candles from a small workshop outside Austin, Texas. The candles were already selling well on Etsy. This was a chance to step onto the world stage.

The owner, Maria, did what many small exporters do. She opened her laptop, typed "international shipping terms" into a search box, and picked something that sounded official.

"FOB Houston," she wrote on the quote.

Free On Board. It felt grown up and professional. The Paris buyer agreed.

Next, the buyer asked her for the HS code for the candles. Maria found a code on an online list that looked close enough. It mentioned "chemical preparations, not elsewhere specified." Candles are chemicals, she thought. Close enough.

Her cousin's friend worked at an air freight company. He offered to book the shipment from Houston to Paris. A week before pickup, he asked a question that stopped everything.

"Who is filing AES for this shipment?"

Maria stared at the message. She had never seen those three letters in her life. The airline would not accept the cargo without an Internal Transaction Number, the ITN that comes from filing Electronic Export Information through the Automated Export System, or AES.

Then the buyer wrote with a different problem. Their customs broker in France was not happy with the HS code. The code described industrial chemicals, not scented candles. That code carried a higher duty and triggered extra safety checks. The broker warned that customs could seize or delay the shipment.

On top of that, the buyer expected Maria to pay all transport to Paris. Maria thought her job ended when the boxes left her warehouse. The buyer thought "FOB Houston" meant delivery to their door.

The order that could make her year now threatened to wreck her cash flow and reputation. At two in the morning she sat at her kitchen table surrounded by printouts, trying to decode words like Incoterms, HS code, AES, and USPPI.

That feeling of confusion is common. Three invisible systems had shown up at once:

- Incoterms, which divide costs and responsibilities between buyer and seller.
- HS codes, which tell customs what the product is.
- Export declarations such as AES, which tell governments what is leaving the country.

If any one of those is wrong or unclear, a "simple" shipment can go sideways.

Think of an international shipment like a long road trip.

- Incoterms are the agreement about who drives which part of the route, who pays for gas, and who is responsible if the car breaks down near the border.
- HS codes are the description of your car and luggage written in a number language that every border guard understands.
- AES filing, for United States exports, is the step where you tell the border officials in advance who is traveling, where they are going, what they are carrying, and whether anything in the trunk needs special permission.

If you get any of those wrong, the trip can stall, cost far more than planned, or never reach the destination.

Before dealing with codes and portals, we need to answer the basic question in any shipment:

Who does what, and who is on the hook when things go wrong?

That is the world of Incoterms.

Section I Takeaway: Trade terms, product classification, and export filings are three pillars of every international shipment. When they are vague or guessed, even a small order can turn into a large problem.

7.2 Incoterms Explained - Who Does What, Pays What, and Takes the Risk

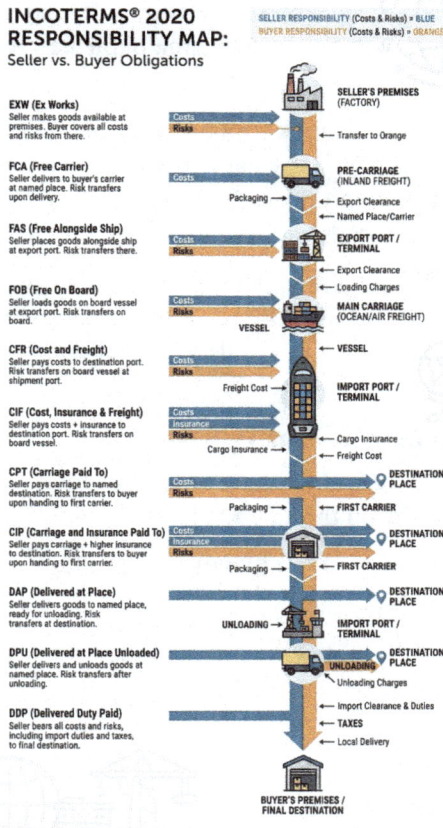

Figure 15: Incoterms

7.2.1 What Are Incoterms?

Incoterms is short for International Commercial Terms. The current version, Incoterms 2020, is a set of three letter trade terms such as FOB or DAP published by the International Chamber of Commerce in Paris.

These terms appear in sales contracts, purchase orders, commercial invoices, and in casual emails where people write things like "FOB Shanghai, as usual."

Each Incoterm answers three questions:

- Who pays for which part of the journey?

- Who carries the risk of loss or damage at each stage?
- Who is responsible for export and import formalities, such as customs clearance and licenses?

Think of them as a shared playbook. If both sides say "CIF Rotterdam, Incoterms 2020," they are pointing to the same published rules, in the same edition, with the same meaning.

Appendix D at the back of the book contains a quick reference table for selected Incoterms, showing who pays for what and where risk transfers. You can use it as a shortcut while working through this chapter, but the explanations that follow here give you the detail you need to use the terms correctly.

Incoterms do not cover everything. They do not decide ownership of the goods in a legal sense, or how you get paid, or what happens if the buyer never pays. They only cover the movement of goods, cost sharing, and risk transfer along the physical route.

7.2.2 The Main Incoterms You Will See

There are eleven Incoterms in Incoterms 2020, but a handful appear most often in practice. We will focus on those.

7.2.2.1 EXW - Ex Works (named place)

Example: EXW Austin workshop.

Under Ex Works, the seller makes the goods available at their premises and does very little else. The buyer:

- Picks up the goods.
- Arranges export clearance.
- Pays for all transport and insurance.
- Bears the risk from the moment they collect the goods.

EXW is misleadingly simple. For international trade it often creates problems, because foreign buyers may not be able to handle export formalities in the seller's country. Many professionals prefer FCA (Free Carrier) instead, where the seller takes responsibility up to a handover point and handles export clearance.

7.2.2.2 FOB - Free On Board (named port of shipment, sea and inland waterway only)

Example: FOB Houston.

Under FOB, the seller:

- Clears the goods for export.

- Delivers them on board the vessel at the named port.

Risk and cost transfer to the buyer when the goods are on board. From that point, the buyer pays ocean freight, insurance, and destination costs and bears the risk for loss or damage.

FOB was designed for bulk and breakbulk cargo that is loaded directly onto a ship. Many people use it loosely for containers and even for air freight. Strictly speaking, FCA is better for containers and non sea transport, but the habit of writing "FOB" is deeply ingrained.

7.2.2.3 CIF - Cost, Insurance and Freight (named port of destination, sea only)

Example: CIF Rotterdam.

Under CIF, the seller:

- Clears the goods for export.
- Pays for transport to the named destination port.
- Provides minimum insurance for the buyer's benefit.

Risk still transfers when the goods are on board at the port of shipment, just as under FOB. The seller pays for the ocean leg and insurance, but the buyer bears the risk during that leg. This subtle point surprises many people.

7.2.2.4 DAP - Delivered At Place (named place of destination)

Example: DAP Paris boutique.

Under DAP, the seller:

- Arranges and pays for main transport.
- Covers origin handling and export clearance.
- Pays for delivery to the named place of destination.

The buyer:

- Handles import customs.
- Pays import duties and taxes.

Risk transfers when the goods are ready for unloading at the agreed place.

DAP is a common choice when the seller wants to offer door delivery but does not want to handle or prepay duties and taxes in the buyer's country.

7.2.2.5 DDP - Delivered Duty Paid (named place of destination)

Example: DDP Berlin warehouse.

Under DDP, the seller takes on almost everything:

- Origin handling and export clearance.
- Main transport.
- Import customs clearance.
- Payment of duties and taxes.
- Delivery to the named place.

Risk transfers when the goods are made available at the destination.

For buyers, DDP is attractive. For sellers, it can be risky if they do not fully understand import rules and tax systems at destination. It is easy to underestimate the time and cost of full door and duty paid delivery.

7.2.2.6 A Quick Word on FCA, CPT, and CIP

Three other terms appear regularly:

- FCA (Free Carrier) is often a better alternative to EXW or FOB for containerized trade. The seller delivers the goods to a named place, such as a terminal, and clears export customs. Risk transfers there.
- CPT (Carriage Paid To) and CIP (Carriage and Insurance Paid To) are similar to CIF but can be used for any mode, not only sea. The seller pays for transport to a named place, and under CIP also for insurance, but risk transfers earlier in the journey.

The key pattern is simple: the C terms (CIF, CIP, CFR, CPT) mean the seller pays for the main carriage, but risk transfers earlier, usually at the point of shipment.

7.2.3 Who Arranges the Forwarder?

Incoterms do not mention freight forwarders by name, but they imply who will hire them.

- Under EXW or FCA at the seller's location, the buyer usually hires the forwarder.
- Under FOB, CFR, CIF, or CPT, the seller typically books the main carriage, though risk allocation differs.
- Under DAP or DDP, the seller often engages a forwarder to manage door delivery.

This matters because the party who hires the forwarder usually receives the most direct communication about delays, options, and costs. They also decide how much information to share with the other side.

7.2.4 Common Mistakes With Incoterms

Several patterns repeat across industries.

- Companies mismatch Incoterms and payment terms. A letter of credit might require certain shipping documents, but the chosen Incoterm gives control of those documents to the other party. The seller then struggles to present what the bank demands and risks not getting paid on time.
- Many firms casually write "FOB" for air freight or container shipments simply because everyone does. In a dispute, that habit makes it harder to prove when damage occurred.
- Sellers sometimes "help" by booking freight even when the Incoterm puts that task on the buyer. When delays or extra charges appear, both sides argue over who owns the problem.
- The most dangerous mistake is using EXW when the foreign buyer has no way to complete export formalities. The truck arrives. Nobody has filed export customs. The truck leaves empty.

7.2.5 Choosing Incoterms Wisely

The right Incoterm can cut costs and reduce conflict.

If you are a buyer that ships large volumes on a trade lane, you might have better freight rates than your suppliers. In that case, you may prefer FOB or FCA so you control the main carriage and enjoy your lower rates.

If you are a seller with a strong relationship with a forwarder, you might offer DAP to make life easier for your customers and differentiate your service, then bake the door to door cost into your price.

Before you quote, ask:

- Who understands export rules in the seller's country?
- Who has stronger freight contracts on this route?
- Who is better equipped to handle customs in the destination country?

Proposing a thoughtful Incoterm is a quiet way to show professionalism. It tells your counterpart that you understand not just your product, but how it moves.

Section II Takeaway: Incoterms divide costs, risk, and paperwork duties. Choosing them on purpose, and matching them to your real capabilities, prevents arguments that can burn profit and relationships.

7.3 HS Codes - The "DNA" of Your Product in Global Trade

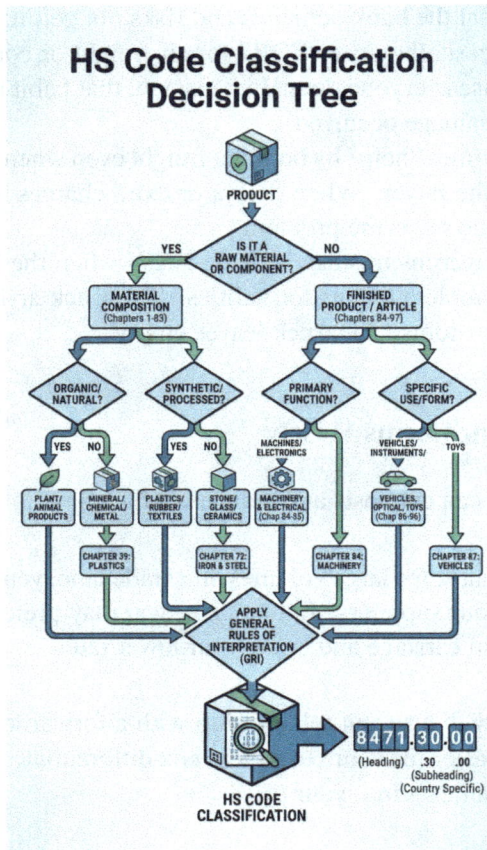

Figure 16: HS Code Classification System

7.3.1 When a T-shirt Becomes a Luxury Blouse

A small apparel brand in Los Angeles specialized in simple cotton T shirts. They imported blanks from Asia, printed designs, and sold online.

To save money, they handled their own customs paperwork. For classification, they skimmed a few online charts and picked an HS code they thought matched "cotton T shirt."

Two years later, United States Customs and Border Protection reviewed their entries.

An officer decided that the cut, fit, and finishing of some "T shirts" looked more like women's blouses according to the official tariff notes. Under that code, the duty rate was 18 percent instead of 6 percent.

The government calculated the difference over hundreds of shipments, added interest, and imposed a penalty for negligence. The bill ran into the tens of thousands of dollars.

A few digits in a number had quietly controlled their duty cost all along.

That is the power of HS codes.

7.3.2 What Are HS Codes?

HS stands for Harmonized Commodity Description and Coding System. It is administered by the World Customs Organization in Brussels and used by more than 200 countries.

The HS is a global system for classifying goods. Each product gets a numeric code that describes its nature and use in a standardized way.[8] [9]

The first six digits of the code are harmonized worldwide. For example, 0901.21 refers to roasted, non decaffeinated coffee, no matter which country you ship to.

Individual countries extend these codes to eight, ten, or more digits for their own tariff and statistical purposes. The United States uses ten digit codes in the Harmonized Tariff Schedule for imports, and another set of ten digit Schedule B codes for exports. The European Union uses TARIC codes.

Think of HS codes like library call numbers. Every book in a large library has a number that tells you the subject and sometimes the format. Librarians in different cities understand the structure. In global trade, customs officers play that role.

7.3.3 Why HS Codes Matter

The HS code on your invoice does a remarkable amount of work behind the scenes.

---

[8]

See the "Selected Sources for Chapter 7 (HS Codes, Tariffs, and Export Declarations)" notes, including WCO materials and U.S. Customs and Border Protection informed compliance publications, for more detailed guidance on HS structure and use.

[9]

See the "Selected Sources for Chapter 7" notes, including WCO materials and U.S. Customs and Border Protection informed compliance publications, for more detailed guidance on HS structure and use.

- It sets the basic import duty rate. One code might be taxed at 5 percent of value, another at 12 percent, another at a specific charge per kilogram.
- It determines whether a product qualifies for benefits under trade agreements. Under USMCA, for example, certain car parts that meet regional value and HS based rules can enter duty free.
- It acts as a trigger for regulatory controls. Certain codes cover weapons, dual use electronics, chemicals, medical devices, food, plants. Those codes can require special licenses, certifications, or inspections.
- It feeds trade statistics. Governments track imports and exports by HS code and use that data to shape economic and foreign policy.

If the HS code is wrong, all of those downstream effects can be wrong as well.

7.3.4 How HS Codes Are Structured

The HS system is organized in chapters, headings, and subheadings.

- The first two digits are the chapter. Chapter 09 covers "Coffee, tea, maté, and spices."
- The first four digits are the heading. 0901 is "Coffee, whether or not roasted or decaffeinated."
- The first six digits are the subheading. 0901.21 is "Roasted, not decaffeinated."

After that, each country adds more digits.

Consider chocolate. Cocoa powder without added sugar generally falls under 1805.00. Chocolate bars with sugar often appear under 1806.32 or a similar extension. The difference between "powder" and "bar" is obvious in daily life, but in the tariff it is encoded in a handful of digits and often results in very different duty rates.

Small changes in classification can mean large changes in cost. Sports footwear under one code might face 8 percent duty, while other footwear under a slightly different code faces 17 percent. A running shoe misclassified as "other footwear" can nearly double your duty bill.

7.3.5 How To Find the Right HS Code

The work of classification starts with knowing your product in detail.

- What materials is it made of, and in what percentages?
- What is its main function?
- How is it used, and by whom?
- Is it sold as a single item, in a set, or as part of a kit?

The more precise your knowledge, the easier the classification.

With that description in hand, you consult official resources. Most customs authorities publish searchable tariff databases. The United States Harmonized Tariff Schedule and the European Union TARIC system let you search by keywords and browse by chapter. For complex questions, the World Customs Organization publishes Explanatory Notes that show how officials interpret different headings.

Customs brokers and experienced forwarders use these tools daily. They also rely on past rulings. In many countries, you can submit a binding ruling request, in which customs reviews your product description and returns a code that becomes legally binding for that product within that jurisdiction.

Classification follows general rules. These include principles such as "the more specific description prevails over the more general" and "goods consisting of different materials are classified according to the material that gives them their essential character." For sets, such as a picnic basket that includes utensils and plates, the item that gives the set its main function drives the code.

If this starts to sound like medicine, that is not an accident. Your product has "symptoms" such as composition, shape, and use. A customs broker is like a doctor who reads those symptoms, consults the manual, and assigns a code. A good diagnosis requires good information from the patient.

7.3.6 What Happens When HS Codes Are Wrong

Wrong codes create three main kinds of pain.

Overpayment, the quiet one. If you classify under a high duty category when a lower one would be correct, you simply pay more tax than you should. Over years and many shipments, that can empty a surprising amount of profit. Some companies have recovered hundreds of thousands of dollars by reclassifying products and filing for refunds.

Underpayment, which attracts attention. If customs believes you chose a cheaper code to save money, they can reclassify the goods, demand back duties for several past years, and add penalties and interest. In extreme intentional cases, they can pursue fraud charges.

Delays. Suspicious or inconsistent codes often trigger inspections. For sensitive goods such as food, chemicals, or electronics, a questionable code can cause the shipment to sit in a warehouse while agencies argue over jurisdiction.

An outdoor gear importer once tried to be clever by classifying portable camping stoves as "other metal articles" instead of as "stoves for cooking." The duty rate under "other metal articles" was lower. For a while, nobody noticed. Then customs audited the entries. The reclassification produced a large back tax bill and a painful fine. The profit from those stoves evaporated.

7.3.7 Case Study: Misclassification and a Demurrage Shock

Now imagine a different variation of the same mistake, this time with much more immediate pain.

A mid sized European electronics importer brought in several containers of home audio equipment from East Asia. On paper, the product was listed under an HS code for "parts and accessories," which carried a relatively low duty rate. In reality, customs believed the goods belonged under a heading for complete consumer electronics, taxed several percentage points higher.

At first, nothing happened. The importer's customs broker filed entries using the code the importer supplied. Containers cleared with only random inspections.

Then, during a period of tight port capacity, customs selected three containers for a detailed review.

Officials pulled the containers aside at the terminal. They opened cartons, compared the goods to catalogues and online listings, and concluded that the declared HS code was wrong. They reclassified the items and calculated higher duties for the three containers, plus back duties for similar entries in the previous year.

While those calculations and discussions took place, the containers sat.

Free time at the terminal expired. Demurrage charges started to accumulate. Because trucks could not pick up the containers until customs released them, no one could move the boxes to cheaper storage. The importer found itself paying:

- Additional duties on past and current shipments.
- Demurrage to the terminal for each extra day the containers occupied yard space.
- Extra brokerage and legal fees to resolve the dispute.

By the end of the episode, demurrage alone had added several thousand euros per container. The total cost of the mistake ran well into six figures.

None of these costs appeared on the original freight quote. They emerged only because an HS code chosen casually years earlier finally collided with a tight port and a stricter customs review.

The importer's eventual fix looked mundane: they hired a specialist to review product classifications, obtained binding rulings for their main product lines, and centralized HS code data so that purchasing, logistics, and brokers all used the same, correct numbers. The dramatic part was how much money was saved by preventing the next demurrage shock.

7.3.7 Working With Forwarders and Brokers on HS Codes

Freight forwarders and customs brokers live in this world every day. They can be invaluable guides, but they are not magicians.

Their role is to review your product information, propose an HS code, explain the duty rate and any special controls, and point out potential issues. They bring experience from similar products and knowledge of how local customs offices interpret borderline cases.

Your role is to provide accurate and detailed descriptions. If you send a one line description such as "plastic item" and guess at a code, a good broker will send the request back. The quality of classification depends on the quality of information you provide.

On new products or large value flows, it is often worth paying for a specialized classification review or a binding ruling. The cost of getting the HS code wrong repeatedly is usually higher than the fee for getting it right once.

7.3.8 Practical Habits To Avoid HS Headaches

Some simple habits go a long way:

- Keep a central list of your products with agreed HS codes, and share it with your forwarders and brokers.
- When you change a product's materials or design, review whether the HS code still fits.
- Avoid copying codes blindly from suppliers without checking whether they are correct for your country and for imports versus exports.
- Document how you arrived at a code, including any rulings or explanatory notes you relied on.

7.3.9 Case Study: U.S. "Trump Tariffs" on China — 2018–2025

In 2018 and 2019, the U.S. government imposed additional tariffs on many imports from China under Section 301 of the Trade Act of 1974. These "Trump tariffs" added duties (often 10% or 25%) on top of normal rates, covering specific HS codes across hundreds of billions of dollars in annual trade. Whether a product was affected depended on:

- Its HS code, and

- Its country of origin (not just the country of export).

Two recurring patterns during that period highlight why HS classification and origin rules matter:

- Many firms discovered that their internal HS-code mappings were incomplete or inconsistent. Some product lines had never been properly classified. Others used codes that seemed "close enough"—until small classification differences produced large cost swings once tariffs applied. Importers rushed to audit and clean up HS assignments, often with help from brokers or legal counsel.
- Some companies practiced "tariff engineering": they adjusted product design, sourcing, or production flows so that finished goods either
    - Fell under HS codes not on the tariff lists, or
    - Qualified under rules of origin for countries other than China.

For example, a firm importing assembled electronics from China might relocate final assembly to Vietnam or Mexico — changing the declared origin. Others might tweak components or packaging so the goods fell under a different HS heading with lower or no additional duty. These maneuvers required careful legal and technical work — showing how much leverage lies in a few digits of the tariff schedule.

From the viewpoint of logistics, sourcing, and freight forwarding, the "Trump tariffs" era reinforced three key lessons:

- HS codes are not mere paperwork: they can determine whether a shipment incurs a modest duty or a steep surcharge.
- Country-of-origin rules can matter as much as shipping routes when structuring sourcing and manufacturing chains.
- Policy shocks can instantly change landed costs — customers need visibility into which products (by HS code) travel on which lanes.

Since 2024, U.S. trade policy has undergone further shifts. Under the second term of Donald J. Trump, the U.S. has expanded tariffs beyond legacy Section 301 lists, introducing a broad "reciprocal tariff" regime.[10]

Key developments by 2025 include:

- A global **baseline 10% tariff** on most imports came into effect on April 5, 2025.

---

[10] Forward-looking descriptions of tariff policy here reflect public proposals and commentary as of the time of writing rather than settled law. For current rules, always consult USTR and customs authority notices in your own country.

- On April 9, 2025, additional **country-specific reciprocal tariffs** began applying — rates vary depending on the trade partner's foreign tariff regime and other factors.
- Tariff complexity increased substantially: overlapping measures such as legacy Section 301 tariffs (on China), the new reciprocal duties, and sector-specific tariffs (e.g. under Section 232) coexist.
- Some exclusions remain in force. For example, certain agricultural products were carved out from the 2025 reciprocal tariffs under a presidential executive order issued in November 2025.

From a supply-chain or logistics planner's perspective, this evolution means the structural lessons from 2018–2019 remain valid — but with greater urgency and complexity:

- HS codes and origin data remain fundamental levers for duty exposure.
- But now risk extends beyond one "China list." Tariffs may apply broadly, across multiple sourcing countries and product categories.
- Exclusions and exemptions (e.g. for some agricultural products) remain uncertain and subject to renegotiation — making tariff exposure volatile.
- Freight forwarders, importers, and planners must embed dynamic scenario planning: consider what happens if a 10%, 25%, or even higher surtax appears on a given HS code from a specific country.
- Diversifying suppliers / production sites across countries and HS classifications becomes even more important as a hedge against policy risk.

Section III Takeaway: HS codes are the DNA of your product in trade systems. They decide duty rates, trigger rules, and feed statistics. Getting them right is a matter of information and discipline, not guesswork.

7.4 Export Declarations - AES and Its Cousins Around the World

7.4.1 Why Every Country Has an Export Declaration System

In Chapter 6 you saw how customs treats imports. Countries also care about what leaves their borders.

Governments track exports in order to:

- Enforce controls on weapons, sensitive technologies, or sanctioned destinations.
- Produce trade statistics.
- Support tax and rebate schemes for exporters.

To do this, they require exporters, or their agents, to file export declarations that list key details of each shipment.

The names differ. In the United States it is the Automated Export System, AES. In the European Union it is the Export Control System. Many other countries have similar portals and rules.

The questions are remarkably similar everywhere: who is sending what, to whom, from where, to where, and for how much.

7.4.2 The Invisible Wall at the Airport

Picture an air cargo terminal at night.

Pallets arrive from trucks and warehouses. Forklifts move them to a buffer zone before the security and customs area. Inside that zone is an invisible wall. On one side, goods are still in domestic circulation. On the other side, they are treated as exports.

No forwarder or airline wants to push cargo across that wall without the correct export filings. Doing so can expose them to fines, seizure of goods, and loss of licenses.

That is why Maria's shipment could not board the plane without an AES filing and an ITN. From the airline's point of view, the absence of an ITN was not a small missing detail. It meant the United States government did not yet know about the export, and loading the cargo would be a violation.

7.4.3 What Are AES, EEI, and ITN?

In the United States:

- AES is the Automated Export System, the platform through which export data is filed.
- EEI is the Electronic Export Information, the actual data set that exporters submit.
- ITN is the Internal Transaction Number, the confirmation code returned by AES once an EEI filing is accepted.

You will see the ITN printed on air waybills and ocean bills of lading or referenced in documents. It is proof to the carrier that export reporting obligations have been met for that shipment.[11]

---

[11]

For current definitions and filing rules, see the U.S. Census Bureau Foreign Trade Regulations (15 CFR Part 30) and U.S. Customs and Border Protection export guidance.

7.4.4 When Is AES Filing Required?

United States export rules change over time, and you should always check current regulations or ask a qualified broker. At a high level, filing is required when:

- The value of goods classified under a single Schedule B number, from one United States Principal Party in Interest to one foreign consignee, exceeds a defined dollar threshold, or
- The goods require an export license or are subject to specific export controls, regardless of value.

Certain destinations and goods are exempt or handled under special rules, but the key idea is that for many commercial shipments, an EEI filing and ITN are mandatory, not optional.

7.4.5 What Data Goes Into an AES Filing?

An EEI filing typically includes:

- Identities and addresses of the exporter or USPPI and of the ultimate consignee.
- The Schedule B or HS code for each product line.
- Quantity and unit of measure.
- Value and currency.
- Country of origin of the goods.
- Export Control Classification Number (ECCN) where applicable.
- License information if the goods are controlled.
- Port of export and method of transport.

Much of this information overlaps with what you already prepare for commercial invoices and packing lists. The export declaration is a structured way to present it to the government.

7.4.6 Who Is Responsible for Filing?

In the United States, the USPPI holds the primary responsibility for ensuring that export information is filed correctly. The USPPI is usually:

- A United States based seller of the goods, or
- The United States buyer of goods that were purchased for export, or
- A foreign entity, in certain cases, if they are physically in the United States and own the goods at the time of export.

The USPPI can authorize a freight forwarder or other agent to file EEI on its behalf, usually through a written power of attorney. The agent then becomes the filer, but the USPPI is still responsible for the truthfulness and completeness of the data.

7.4.7 How Forwarders File AES in Practice

In practice, many exporters never log in to AESDirect themselves. Their forwarder does it.

The exporter provides:

- A commercial invoice and packing list.
- Exporter and consignee details.
- HS or Schedule B codes and values.
- Any license information for controlled goods.

The forwarder:

- Enters the data into AESDirect or another approved system.
- Receives the ITN.
- Includes that ITN on the transportation documents.

Forwarders build checklists to make sure they collect all required data. Good ones will not accept vague product descriptions or missing values. If they press you for detail, it is not bureaucracy for its own sake. It is how they keep you and themselves compliant.

7.4.8 Practical Habits for United States Exporters

A few simple habits reduce headaches:

- Ask your forwarder or broker to explain when your shipments require EEI filings and when they do not.
- Keep a clean record of your Schedule B and HS codes.
- Make sure your commercial invoices show exporter, consignee, description, quantity, and value clearly.
- Give your forwarder limited powers of attorney so they can file on your behalf.
- For controlled or sensitive products, work with an export compliance specialist rather than guessing.

If you export from another country, the names will change, but you can expect a similar pattern: an export declaration system, thresholds for filing, and shared responsibility between exporter and forwarder.

Section IV Takeaway: Export declarations such as AES let governments see what leaves the country. Even if a forwarder files the data, exporters remain responsible for its accuracy. Treat export reporting as part of your shipment design, not as an afterthought.

7.5 Putting It All Together - From Candle Idea to Customs Clearance

Let us return to Maria and her order of scented candles to Paris.

In the "bad" version of the story, she picked "FOB Houston" from an internet search, guessed an HS code from a list, and had never heard of AES. The buyer assumed door delivery. French customs saw a code for chemical preparations, not candles, and raised safety concerns. The airline refused to load the shipment without an ITN. Everyone was upset.

Now picture the "good" version, using the concepts from this chapter.

Before confirming the order, Maria calls a freight forwarder in Houston. She explains that the buyer is a boutique in central Paris with no logistics department of its own.

The forwarder walks her through options. Since the buyer can handle local customs and taxes in France but needs help with transport, they settle on DAP Paris. That means Maria will be responsible for transport to the boutique's door, but the buyer will pay duties and French VAT.

The forwarder's quote reflects those responsibilities clearly. It includes pickup at Maria's warehouse, air freight to Paris, and final delivery by a local carrier.

Next, the forwarder introduces Maria to a customs broker. She sends product descriptions, photos of the candles and labels, and a list of ingredients and packaging materials. The broker identifies the proper HS code for scented candles used for domestic purposes and checks the duty rate and any labeling rules for France under European Union law.

They discover that certain fragrances above a threshold require a specific warning symbol on the packaging. Maria adjusts her labels. That small change avoids a hold in Paris.

As the shipment date approaches, the forwarder prepares the EEI filing through AESDirect. Maria, as the USPPI, signs a power of attorney authorizing the forwarder to file on her behalf.

The forwarder uses the correct Schedule B code, the proper value, and accurate exporter and consignee information. The system returns an ITN. The forwarder prints the ITN on the air waybill and includes it in the documentation pack.

The candles fly to Paris, clear customs with minimal delay, and arrive at the boutique in time for the store's spring launch. The buyer knows exactly what portion of the cost they are paying, and Maria knows exactly where her responsibility ended.

Same product. Same people. The difference is that the invisible rules were finally visible.

7.5.1 Three Questions for Every International Shipment

You can simplify all of this into three questions that you ask at the start of any deal:

- Who does what, and who pays for which part of the journey? Answer that with an Incoterm and a named place. For example: FCA Dallas terminal, DAP Hamburg warehouse, or DDP Ottawa.
- What exactly are we shipping in customs language? Answer that with a precise HS code and a clear product description.
- What does the government know about this shipment? For United States exports, answer that with an AES filing, EEI data, and an ITN when required. For other countries, the answer is whatever export declaration your own government requires.

If you can answer those three questions confidently, you are ahead of many companies larger than yours.

7.5.2 How Freight Forwarders Connect the Dots

Good freight forwarders live at the intersection of these three questions.

As advisors, they explain the pros and cons of different Incoterms, highlight common traps, and suggest terms that match your capabilities.

As doers, they book carriers, coordinate trucking and warehousing, file AES if authorized, or handle the equivalent export declaration in other countries, and move documents between buyer, seller, customs, airlines, and ocean lines.

As a safety net, they spot mismatches before they blow up. If your invoice says DAP but you refuse to pay for destination trucking, the forwarder will ask you to resolve it before departure. If your HS code for a lithium battery sounds off, they will question it. If no one has mentioned AES or another export declaration for a USD 20,000 shipment, they will ask who is filing.

You do not need to know everything a forwarder knows. You do need enough understanding to have a clear, specific conversation. That is how you get real value from their expertise.

7.5.3 A Simple Checklist

For your next international shipment, try this one page checklist:

- Incoterm and named place agreed in writing.

- Roles and responsibilities understood for export, main transport, import, and final delivery.
- HS code confirmed with a broker or forwarder, and recorded in your product list.
- Commercial invoice and packing list prepared with clear descriptions, quantities, and values.
- Export declaration requirements checked and, if needed, a filing plan agreed with your forwarder.
- Customs broker selected at destination, or buyer confirmed as responsible.

Section V Takeaway: Incoterms, HS codes, and export declarations look technical from a distance. Up close, they are structured ways of answering three human questions: who does what, what are we really shipping, and who needs to know. Get those answers right and you dramatically raise the odds that your shipment leaves on time, clears customs, and arrives more or less as planned.

Field Guide: Rules of the Game

Key concepts

- Incoterms define who pays for which parts of the journey and where risk transfers between seller and buyer.
- HS codes are the product's "DNA" in trade systems, determining duty rates and triggering regulatory rules.
- Export declarations such as AES filings are how governments see what leaves the country, and responsibility for them cannot be outsourced completely.
- Country of origin and classification interact with trade policies such as Section 301 tariffs and any future "reciprocal" tariffs.
- Freight forwarders and customs brokers operate in this rules space every day and are critical partners.

Common mistakes

- Picking Incoterms from a drop down or a blog post without aligning them with real capabilities and responsibilities.
- Copying HS codes from suppliers or internet lists without checking whether they are correct for your product and your country.
- Treating export and import filings as "paperwork someone else handles," then being surprised when fines or shipment holds arrive.
- Using EXW when a foreign buyer has no way to handle export formalities in your country.

- Letting sales teams write Incoterms on quotes that operations and finance cannot actually support.

Warning signs

- Contracts and invoices that mention Incoterms without naming a specific place (for example just "FOB" with no port).
- Internal product lists that lack HS codes, or that show different codes for similar items with no explanation.
- Frequent customs holds, repeated requests for additional information, or demurrage and detention bills tied to documentation issues.
- Confusion inside your company about who is the USPPI or who files export declarations.

Practical shortcuts

- For each major product, create a one page record showing HS code, origin, and any special rules; use that sheet for both quoting and customs.
- Before agreeing to an Incoterm, ask three questions: who knows export rules at origin, who has the best freight contracts on the lane, and who is best placed to handle customs at destination.
- Treat export declarations as a checklist item in your shipment planning process, not as a separate afterthought; a simple template shared with your forwarder reduces missed data and filing surprises.
- When trade policy shifts, such as new tariffs on specific HS codes or origins, use your classification data to quickly see which SKUs and lanes are exposed instead of guessing.

If You Only Remember Three Things

1. Incoterms, HS codes, and export declarations are not paperwork trivia; together they decide who pays, who carries risk, and whether your shipment is even allowed to move.
2. Guessing at classification or leaving origin and destination responsibilities vague rarely saves time; it usually reappears as delays, fines, or demurrage and detention bills.
3. A forwarder or broker is most useful when you treat them as a rules advisor and planning partner, not just as someone who fills out forms once you are already committed.

Chapter 8: Cold Chain Logistics

8.1 The Ice Cream that Never Melted (and the Vaccine that Could Not)

In 2013, a small clinic in northern Mozambique received its first shipment of rotavirus vaccines. The nurse in charge, Ana, had been talking about this day for months. Rotavirus kills hundreds of thousands of children every year through severe diarrhea. For many in her district, these vials were the difference between growing up and never reaching school age.

The vaccines started life thousands of kilometers away in a pharmaceutical plant in Europe. They rode inside a refrigerated truck to an airport, crossed continents by air, passed through customs at a large African hub, spent a night in a government cold room, then continued by truck along rough roads. The last stretch was on the back of a motorbike, inside a small insulated box with frozen ice packs, bouncing over red dirt tracks in 35 degree heat.

When the shipment finally arrived, Ana did not look at the labels first. She went straight to a tiny square on each vial called a vaccine vial monitor. This little sticker changes color if the vial has been too warm for too long. If it is dark, the contents are no longer safe. It is no longer medicine. It is expensive, dangerous water.

Every monitor she checked was still in the safe zone. The cold chain had held.

If you have ever eaten strawberries in winter, bought sushi in a landlocked city, or taken an injection that had to stay in the fridge, you have already trusted that same kind of invisible system with your health. Your ice cream, your salad, your insulin, all rely on a chain of people and machines that guard one simple thing: temperature.

This chapter unpacks that system. We will look at what cold chain logistics actually is, how it keeps food and medicine safe, how it differs from normal freight, what can go wrong, and how professionals reduce those risks.

Every temperature sensitive product has a safe band. For many vaccines it is between plus 2 and plus 8 degrees Celsius, and for many frozen foods it is minus 18 degrees or colder.[12] If products spend too long outside their band, quality and safety drop in ways that no later cooling or reheating can fix.

Cold chain logistics is the global effort to keep products inside that band from factory or farm all the way to your kitchen or clinic. When it works, it feels routine. When it fails, people get sick, businesses lose money, and regulators start asking hard questions.

Now that the stakes are clear, from a village clinic to your freezer at home, we can define what the cold chain is and how it differs from ordinary shipping.

Cold chain logistics is the invisible system that lets perishable products survive long, complicated journeys without spoiling or becoming dangerous. Every time you eat imported fresh food or take a refrigerated medicine, you are quietly betting that system got it right.

12

These commonly cited ranges reflect WHO vaccine storage guidance and food safety standards from national regulators for chilled and frozen products.

8.2 What Is Cold Chain Logistics and Why It Matters

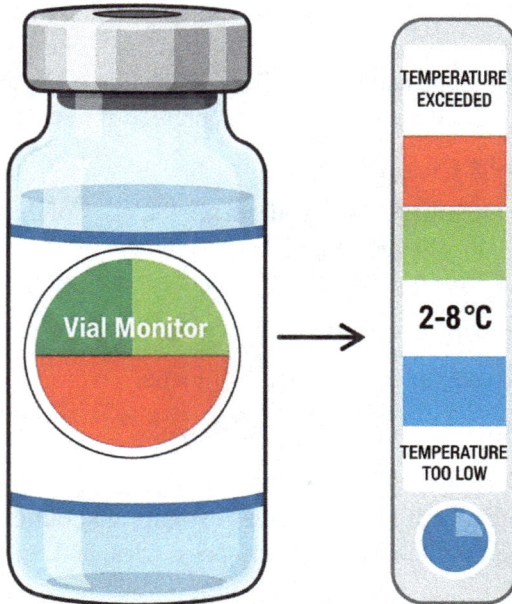

Figure 17: Temperature Monitoring System

8.2.1 Defining the Cold Chain

Cold chain logistics is the temperature controlled part of the supply chain. It is the way the world moves and stores products that can be ruined, weakened, or made unsafe if they get too warm or too cold.

This includes perishable foods, temperature sensitive medicines, and many laboratory and industrial materials. It is not just about keeping things cold. It is about keeping them inside a specific temperature band from start to finish.

The "chain" in cold chain is every link in the journey. A typical path might be a farm or factory, a pre cooling stage, a cold warehouse, a refrigerated truck, a port terminal, a refrigerated container on a ship, another terminal, another truck, a distribution center, and finally a store or hospital. For the chain to work, that temperature band must be respected at every step. If one link breaks, the whole chain is considered broken, no matter how well the other parts worked.

A good mental picture is a relay race with a fragile glass ornament instead of a baton. Each runner must pass it carefully. If even one person drops it, the ornament shatters and the team loses. For cold chain goods, temperature is that glass. You cannot tape it back together and pretend it never broke.

8.2.2 Typical Cold Chain Cargoes

Walk through any supermarket and you can see the work of the cold chain. Fresh berries, bags of salad, shrink wrapped meat, blocks of cheese, tubs of yogurt, and freezers full of frozen pizza and ice cream all depend on it.

In food, cold chain cargo includes:

- Fresh fruits and vegetables such as blueberries, lettuce, grapes, and asparagus.
- Chilled meat and poultry.
- Fresh and frozen fish and seafood.
- Dairy products such as milk, cheese, yogurt, and butter.
- Frozen products such as ice cream, peas, fries, and ready meals.

In pharmaceuticals and health care, it includes:

- Vaccines that must stay between plus 2 and plus 8 degrees.
- Some biologic drugs that lose effectiveness if frozen.
- Certain diagnostic reagents and laboratory materials.

In industry, cold chain extends to:

- Temperature sensitive chemicals.
- Some adhesives and resins.
- Specialty films and materials that warp or degrade if exposed to heat.

All of these products have a "no go" zone. Above or below certain temperatures, they may be unsafe, ineffective, or unsellable.

8.2.3 Temperature Ranges and Stability

Different products have different comfort zones:

- Fresh leafy vegetables might prefer 0 to 4 degrees Celsius.
- Bananas and some tropical fruits suffer if cooled below about 12 degrees.

- Standard frozen food is stored at around minus 18 degrees or colder.
- Many vaccines need plus 2 to plus 8 degrees.

Two numbers matter:

- The target range, where quality is maintained.
- The time the product can survive outside that range before quality drops to an unacceptable level.

Cold chain planners think in terms of cumulative exposure. A crate of yogurt that sits at room temperature for six hours during unloading and customs inspection may still be cold by the time it reaches a store, but its shelf life has silently shortened. The damage is cumulative and invisible until the product spoils early at home.

8.2.4 What Happens When the Cold Chain Fails

When temperature control fails, consequences appear in several ways:

- Food spoils early or grows harmful bacteria.
- Vaccines and biologics lose potency, sometimes without obvious visual change.
- Cosmetics and chemicals separate, crystallize, or change texture.

A supermarket might see higher levels of returns and waste. A hospital might quietly throw away a batch of drugs and re order at high cost. In worst cases, people get sick from contaminated food or from medicines that do not work.

Cold chain failures also carry legal and reputational risk. Food safety authorities and drug regulators expect traceability. They want to see that products were kept within required ranges or, if they were not, that the affected batch was removed from sale.

8.2.5 Why Freight Forwarders Are Critical in Cold Chain Logistics

Cold chain forwarders do more than book reefers and fridges. They:

- Design routes that minimize exposure to heat and handling.
- Choose carriers and ports with strong cold chain infrastructure.
- Check that warehouses and trucks have reliable temperature control and backup power.
- Coordinate documentation for health and safety regulations.
- Arrange monitoring such as data loggers or real time sensors.

They think about path, timing, and protection in a joined up way. For a vaccine shipment or a high value seafood load, that planning can be the difference between a routine delivery and a costly recall.

8.3 Cold Chain Infrastructure: Reefers, Warehouses, and Monitoring

8.3.1 Refrigerated Containers (Reefers) - The Moving Fridges of the Sea

Refrigerated containers, or reefers, look like regular containers from a distance but have insulated walls and a built in refrigeration unit. They plug into power sources on ships, in ports, and sometimes on trucks and trains.

Key features:

- Temperature control within a set range.
- Air circulation to keep temperature stable throughout the load.
- Alarms and data logging for temperature deviations.

Reefers carry everything from frozen meat and fish to bananas and pharmaceuticals. Shipping lines invest heavily in them because they command higher rates and serve sticky, repeat business such as supermarket supply contracts.

8.3.2 Temperature Controlled Trucks and Vans

On land, refrigerated trucks and vans move goods between farms, factories, ports, warehouses, and stores.

They vary from small delivery vans serving city centers to articulated trucks with multi compartment trailers that carry different products at different temperatures.

Things that matter:

- Pre cooling the truck body before loading.
- Fast loading and unloading to reduce door open time.
- Regular maintenance of refrigeration units and seals.

8.3.3 Temperature Controlled Warehouses and Cross Docking Facilities

Cold stores and temperature controlled warehouses provide:

- Chilled and frozen chambers at different set points.
- Dock areas with insulated doors.
- Racking and handling equipment suited to low temperatures.

Some facilities specialize in quick "cross docking," where goods that arrive in the morning leave again the same day with minimal storage time. Others hold stock for weeks or months.

8.3.4 Port and Terminal Requirements for Cold Chain

Ports that handle significant cold chain volumes need:

- Plug in points for reefers in yards and on vessels.
- Backup generators or dual power feeds.
- Procedures for monitoring reefers and responding to alarms.

In some disruptions, such as storms or power outages, reefer racks and cold stores are priority loads for backup power because of the high value and sensitivity of their contents.

8.3.5 Monitoring Technologies: Data Loggers, Sensors, and Tracking

Monitoring is as important as machines.

Simple data loggers record the temperature inside a pallet or container over time. At destination, staff download the log. If the trace shows that the product stayed within limits, they release the goods. If it shows long deviations, they may hold or discard the shipment.

More advanced systems use:

- Sensors that send real time data via cellular or satellite networks.
- GPS tracking of reefers and trucks.
- Alerts when temperature moves outside a set band or when doors open unexpectedly.

For high value cargo and strict regulations, shippers and forwarders increasingly layer two protections:

- Physical temperature control.
- Proof that the control actually worked.

8.3.6 Infrastructure Choices, Shipping Costs, and Forwarder Selection

Better infrastructure costs more. A modern cold store with redundant power, trained staff, and digital monitoring charges higher fees than a basic warehouse with a few old fridges.

Forwarders who specialize in cold chain know which facilities deliver real value and which ones only claim to. They also know where you can safely save money by accepting a slightly simpler facility without raising risk too far.

In practice, cold chain customers rarely pick the very cheapest option. They pick the option that balances cost with confidence that the product will reach customers in good condition.

8.4 Managing Risk in a Temperature Controlled Supply Chain

8.4.1 Common Cold Chain Risks

Common risk points include:

- Long truck waits in open yards during hot weather.
- Power failures at cold stores or ports.
- Customs holds without access to cold storage.
- Poor loading that blocks air circulation in a reefer.
- Incorrect temperature set points or units (for example, Fahrenheit instead of Celsius).

Many of these are human problems as much as technical ones. A forgotten door, a mis set dial, or a delayed truck can undo expensive investments in hardware.

8.4.2 How Freight Forwarders Design Cold Chain Routing and Contingency Plans

Cold chain forwarders manage risk by:

- Choosing routes with fewer handoffs where possible.
- Avoiding ports and airports with a history of long dwell times for reefers.
- Building realistic transit schedules that include time for customs and inspections.
- Pre arranging backup options such as alternate flights or ports.

They may also require:

- Confirmation that destination warehouses can receive and store loads on arrival.
- Special handling codes on air waybills and bills of lading to flag temperature needs.
- Agreements with carriers about what happens if a reefer unit fails in transit.

8.4.3 Documentation and Regulatory Requirements for Food and Pharma

Cold chain shipments often have extra documentation:

- Health or sanitary certificates for meat and dairy.
- Phytosanitary certificates for plant products.
- Certificates of analysis and batch release documents for pharmaceuticals.
- Temperature mapping and validation records for new routes.

Regulators expect companies to show not just that they intended to keep products cold, but that they tested systems and routes to prove they could.

8.4.4 Incoterms, HS Codes, and Added Cold Chain Constraints

All the rules from Chapter 7 still apply in cold chain logistics, with extra twists.

- Incoterms decide who carries the temperature risk on each leg.
- HS codes trigger health and safety rules for foods and medicines.
- Export declarations often ask about controlled drugs or biologics.

If a shipment of frozen fish is sold under CIF Rotterdam, the seller pays for the ocean freight and insurance, but risk passes at loading. Who bears the cost if a reefer unit fails halfway through the voyage? If a vaccine shipment under DDP London spoils in customs, does the seller or buyer carry that loss? Clarity in contracts matters more when failure means wasted product and regulatory trouble, not just delay.

8.4.5 Small Process Improvements with Big Impacts

Improving cold chain performance does not always require enormous investment. Small changes can have large effects:

- Reducing truck waiting time at the farm gate or factory by better scheduling.
- Training staff to load pallets in ways that allow airflow.
- Adding simple shade structures where trucks queue in hot climates.
- Using low cost data loggers in pallets to detect where problems most often occur.

Improvement resembles a speedrun in a game. You look at the replay, see where time or health was lost, and plan a better path. The difference here is that the stakes are not virtual trophies but real products and real health.

8.5 Bringing It All Together: Thinking Like a Cold Chain Professional

8.5.1 A Simple Framework: Product, Path, Protection

Cold chain professionals often reduce a complex operation to three words: Product, Path, Protection.

Product comes first. What exactly are you moving? Is it fresh salmon, frozen peas, insulin, or a laboratory enzyme? What temperature range does it need, and for how long can it stay within that range before quality drops? Does it hate freezing, like some tropical fruit, or can it sit happily at minus 18 degrees for months? Without precise product knowledge, even the best logistics plan may fail.

Path is the journey the product will take from origin to destination. Which farms, factories, warehouses, ports, and airports will it pass through? How many handoffs are there? A simple path might be farm, pre cooler, cold store, reefer truck, port, reefer container, destination port, distribution center, store. A complex pharmaceutical path might add contract packers, quality release sites, and regional warehouses. Each extra step is a potential weak point, especially where climate is hot or congestion is common.

Protection is everything you do to guard the product along that path. It includes reefers, refrigerated trucks, cold rooms, packaging, sensors, documentation, and backup plans for when flights are canceled or ports close.

8.5.2 Mini Case: Exporting Fresh Mangoes from a Small Farm

Picture a small mango grower in Maharashtra, India, whose fruit has been sold only in domestic markets. A European supermarket chain is interested but wants high quality Alphonso mangoes on its shelves, with good appearance and taste, and at least a week of remaining shelf life for customers.

Product first. Mangoes are living fruit. They keep respiring after harvest and produce heat. Many varieties suffer chilling injury if they are stored too cold, below about 7 degrees Celsius. Their ideal range for export may sit around 10 to 13 degrees, depending on maturity and variety.[13] Too warm and they over ripen before arrival. Too cold and they develop brown patches and off flavors.

Next is the path. The mangoes are harvested in orchards, brought to a pre cooling center, then to a cold warehouse near Mumbai. From there they go by reefer truck to the port, into a reefer container for the sea leg to Europe, then through a European port, into a cold warehouse, on to a supermarket distribution center, and finally on chilled trucks to individual stores.

Finally comes protection. The forwarder helps arrange rapid pre cooling after harvest to remove field heat. Cartons are designed to allow good airflow. Temperature is set to the correct range in the reefer. Data loggers are placed in a few cartons. The forwarder chooses a shipping line with direct service and good reefer records and avoids a port known for weekend congestion. All export paperwork, including plant health certificates and HS codes, is checked and pre cleared where possible to avoid holds in Europe.

13

Typical mango and other tropical fruit temperature bands are drawn from export handling guidance published by FAO and national horticulture and food safety agencies.

If any of those choices are wrong, the result shows up quickly. No pre cooling and the mangoes arrive soft. Wrong temperature and they show chilling injury. A customs delay without cold storage and mold appears on the fruit. With the right Product, Path, and Protection decisions, however, that small farm can sell into a premium European market at a good price.

8.5.3 Why Cold Chain Matters for Your Business and Career

Cold chain logistics touches food security, public health, and everyday shopping baskets.

For small business owners, understanding cold chain basics can open new doors. A cheesemaker in Wisconsin, a seafood cooperative in Senegal, or a juice producer in Brazil can reach distant markets if they respect temperature rules, invest wisely in packaging and partners, and resist the temptation to cut corners.

For early career professionals and students, cold chain offers a field where logistics knowledge meets technology, regulation, and science. Roles in cold chain freight forwarding, quality management, operations, and supply chain design are growing worldwide. Employers in food, pharmaceuticals, and ecommerce all need people who understand how to move sensitive products safely and efficiently.

Thinking like a cold chain professional means always asking three questions: what does this product truly need, where along its journey is the chain most likely to break, and how can we protect it better without blowing up costs? If you can answer those questions clearly, you will already be ahead of many people working in logistics today.

8.6 Chapter 8 - Summary Takeaways

Cold chain logistics is the temperature controlled supply chain that keeps perishable and sensitive products safe and effective from origin to destination.

It differs from standard freight because even short temperature mistakes can destroy product value and create health and legal risks. Once a vaccine overheats or a frozen product thaws, cooling it again does not restore its original quality.

The cold chain relies on physical infrastructure such as refrigerated containers, cold trucks, temperature controlled warehouses, and port facilities with reliable power and monitoring. It also depends on digital tools, from simple data loggers to real time sensors and GPS tracking.

Freight forwarders specializing in cold chain plan routes with temperature and risk in mind, coordinate infrastructure and documentation, and prepare contingency plans so that delays and surprises do not automatically turn into losses.

They help shippers balance safety, compliance, and cost.

With the right planning and partners, businesses of any size can use cold chain logistics to reach new markets and protect the people who consume their products. Every perfectly frozen ice cream bar in a hot city and every safe vaccine delivered to a remote clinic is proof that the cold chain, quietly and constantly, is working.

Field Guide: Cold Chain Logistics

Key concepts

- Cold chain logistics is about keeping products within specific temperature bands from origin to final delivery.
- Different products have different ideal ranges and tolerances; some hate freezing, others must be kept frozen.
- Product, Path, Protection is a useful framework: know the product's needs, map the journey, and design protection at each step.
- Cold chain failures can be invisible at first but show up as lost shelf life, spoilage, or reduced drug efficacy.
- Monitoring and documentation (data loggers, temperature maps, validation records) are as important as hardware.

Common mistakes

- Treating refrigerated transport as a generic service without specifying precise temperature ranges and limits.
- Failing to pre cool product or equipment, so goods spend long periods above target temperature before entering the cold chain.
- Leaving cold chain routing decisions to generic forwarding processes that ignore handoff times and likely delays.
- Assuming that any warehouse or port can handle reefer cargo without checking power reliability, plug in points, and procedures.
- Skipping or under funding temperature monitoring because "we have never had a problem."

Warning signs

- Frequent alarms or unusual temperature traces on data loggers, even if products still appear usable.
- Long truck dwell times at farms, factories, or ports with reefers sitting in the sun and engines cycling hard.
- Repeated customer complaints about quality or short shelf life for chilled or frozen products.

- Cold rooms or reefer racks operating near capacity with no backup power plan.
- Documentation gaps such as missing health certificates, incomplete temperature mapping, or inconsistent labels.

Practical shortcuts

- For any new cold chain lane, run a small pilot shipment with data loggers in multiple positions; review the traces before scaling up.
- Simplify paths where possible: fewer handoffs and shorter dwell times in hot environments are usually worth a slightly higher rate.
- Work only with partners (forwarders, warehouses, carriers) who can show clear procedures and records for handling your specific temperature range.
- When in doubt, prioritize product integrity over marginal savings; the cost of a ruined shipment or recall is almost always higher than the extra cost of a more conservative plan.

If You Only Remember Three Things

1. Cold chain shipments are about time in range, not just time in transit; a few bad hours at the wrong temperature can undo an otherwise perfect plan.
2. Product, Path, Protection is a simple way to design and audit cold chain routes: know the product's needs, map each step, and make sure protection exists where the journey is weakest.
3. Monitoring and documentation are part of the product, not optional extras; regulators and customers will judge you on records as well as results.

Chapter 9: Freight Brokers and the Edges of the Network

Global context note In this chapter, we use the United States concept of a "freight broker" as a clear example: a company that is separately licensed, for example by the FMCSA, to arrange road freight without operating trucks itself. That strict legal distinction between "freight broker" and "freight forwarder" is strongest in North America. In much of Europe and Asia, forwarders routinely arrange domestic trucking and play a broker like role without a separate broker license, and local laws use different terminology. The underlying function, matching shippers with trucking capacity and managing that relationship, exists almost everywhere, even if job titles and regulations differ.

9.1 Why Freight Brokers Matter in Everyday Logistics

Imagine a container that has just cleared customs at a busy port late on a Friday afternoon. Storage charges start the next morning. The consignee expects delivery at a distribution center on Monday, and missing the delivery window means contractual penalties.

The local trucking company that normally handles this lane is already fully booked. Dispatchers are heading home. Terminal appointment slots are scarce. Somewhere, a shipper or freight forwarder is staring at a schedule and a growing list of costs, wondering how to find a truck that can legally, safely, and reliably move that container on time.

When that situation ends well, there is usually a freight broker in the background.

This chapter is about that often invisible role. You will see:

Who freight brokers are, and who they are not. The different types of brokers, from classic truckload brokers to digital platforms. How brokers fit with freight forwarders, carriers, and 3PLs. When it makes sense for a shipper or forwarder to call a broker.

If trucks are like taxis, a freight broker is like the dispatcher or the ride hailing app that connects people who need a ride with drivers who have a vehicle and time. The broker does not own the truck, but without that matchmaker, many shipments would sit, waiting, while costs quietly pile up.

By the end of this chapter you will know exactly what it means when someone says, "I will call a broker I trust," and how that one call can keep a supply chain, and a hard-won customer relationship, intact.

Figure 18: Freight Broker as Matchmaker

9.2 What Is a Freight Broker in the Logistics Ecosystem?

In earlier chapters we met most of the main characters in global logistics. It helps to bring them back on stage for a moment.

The shipper is the party that owns the goods and needs them moved. The carrier owns and operates the actual vehicle, the ship, the plane, or the train that moves the goods. The freight forwarder organizes international shipments from origin to destination, often across several transport modes. The customs broker handles customs clearance, taxes, and regulatory paperwork.

So where does a freight broker fit into this cast?

A freight broker sits between shippers and trucking companies. Their world is primarily road freight. They do not operate vessels across oceans or aircraft across continents. Their specialty is trucks, from short port drayage moves to long haul trips crossing several states or countries.

If you drew it on a whiteboard, it would look like this:

Shipper → [Freight Broker] → Trucking Company

In parallel, especially in international trade, you might also have:

Shipper → [Freight Forwarder] → Ocean or Air Carriers → [Freight Broker] → Trucking Company

The freight broker's core function is simple to describe, although hard to execute well: find a safe, reliable truck for a specific load, within a specific time window, at an acceptable price.

9.2.1 A Working Definition

A freight broker is a licensed intermediary that matches shippers who have loads with motor carriers who have trucks and drivers. In the United States, for example, brokers are regulated by the Federal Motor Carrier Safety Administration (FMCSA) and must hold a broker authority and a surety bond.

Crucially, the broker does not physically move the freight. They do not drive the truck. They typically never take possession of the goods. They arrange the movement and manage the information and commercial commitments around it.

This is different from a freight forwarder. A forwarder may store, pack, and consolidate shipments. They may hold the goods in a warehouse, label them, and issue their own house bill of lading for an international shipment. They may be legally responsible as a carrier for certain parts of the journey.

A freight broker, in its classic form, does not do that. They focus on arranging a single leg of road transport. They may work hand-in-hand with a forwarder who is managing the bigger international puzzle.

You can think of it this way:

A freight forwarder is a travel organizer and tour manager who designs the whole trip, including flights, hotels, transfers, and visas. A freight broker is the ticket agent for one specific bus ride from the airport to the hotel.

Both matter. They simply operate at different levels of the journey.

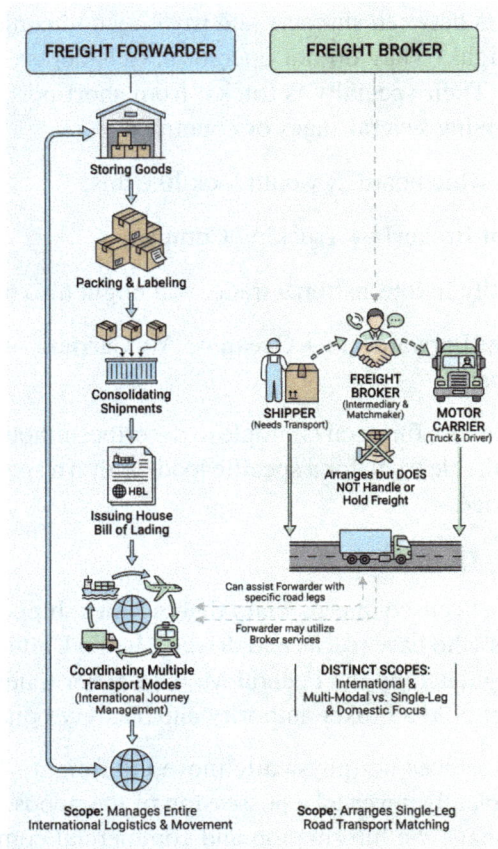

Figure 19: Logistics Ecosystem Diagram

9.2.2 How Brokers Make Money: The Margin Game

Freight brokers work on margin.

They "buy" transport capacity from a carrier at one rate, then "sell" that capacity to the shipper at a slightly higher rate. The difference between these two numbers is the broker's gross margin on that load.

For example, a broker might call a small trucking company and ask for a rate from Port Newark to a distribution center near Allentown, Pennsylvania. The carrier might say:

"We can pull that container tomorrow and deliver Monday for 1,000 dollars, all in."

The broker then quotes the forwarder or shipper:

"Your all-in rate is 1,200 dollars."

The 200 dollar difference is the broker's gross margin. From that margin, they pay their staff, their software, their rent, their taxes, and hopefully keep some profit.

That margin is not guaranteed. If the driver arrives at the port and waits four hours in a queue, the carrier may charge extra waiting time. If the port suddenly imposes a chassis fee, or the destination DC changes the delivery appointment, costs can rise. If the broker misjudges the market and offers a rate that is too low, they may have to top up the carrier's payment out of their own pocket to keep the relationship.

Good brokers do not get rich on one magical high-margin load. They survive and grow by handling many loads efficiently, knowing their lanes, reading market conditions, and managing the gap between what carriers need to earn and what shippers are willing to pay.

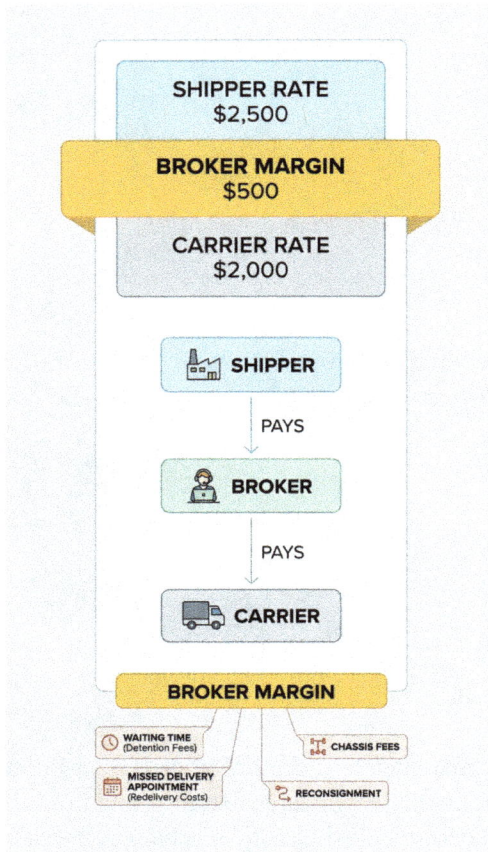

Figure 20: Broker Margin Concept

9.2.3 Why Shippers and Forwarders Use Freight Brokers

If a shipper could simply call a carrier directly, why involve a middleman at all?

The short answer is speed, reach, and flexibility.

A shipper that runs dozens of full-truckload shipments a day between the same few locations might have long-term contracts with a handful of large carriers. That system works well for predictable, stable freight.

Real life is rarely that tidy.

Retail promotions spike demand unexpectedly. A factory in a rural town has a breakdown and suddenly needs urgent parts delivered. A vessel arrives late, so several containers clear customs at once and must leave the port quickly to avoid demurrage.

Shippers and forwarders do not always have the time or resources to call twenty different trucking companies and negotiate a one-off rate for each of these surprises. A broker already maintains a network of hundreds, sometimes thousands, of carriers, including many small operators that a shipper would never find or vet on their own.

Brokers also have access to "load boards." These are online marketplaces where brokers post available shipments and carriers check for loads that match their equipment and routes. In North America, boards like DAT and Truckstop have been around since the 1990s. A broker can post a load and get calls from carriers within minutes.

This reach matters especially on awkward lanes. Moving freight from Chicago to Dallas is simple. Both ends are busy freight markets with lots of carriers. Moving freight from a small town in northern Wisconsin to a specialty retailer in western Nebraska is much harder. A broker who knows regional carriers can find that one truck that happens to be empty near the pickup location and wants to go in that general direction.

A useful analogy is a talent agent for actors. The agent tracks who is available, who is good at which roles, and what rates they expect. The agent connects producers, who have budgets and schedules, with actors, who have skills and time. A freight broker does the same, but for trucks.

9.2.4 Reliability, Safety, and Carrier Vetting

Connecting people is not enough. The carriers on the other side of the phone have to be safe and legitimate. A single bad choice can cause cargo damage, regulatory fines, injury, or worse.

Good brokers spend significant effort on vetting their carrier base.

In the United States, that starts with checking FMCSA records: Does the carrier have active operating authority? What is their safety rating? Have they had serious violations or crashes? Brokers also request certificates of insurance to confirm that liability and cargo coverage meet agreed minimums, for example 1 million dollars in liability and 100,000 dollars for cargo.

They store details about equipment types and capabilities: which carriers have refrigerated trailers, which can legally carry hazardous materials, which run flatbeds, and which are reliable at ports with complex appointment systems.

In recent years, fraud has become a bigger risk. "Double brokering" is a common problem. In this scam, a carrier that accepts a load from a broker re-brokers that load to a third party without permission, takes payment from the original broker, and never pays the actual carrier. Identity theft also occurs when criminals pose as legitimate carriers using stolen credentials.

Because of this, serious brokers run strict checks before giving a carrier their first load and monitor performance over time. They may have internal "do not use" lists for carriers with repeated late deliveries, questionable paperwork, or safety red flags.

Forwarders care deeply about this. When a forwarder hires a broker to move containers away from a port, the forwarder's name is the one the shipper sees on all the documents. If the truck never shows up, or if the driver damages the cargo, the shipper rarely blames "some broker." They blame the forwarder. So most forwarders keep short lists of trusted brokers in each region and stick with them.

A freight broker is only as valuable as their ability to find safe, reliable trucks quickly, again and again.

9.3 Types of Freight Brokers: TL, LTL, Niche, and Digital

Just as not all doctors are surgeons, not all freight brokers focus on the same kind of freight. The type of broker you talk to depends heavily on what you are shipping and how.

9.3.1 The Basic Divide: Truckload vs Less-than-Truckload

9.3.1.1 Truckload Brokers

Truckload, often shortened to TL, refers to shipments that fill an entire truck by weight, volume, or by using up the legal weight limit. Usually there is one pickup and one delivery, with no transfers in between.

Typical examples include:

A factory shipping 26 pallets of canned drinks from its plant to a supermarket distribution center. A forwarder moving a full 40-foot container from an ocean terminal to an inland warehouse.

Most of the freight that moves out of ports and large DCs travels as full truckloads.

Truckload brokers specialize in this type of move. They think in rates per mile or per kilometer. They monitor daily spot market conditions. They often book loads for same-day or next-day pickup.

In Maya's case, the broker the forwarder called was working as a truckload broker. They were finding a single truck and chassis to pick up a single import container and drive it straight to a single destination.

9.3.1.2 LTL Brokers

LTL stands for less-than-truckload. These are shipments that do not fill a truck. Think of one, two, or maybe six pallets at a time. Many small and midsize businesses ship this way.

Instead of putting one company's goods in a trailer, LTL carriers consolidate freight from many customers into shared trucks. They run hub-and-spoke networks. Freight goes from the origin terminal to a regional hub, maybe changes trailers once or twice, then travels to a destination terminal that does local delivery.

Forwarders consolidate small international shipments into containers or air pallets. LTL carriers and LTL brokers do something similar, but within domestic road freight.

For example, a Chicago based ecommerce seller might ship three pallets of rugs each week to an Atlanta fulfillment center. Hiring a full truck for those three pallets would be wasteful and expensive. An LTL broker can compare rates from several LTL carriers, choose a service level, and arrange pickup and delivery on shared trucks.

A simple comparison helps:

TL is like hiring a taxi to take just you and your luggage from the airport to your hotel. LTL is more like a shared shuttle or bus. You travel with others and split the cost, but the route includes extra stops and sometimes takes longer.

Some brokers handle both TL and LTL. Others focus heavily on one side.

9.3.2 Niche and Specialized Brokers

Certain types of freight need more than a truck and a driver. They need specific equipment, training, or permits. Many brokers carve out niches around these needs.

9.3.2.1 Refrigerated Brokers

Refrigerated trailers, often called reefers, move perishable goods. That includes frozen meat, fresh produce, dairy, pharmaceuticals, and flowers.

Temperature control is not a detail. If a load of berries sits on a hot loading dock for two hours, or if the trailer temperature is set incorrectly for a vaccine, the entire shipment can be lost.

Reefer brokers understand:

Required temperature ranges. Pre-cooling procedures for trailers. How long particular products can travel before quality suffers. Which carriers maintain their reefers properly and have reliable monitoring systems.

During the extreme European heatwave in 2019, for example, many produce shippers leaned heavily on specialized brokers who could locate reefers with strong cooling units and drivers who knew how to handle sensitive loads. A mistake was not just late fruit. It was melted chocolate, spoiled meat, and thousands of euros in waste.

9.3.2.2 Flatbed and Oversize-load Brokers

Construction companies, steel mills, and machinery manufacturers rarely ship goods on regular box trailers. They use flatbeds, step-decks, and other open-deck equipment.

Oversize or overweight loads, such as transformers, industrial presses, or wind turbine blades, need permits from each state or country they cross. Many need escort vehicles and careful route planning to avoid low bridges, tunnels, or roads with weight restrictions.

Flatbed and heavy-haul brokers understand:

Permit rules in different jurisdictions. How to schedule escorts. Which carriers own specialized trailers such as extendable flatbeds or multi-axle lowboys.

If you have ever seen a 60 meter turbine blade crawling along a highway between two pilot cars, there is almost certainly a specialized broker behind that move.

9.3.2.3 Hazmat Brokers

Hazardous materials, or hazmat, include fuels, industrial chemicals, gases, and many other substances classified as dangerous goods.

Moving hazmat requires:

Drivers with specific certifications. Vehicles with appropriate equipment and signage. Compliance with regulations such as ADR in Europe or U.S. Department of Transportation rules. Higher insurance coverage.

A mistake here does not mean a few damaged boxes. It can mean explosions, toxic leaks, and serious legal consequences. Hazmat brokers build small, carefully checked carrier networks and treat each move with tight controls.

9.3.2.4 Drayage Brokers

Drayage refers to short-distance trucking between ports, rail terminals, and nearby warehouses. The distance might be only 20 or 50 kilometers, but the complexity can be high.

Port drayage involves:

Dealing with terminal appointment systems. Understanding free time, demurrage, and detention rules. Finding drivers with the right port access credentials. Managing chassis availability in markets like the United States where chassis can be a separate asset.

Drayage is often the weak link in an otherwise polished international supply chain. Ships arrive, containers stack up, and if drayage capacity is tight, everything downstream suffers. That is why many forwarders rely heavily on drayage brokers around busy ports such as Los Angeles, Rotterdam, or Singapore.

9.3.3 Digital Freight Brokers and Platforms

In the past decade, a new breed of broker has emerged: digital freight platforms.

These companies use websites and mobile apps to match loads and trucks. Some people casually describe them as "Uber for trucks." The comparison is not perfect, but it helps.

Digital brokers offer:

Instant or near-instant rate quotes based on algorithms that read market conditions. Online booking, where a shipper can click to confirm a load without talking to a person. Mobile apps for drivers to accept loads, see instructions, and upload photos or proof-of-delivery documents. Real-time tracking based on GPS, so shippers and forwarders see where their loads are on a map.

Large players in this space include Convoy in the United States (before it shut down and had assets acquired in 2023), Uber Freight, and various regional platforms in Europe, India, and Latin America.

These tools change expectations. They push traditional brokers to provide more visibility, more structured data, and quicker responses.

Digital platforms are not perfect. They handle standard dry-van and some reefer loads well, especially on common lanes. They often struggle with complex projects, highly specialized freight, or situations that need deep local knowledge and negotiation. Behind their screens, they still employ human operators for problem-solving and relationship management.

9.3.4 Matching Broker Types to Supply Chain Needs

Each type of broker tends to match a certain profile of customer and cargo.

Truckload brokers work with manufacturers, retailers, and forwarders that move many full truckloads between factories, ports, and distribution centers.

LTL brokers support small and midsize firms that ship a few pallets at a time but need national coverage without building their own carrier contracts.

Specialized brokers serve industries with strict requirements, such as food producers who need reefers, chemical companies who need hazmat expertise, and construction firms who ship heavy or oversized equipment.

Digital brokers and platforms attract shippers that value speed and transparency, and that are comfortable managing freight through screens rather than only through phone calls.

For freight forwarders, TL and drayage brokers are essential partners for inland legs to and from ports, airports, and rail terminals. Specialized brokers help forwarders cover cargo that has product-specific rules, like temperature or hazardous classifications.

There is no single "best" broker type for everyone. The right choice depends on what you ship, how often, how urgent it is, and how predictable your flows are.

9.4 How a Freight Broker Actually Works: From Phone Call to POD

So far we have talked about what brokers are and the types that exist. Now it helps to walk through what they actually do when a load appears, hour by hour.

To make this concrete, we will follow Maya, a logistics manager for a national retail chain who relies on a freight forwarder to handle her import containers.

9.4.1 Step 1: Getting the Load

The process usually starts with a phone call or an email from a shipper or forwarder.

To quote and plan a move, a broker needs several key details:

Origin and destination addresses. Pickup and delivery windows. Cargo description, weight, dimensions, and number of pallets. Special requirements such as refrigeration, hazmat, liftgate service, or tarps. Contact information at pickup and delivery locations.

If an international shipment is involved, the broker also needs to know who is responsible for what, based on Incoterms. For example, if the buyer is responsible from the port onward, the broker's customer might be the buyer's forwarder rather than the original seller.

In Maya's situation, her forwarder emailed the broker:

"Need 1 x 40-foot container dray from Port Newark to XYZ Retail DC, near Allentown. Pickup window: Saturday 08:00 to 13:00. Delivery by Monday 10:00. Non-hazmat, dry, about 20 tons. Standard chassis."

With that, the clock started ticking.

9.4.2 Step 2: Quoting the Load

To build a rate, the broker considers several factors:

Distance and route. A 130-mile port dray that crosses busy bridges may cost more per mile than a 400-mile highway run through open countryside. Market conditions. Before major holidays or during produce seasons, trucks get scarce in some areas and rates rise. Fuel prices. Many rates include a fuel surcharge, which moves with diesel prices. Tolls and fees. Bridges, tunnels, port access, and chassis may add fixed costs. Accessorials. These are extra services or situations, such as waiting time, extra stops, or weekend deliveries.

Brokers look at historical data from their own systems and at current spot market indicators. Then they decide what rate to offer the shipper or forwarder, including their target margin.

In our example, the broker replied:

"All-in rate 1,200 dollars. Includes standard free time at the terminal and one hour free waiting at destination. Detention after that billed at standard rates."

The forwarder checked this against expected budgets and quickly accepted. Speed matters. If the broker delays too long in quoting, the shipper may call someone else.

9.4.3 Step 3: Sourcing a Carrier

Now the real matchmaking begins.

The broker needs to find a carrier that can do the job, at a cost that leaves room for margin, with a level of reliability the broker is willing to stake their reputation on.

They start with their internal carrier database. Many brokers maintain "preferred carriers" for each lane or region. If that does not yield a result, they post the load to one or more load boards, listing key details and inviting carriers to call or bid.

Suppose the broker hears back from three carriers.

Carrier A has a strong track record with this broker. They quote 950 dollars. Carrier B is new to the broker, with minimal safety data. They quote 800 dollars.

Carrier C is a small drayage company that has done a few good jobs for this broker before. They quote 900 dollars.

The broker weighs price, safety records, on-time performance scores, and how tight capacity feels in that port today.

Choosing Carrier B purely for price might add 100 dollars to the broker's margin on paper, but if the carrier fails to show up, the broker could lose the forwarder's trust and potentially the entire relationship.

Most seasoned brokers would choose Carrier C, balancing a fair cost with known reliability. That still leaves 300 dollars of gross margin on a 1,200 dollar job, which is healthy for a complex, time-sensitive drayage move.

9.4.4 Step 4: Confirming the Load

Once the carrier is selected, the broker sends a "rate confirmation" to the carrier. This document lists:

Pickup and delivery addresses. Contact names and phone numbers. Agreed rate and what it includes. Any special instructions, such as "must pull from terminal X" or "delivery appointment at 09:00 Monday, check in 30 minutes early."

The carrier signs or otherwise accepts this rate confirmation. This is the contract between broker and carrier.

The broker also confirms details with the customer, the shipper or forwarder. They may send a load confirmation or simply a clear email that includes pickup window, ETA, and key references such as container number, booking number, or purchase order.

Legally, the broker is a separate party from the carrier. The carrier is the one that issues the bill of lading at pickup. The shipper usually signs that bill of lading as proof that the goods were handed over in good condition.

So the paperwork web looks like this:

Shipper or forwarder has a service agreement with the broker. Broker has a rate confirmation agreement with the carrier. Shipper and carrier interact through the bill of lading at pickup and the proof of delivery at the end.

9.4.5 Step 5: Execution and Tracking

On the day of pickup, the broker's job is to keep everyone informed and to intervene if things go off track.

The carrier's dispatcher tells the broker when the driver is on the way to the port. In many cases, the broker can see this in real time through GPS integrations or the carrier's telematics. At a minimum, the broker gets phone or text updates.

If the port is congested, cranes go down, or a sudden security alert halts gate operations, the broker must relay this to the forwarder and, if necessary, renegotiate appointment times with the destination.

For forwarders, this information flows into their broader visibility systems. They may be tracking vessels, containers, customs clearance, and inland trucks all together. The broker's updates are a critical piece of that puzzle.

A useful picture is air traffic control for one truckload. The air traffic controller does not fly the plane, but tracks its position, watches for conflicts, and coordinates with pilots and other controllers to keep things safe and on schedule. The broker plays a similar role for each load they manage.

9.4.6 Step 6: Delivery, POD, and Invoicing

At the delivery point, the driver hands over the goods or the container and obtains a proof of delivery, usually a signed delivery receipt or a signed copy of the bill of lading.

Many carriers now use mobile apps to take a photo of the signed document and send it instantly to the broker. Others email scans or even fax them, though fax is fading.

The broker checks the documents and confirms that the service was completed as agreed. They verify any accessorial charges, such as extra waiting time, that the carrier wants to bill.

Then the broker sends an invoice to the customer for 1,200 dollars and logs the carrier's bill for 900 or 950 or whatever was agreed. Payment terms can vary. Brokers might pay carriers within 30 days and get paid by customers in 45, which means they carry some cash risk.

If extra costs have eaten into the margin, the broker sees it on that single load profit and loss statement. Multiply that by hundreds or thousands of loads per month and you get a sense of the real business of brokerage: a constant balancing act between service, risk, and thin margins.

9.5 Freight Forwarder vs Freight Broker vs 3PL: How They Work Together

Now that you have a feel for a broker's day, it helps to zoom back out and see how brokers fit alongside freight forwarders and third-party logistics providers, often called 3PLs.

9.5.1 Clear Definitions Side by Side

A freight broker focuses on arranging road freight, usually domestic or regional. Their typical scope is a single leg of a journey, such as port to warehouse. They do not take possession of the goods and usually do not operate warehouses.

A freight forwarder designs and manages end-to-end international shipments. They coordinate multiple legs and modes, from truck pick-up at a factory to vessel or aircraft booking, customs clearance, and final delivery. They often handle export and import documents, consolidate shipments, and may own or lease warehouse space.

A 3PL is a broader outsourced logistics provider. A 3PL might design and operate distribution centers, manage inventory, run domestic transportation planning, and sometimes include forwarding and brokerage services within one contract. They often work on multi-year agreements with large shippers, acting almost like the shipper's logistics department.

The lines can blur, because some companies hold all three roles in different situations, but the core focus of each is different.

9.5.2 An Analogy from Music

Think of a large international concert tour.

The tour manager is like the freight forwarder. They plan the route from city to city and country to country. They book flights, arrange visas, and make sure the band and crew have hotels and equipment at each stop.

The booking agent for local transportation in each city is like the freight broker. They arrange buses to move people from the airport to the venue, trucks to move equipment from warehouse to stage, and sometimes local drivers with special knowledge of tricky streets.

The event management company that handles the whole production, including staging, local crew, storage, and security, is like a 3PL. They may subcontract forwarders and brokers, but from the band's perspective, they are the main point of contact.

The musicians, finally, are the carriers. They are the ones who actually perform, or in logistics terms, actually move the cargo.

9.5.3 How Forwarders Use Freight Brokers

Freight forwarders rarely run their own trucking fleets in every country. It is expensive and complicated. Instead, they design the overall route, then plug in trucking capacity at origin and destination.

Those inland legs are often called pre-carriage and on-carriage.

Pre-carriage is the move from the factory or warehouse to the port or airport at origin. On-carriage is the move from the port or airport at destination to the final warehouse or consignee.

Forwarders could build direct relationships with hundreds of small and midsize carriers for these legs. Some do, especially on key lanes. Many others choose to work with brokers who already manage those carrier networks. It is a classic "buy vs build" decision.

Consider a shipment of auto parts from a plant near Wrocław in Poland to a retailer's DC near Valencia in Spain.

A forwarder in Poland might:

Arrange a local truck (possibly via a Polish broker) to pick up pallets from the plant and deliver them to the Port of Gdańsk. Book an ocean feeder to a main port, then a larger vessel to Barcelona. Work with their Spanish office or partner to arrange customs clearance. Have that Spanish office hire a local broker to book trucks from Barcelona port to regional distribution centers in Spain.

From the shipper's point of view, they are dealing with a forwarder handling the whole move. Under the surface, several brokers and many carriers may have played a part.

9.5.4 How 3PLs Fit In

A 3PL often acts as a logistics architect and operator for a shipper. A large retailer, for instance, might contract a 3PL to:

Operate multiple warehouses. Manage inventory and order picking. Plan and execute transportation from DCs to stores or to end customers.

To achieve this, the 3PL might:

Use its own trucking fleet for some lanes. Use its own in-house brokerage division for additional road capacity. Use its own forwarding division for international shipments.

Companies like DHL Supply Chain, XPO, and Kuehne + Nagel have multiple legal entities within the same corporate group. One entity might be a registered freight forwarder, another a licensed broker, another a carrier.

From the outside, it can be confusing. What matters is understanding which legal role is being played on each leg of your shipment, because that affects who holds responsibility and what rules apply.

9.5.5 Incoterms and Who Hires Whom

Incoterms, which we covered earlier in the book, describe who is responsible for transport, risk, and cost at different points of an international move.

Those responsibilities strongly influence where brokers and forwarders step in.

Under FOB (Free On Board) at the origin port, the seller delivers the goods to the port in their country and clears export customs. From that point, the buyer is responsible. Usually the buyer or their forwarder arranges the ocean freight and the inland haul at destination, often hiring a broker for the trucking leg.

Under CFR or CIF, the seller pays for main carriage to the destination port. The buyer often takes over from that port onward. Once again, a local broker on the buyer's side might handle the onward trucking.

Under DDP (Delivered Duty Paid), the seller is responsible for getting the goods all the way to the buyer's door, including import customs and taxes. In that case, the seller's forwarder often manages the entire chain and hires brokers and carriers in the buyer's country to perform inland legs.

Visualizing a timeline helps. From left to right: factory, origin truck, origin port, vessel, destination port, destination truck, final warehouse. At different points, control passes from supplier to buyer based on Incoterms. Forwarders, brokers, and carriers plug into those points based on who is paying and who holds risk at each stage.

9.5.6 Common Collaboration Patterns

Three patterns appear again and again in modern trade.

Pattern 1: Classic import. A retailer in Country B buys goods FOB from a supplier in Country A. The retailer hires a forwarder in Country B. That forwarder books the vessel, handles customs on arrival, and hires a drayage broker to move containers from the port to the retailer's DCs.

Pattern 2: Exporter using a 3PL. A manufacturer outsources its finished goods warehouse to a 3PL. The 3PL receives goods from the factory, stores them, and ships orders. For international orders, the 3PL works with a forwarder to book ocean or air freight, and uses internal or external brokers to move freight to ports and to domestic customers.

Pattern 3: E-commerce brand with digital brokers. A direct-to-consumer brand imports small batches by air using a forwarder. For domestic deliveries to Amazon facilities or regional fulfillment centers, the brand's logistics team connects directly to a digital freight platform. They get instant quotes and book truckloads online, often without talking to a human broker unless something goes wrong.

In each case, freight brokers are solving road-transport puzzles, while forwarders and 3PLs design and manage the broader network.

9.6 When Should You Use a Freight Broker, Forwarder, or 3PL?

Understanding all these roles is useful only if you can act on it. The good news is that a simple set of rules will guide most decisions.

9.6.1 A Simple Decision Guide

If your shipment is domestic, moves only by road, and is relatively straightforward, your first call can be to a freight broker. They can arrange TL or LTL capacity and handle the day-to-day details of matching loads with trucks.

If your shipment crosses borders by ocean or air, you should start with a freight forwarder. The forwarder understands customs, international carriers, and multimodal handoffs. They will often hire brokers for inland trucking at origin and destination, so you do not have to.

If your business needs ongoing warehousing, regular distribution, and someone to manage your logistics strategy, a 3PL becomes attractive. They can design your network and then, within that, act as a forwarder, a broker, and sometimes a carrier.

You do not need to know the name of every trucking company in your country. You do need to know which kind of partner to call first.

9.6.2 Evaluating a Freight Broker

Not all brokers are created equal. Price is important, but it should not be the only factor.

When you talk with a potential broker, ask questions such as:

How long have you been operating on the lanes that matter to me? How do you vet your carriers? Which safety and insurance checks do you perform before you give them loads? Can you share references from customers with similar freight? What technology do you use for tracking and communication? Will I get proactive updates or will I need to chase you? How do you handle claims if cargo is damaged or lost? What happens when a carrier fails to show up?

Be wary of rates that are dramatically lower than others. Underpriced loads often attract less reliable carriers or cut corners around safety and service. Also be wary if a broker seems vague about their operating authority, cannot explain their carrier vetting process, or is already slow to respond before you even give them business.

Communication is a leading indicator. If they will not answer emails and calls before they land your freight, they are unlikely to suddenly become responsive afterwards.

9.6.3 Building Strong Partnerships Between Forwarders and Brokers

Forwarders and brokers work best together when they understand each other's constraints.

Forwarders should look for brokers who:

Know port and rail terminal operations, including appointment systems and free-time rules. Understand the types of cargo the forwarder typically handles, such as reefer goods or high-value electronics. Can commit to response times on quotes and clear escalation paths when something goes wrong.

Brokers should learn:

The forwarder's cutoffs with ports, airlines, and rail operators. If a container misses a gate-in time, it can miss an entire vessel. Documentation cycles. For example, when customs exams or holds are likely, and how that affects trucking windows.

Brokers that offer transparent pricing, clear invoices, and timely status updates become trusted parts of a forwarder's toolkit. Forwarders that share realistic forecasts, give early warning of special projects, and pay on time become preferred customers for brokers and, by extension, for the carriers they bring into the picture.

9.7 The Future of Freight Brokerage and Returning to Maya

9.7.1 Digitalization and the "Uberization" of Trucking

Freight brokerage is changing rapidly.

Transportation management systems, known as TMS software, are now standard at many brokers. Digital load boards provide real-time pricing signals. Brokers integrate directly with carrier GPS systems and driver apps. Algorithms suggest which carrier is most likely to accept a load at what rate.

Dynamic pricing, where rates adjust hour by hour based on supply and demand, is spreading. Shippers and forwarders expect self-service portals, online tracking, and electronic documents instead of faxed pages and phone calls.

Traditional brokers face pressure to modernize. Many are responding by combining their relationship skills with new tools. Others are being squeezed out by larger, more tech-savvy competitors.

Despite all this, humans still matter. A snowstorm that closes highways, a labor strike that shuts a port, or an earthquake that damages infrastructure are not easily handled by algorithms alone. When things go wrong, shippers still want a person who understands the context, can negotiate with carriers, and can make judgment calls.

9.7.2 Sustainability and Compliance Pressures

Environmental and regulatory pressures are shaping brokers' work as well.

Many large shippers now track the carbon footprint of their transport. They ask brokers to provide information about carrier fuel efficiency, equipment age, and options to shift some freight to lower-emission modes such as intermodal rail.

Governments keep tightening rules on driver working hours, emissions standards, and safety equipment. Compliance is no longer optional.

In this environment, brokers help shippers and forwarders find carriers that meet stricter standards, whether that means Euro 6 trucks in Europe, California's emissions rules in the United States, or local regulations elsewhere. They also help design routes and mode combinations that balance cost, speed, and sustainability.

9.7.3 Closing the Loop: Maya's Friday Afternoon

Return to that Friday afternoon in New Jersey.

Maya put down her phone after her forwarder said, "I will call a broker I trust." For her, the story skipped straight from that sentence to seeing a truck pull into the retailer's DC on Monday morning.

What actually happened in between looked more like this.

At 4:10 p.m., the broker's operations team pulled up internal data on carriers that serve Port Newark. They checked which ones had drivers who liked weekend work and who had delivered before to that particular retailer's DC, which was known for tight appointment windows.

By 4:15, they had posted the load to a regional load board and were already getting responses. They checked each carrier's FMCSA safety status and insurance, looked at recent on-time performance in their TMS, and chose a drayage carrier that had a clean record and a driver finishing a run only 15 miles from the port.

At 4:20, the broker sent a rate confirmation to the carrier and a load confirmation to the forwarder. The driver received instructions on a mobile app with the container number, terminal details, and delivery ETA.

On Saturday morning, the driver fought through a busy terminal, waited longer than expected at the gate, and pulled the container. The broker monitored progress and twice updated the forwarder, who updated Maya.

On Monday at 9:37 a.m., the driver backed up to the dock door at the DC, the staff unloaded the pallets, and someone in the warehouse signed a proof of delivery.

A few days later, Maya saw a line on an invoice: "Port drayage, Newark to DC, 1,200 dollars."

For her, that line was a cost. For the broker, it was the visible tip of a job that involved data checks, risk calculations, relationship calls, and tight coordination in a crowded port.

Next time you pass a truck on the highway or see a container stacked at a terminal, it is worth remembering that many of those trucks and containers did not end up where they are by accident. Somewhere, often in a modest office filled with phones and screens, a broker was making sure a truck and a load met each other on time.

9.7.4 Case Study: When Truck Capacity Disappears

In 2017, a large consumer goods company in the United States learned what a trucking capacity crunch feels like from the inside.[14]

The company ran several factories in the Midwest and shipped full truckloads of toiletries and cleaning products to distribution centers across the country. For years, truck capacity felt abundant. Procurement focused almost entirely on getting a slightly lower rate per mile from carriers and brokers.

Then, a combination of factors hit at once:

- New electronic logging device (ELD) rules tightened enforcement of driver hours of service limits.

---

[14]

This composite example reflects the well documented tight truckload market following the rollout of Electronic Logging Device (ELD) enforcement and strong freight demand in 2017–2018; see FMCSA ELD rule materials and industry analyses from ATA and trade press.

- A strong economy pulled drivers into competing sectors such as construction.
- Hurricanes disrupted capacity in the Southeast, pulling trucks away from the Midwest to support relief efforts.

Over a few months, the company's long standing carriers and brokers began saying a word procurement was not used to hearing: "no."

Loads that once received several bids now attracted none. When trucks were available, rates were far higher than contracted prices. Some carriers simply refused to honor old rates, preferring to take better paying spot loads elsewhere.

The company's outbound planners watched as:

- Trailers loaded with finished goods sat in yard spots for days waiting for a driver.
- Orders to key retailers were missed or shipped partial.
- Inventory built up in factories even as store shelves for some items thinned.

At first, managers blamed individual brokers and carriers. "Why are you abandoning us?" But capacity crunches are market phenomena, not personal decisions. Everyone in the industry was short of drivers and equipment.

With help from a senior broker, the company shifted tactics.

- They created a "must move" list of critical lanes and products and communicated it clearly to brokers and carriers. Non essential loads were allowed to slip or to use slower intermodal options.
- They accepted temporary rate increases on that must move list in exchange for capacity commitments and daily status calls.
- They began using a mix of brokers instead of relying almost entirely on direct carrier contracts, gaining access to smaller carriers that the brokers knew and trusted.
- Longer term, they redesigned their network to add a few regional mixing centers, reducing the average length of haul and making it easier to cover loads with local or regional carriers.

The crisis lasted months, not days. There was no magic tap that could be turned back on. What changed was the company's understanding of how fragile "cheap trucking" can be when the wider system is tight.

For forwarders and shippers, the lesson is that trucking capacity can disappear suddenly due to regulation, weather, or demand spikes. When it does, the relationships and information channels you have built with brokers and carriers matter far more than the last half cent per mile you squeezed out of a rate bid.

9.7.5 Quick Recap

To fix the key points in your memory, keep this short list in mind:

- A freight broker connects shippers and trucking carriers, primarily for road freight, and usually does not touch the cargo.
- Brokers earn money on the spread between what they pay carriers and what they charge shippers, but they earn their keep through speed, flexibility, and careful vetting of carriers.
- There are many types of brokers: TL, LTL, specialized (such as reefer, hazmat, oversize, and drayage), and digital platforms that use apps and algorithms.
- Freight forwarders design and manage international, multimodal journeys and often hire brokers for inland truck legs at origin and destination.
- 3PLs provide broader outsourced logistics, including warehousing and transportation management, and may contain forwarding and brokerage functions under one roof.
- Incoterms and shipment design determine who is responsible for which legs of a move, and therefore which mix of forwarders, brokers, 3PLs, and carriers you will work with.

One last image. Think of global logistics as an orchestra.

The freight forwarder is the conductor who holds the score for the whole performance. The freight broker is the agent who finds the right musicians for each part, especially the ones who play on the road. The 3PL is the organizer that books the concert hall, manages rehearsals, and sells the tickets. The carriers are the musicians, playing the notes that everyone else has arranged.

Without the broker, many of the right musicians would never make it to the stage, at least not on time or at the right price. Understanding that quiet role will help you design smarter, more resilient logistics for your own business or career.

Field Guide: Freight Brokers and Truck Capacity

Key concepts

- Freight brokers match shippers and trucking carriers, usually without owning trucks, and earn a margin on each load.
- Brokers specialize by freight type and lane, from port drayage to long haul dry van, reefers, flatbeds, and LTL consolidation.
- Reliable brokers vet carriers for safety, insurance, and service quality, not just price.

- Forwarders often rely on brokers to cover inland legs at origin and destination, especially in volatile markets.
- Capacity cycles in trucking can swing quickly; relationships and information flow are as important as rate levels.

Common mistakes

- Treating brokers as interchangeable spot rate vendors with no long term partnership.
- Awarding freight solely on lowest rate and then being surprised by no shows, damage, or poor communication.
- Failing to share realistic forecasts and priorities with brokers, leaving them to guess which loads really matter.
- Using one broker for everything and assuming they can cover any lane or freight type equally well.
- Ignoring compliance and safety signals in favor of small rate savings.

Warning signs

- Frequent last minute pleas for trucks on loads that were visible days in advance.
- A pattern of missed pickup appointments, blown delivery windows, or incomplete status updates.
- Brokers that cannot clearly explain how they vet carriers or what authority they operate under.
- Invoices that do not match agreed rates or that hide key accessorials and surcharges.
- Heavy reliance on one or two carriers or brokers in a region with no tested backups.

Practical shortcuts

- Keep a simple scorecard for your main brokers: on time pickup, on time delivery, communication quality, and claim handling, not just price.
- Segment your freight into "must move" and "flexible" and tell brokers which is which so they can allocate capacity intelligently in tight markets.
- Use more than one broker on critical regions or freight types so that you are not exposed if one network hits a limit.
- Review carrier and broker performance jointly with your forwarder at least once a year to align lanes, expectations, and rates.

If You Only Remember Three Things

1. Freight brokers are the specialists of truck capacity, connecting loads and carriers in a volatile, fragmented market that most shippers cannot navi-

gate alone.

2. The value of a broker lies as much in carrier vetting, problem solving, and communication as in the rate per mile on any single load.

3. In a crunch, the relationships and information you have built with brokers and carriers matter more than the last cent you shaved off a rate sheet.

Chapter 10: Top Paying Supply Chain Jobs and Careers

10.1 The 5 Dollar T Shirt and the 150,000 Dollar Career

A college student in Liverpool once held up a bright blue T shirt in a discount store and laughed at the price tag. Five dollars. Cheaper than a sandwich. The label said, in tiny letters, "Made in Bangladesh."

A week later that same student sat in a guest lecture about global logistics. The speaker pulled up a slide of a cotton field in Texas and said, "Some of you are wearing T shirts that have already paid for a few people's salaries on this slide."

He traced the journey.

Cotton grown in Texas, picked, baled, and shipped in bulk to a spinning mill in Gujarat. Yarn sent to a fabric factory in Dhaka. Fabric cut and sewn in a garment plant outside the city, then packed into cardboard boxes. A freight forwarder in Chittagong booked space on a container ship and arranged export customs clearance. Containers loaded at the port, crossed the Indian Ocean, passed through the Suez Canal, and reached the Port of Felixstowe.

There, a terminal planner decided which crane would unload that specific container and where it would sit in the yard. A customs broker in the United Kingdom submitted electronic entries, matched HS codes to the correct duty rates, and cleared the load. A truck picked up the container and hauled it to a distribution center. A logistics manager who might never touch a box in their daily work had already designed that warehouse network, chosen that carrier, and agreed on delivery times and penalties.

Weeks later, the box arrived at that discount store in Liverpool. The shirt went on a hanger. Price: 5 dollars.

Behind that price, at least half a dozen people along the way were making more than 80,000 dollars a year. Some crossed 150,000 dollars once bonuses and stock options were counted. None of them were sewing the shirt or driving the truck. They were planners, negotiators, problem solvers, and risk managers.

Most shoppers never think about them. They see a cheap shirt, not a quiet six figure career.

Global logistics and supply chains move tens of trillions of dollars of goods every year. In this world, experienced supply chain managers, logistics directors, and senior freight forwarding leaders in major markets such as the United States or Western Europe often earn total annual compensation somewhere in the broad range of 80,000 to 130,000 dollars or more. Actual salaries vary widely by country, city, industry, company size, and cost of living, but the pattern is clear. When value moves, there is room for people who know how to move it safely and cheaply to be well paid.

You rarely see these careers on television. There is no prime time drama about a customs classification dispute, or a romantic comedy set in a container yard. Most of the interesting action happens in warehouses, port control rooms, and spreadsheet tabs. The work is essential yet almost invisible. People only pay attention when things break, like during the COVID 19 pandemic, when ships waited outside ports for weeks and supermarkets ran out of basics.

For the people who understand how this logistics system works, that invisibility is an advantage. They can earn well, work with companies on every continent, and move between industries such as fashion, electronics, retail, and humanitarian aid.

In this world, supply chain professionals design how goods move. They decide which suppliers to use, which ports and carriers to trust, and how much to spend on speed versus risk. The more you master the rules covered in this book, from the forwarding steps in Chapter 2 to the cost and Incoterm ideas in Chapters 6 and 7, the more room you have to shape results and earn well.

If this world is so important and often well paid, the next question is obvious: where exactly are the highest earning roles, and what do the people in them actually do all day?

The rest of this chapter pulls back that curtain.

Figure 21: Supply Chain Decision Making

10.2 Where the Money Is: Top Paying Supply Chain Jobs

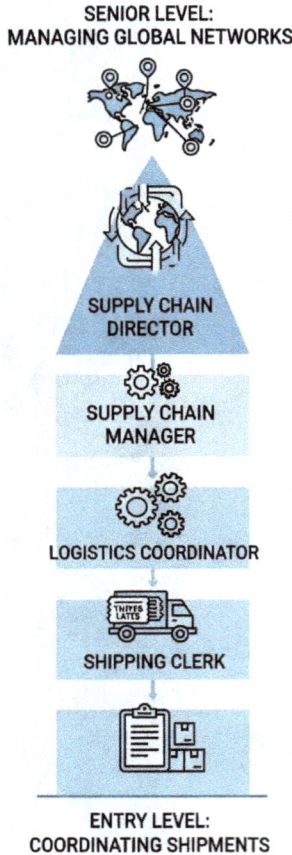

Figure 22: Supply Chain Career Progression

Salaries look different in Shanghai, Rotterdam, Lagos, and Chicago, but the pattern is similar. Early in a career, people work in support roles. They coordinate shipments, handle paperwork, and track containers. Mid career brings specialist or manager roles. Senior people run departments, negotiate contracts worth millions, and design entire networks.

This section does not list every job title in the industry. Instead, it highlights roles that often sit in the better paid band and that make heavy use of the ideas in this book.

10.2.1 Supply Chain Manager and Supply Chain Director

Supply chain managers and directors sit inside manufacturers, retailers, and brand owners. They have broad responsibility for how materials and finished goods flow through the business.

Typical responsibilities include:

- Designing and improving the supply chain network: where to place factories, warehouses, and suppliers.
- Planning inventory levels and replenishment strategies.
- Selecting and managing logistics partners, such as forwarders, 3PLs, and carriers.
- Coordinating with sales, finance, and production to align supply and demand.

At larger companies, directors and heads of supply chain often manage teams across multiple countries. Their decisions affect service levels to customers, working capital, and profitability.

10.2.2 Logistics Director or Head of Logistics

Logistics leaders focus more narrowly on the movement and storage of goods.

They:

- Oversee warehousing and distribution center operations.
- Manage transport contracts and routing between sites.
- Set policies for packaging, labeling, and returns.
- Work closely with forwarders and carriers on performance and cost.

In a retail chain, the head of logistics might be responsible for every shipment from distribution centers to stores. In an industrial company, they might handle inbound components and outbound finished goods worldwide.

10.2.3 Freight Forwarding Operations Manager or Branch Manager

Inside a freight forwarder, operations managers and branch managers are the people who turn global trade into a working daily business.

An operations manager typically:

- Leads teams that handle bookings, documentation, and customer service.
- Ensures shipments are handled correctly and on time.
- Resolves issues with carriers, customs, and ports.

A branch manager or country manager:

- Owns the profit and loss for a local office.

- Manages sales, operations, and administration.
- Builds relationships with key customers and overseas offices.

Forwarding leadership roles reward people who combine technical knowledge of trade with strong people and commercial skills.

10.2.4 Procurement Manager and Strategic Sourcing Manager

Procurement and sourcing managers decide which suppliers a company uses and on what terms.

They:

- Run tenders for raw materials and components.
- Negotiate contracts with suppliers and logistics providers.
- Evaluate total landed cost, not just purchase price.

Because they control large spend, their decisions have big financial impact. People who can weigh supplier risk, logistics constraints, and currency exposure alongside price become valuable quickly.

10.2.5 High Pay Roles in Ports and Network Design

Ports, terminals, and large logistics companies employ specialists in network design and engineering.

Examples include:

- Network planners who decide where to place distribution centers and which routes to operate.
- Port operations managers who optimize cranes, yard flows, and berth planning.
- Intermodal network designers who integrate road, rail, and barge services.

These roles often require strong quantitative and systems skills. They sit at the intersection of operations, finance, and strategy and can be well compensated, especially in major hubs.

10.2.6 Niche Areas: Cold Chain, Project Cargo, and Dangerous Goods

Specialized areas pay well because they are harder to master and riskier to get wrong.

Cold chain managers design and run temperature controlled networks for food and pharmaceuticals. Project cargo specialists handle one off moves of oversized or heavy equipment, such as turbines and refinery modules. Dangerous goods experts make sure hazardous materials move safely and compliantly.

In all three cases, deep technical knowledge and careful planning are essential. Mistakes can destroy cargo, harm people, or cause regulatory trouble. Employers pay for people who can avoid those outcomes.

10.2.7 Why Technical Plus Business Skills Pay Best

Across all these roles, a pattern appears. The best paid people are not pure technicians and not pure generalists. They combine:

- Technical understanding of trade, transport, and regulation.
- Comfort with data and financials.
- The ability to explain options and trade offs to non specialists.

Someone who can talk to both an engineer and a finance director and make each feel understood will usually move faster in this field than someone who speaks only one of those languages.

10.3 Careers Inside Freight Forwarding and Port Logistics

The previous section surveyed roles across many types of employers. This section zooms in on two settings that appear constantly in this book: freight forwarders and ports.

10.3.1 Life Inside a Freight Forwarder

At entry level, people inside forwarders often start as:

- Operations coordinators.
- Documentation clerks.
- Customer service representatives.

Their days are full of concrete tasks:

- Booking space with carriers.
- Issuing bills of lading and air waybills.
- Checking that commercial invoices and packing lists match reality.
- Updating customers when shipments clear or encounter problems.

It can feel repetitive at first, but it is one of the fastest ways to learn how trade really works. You see dozens of shipments, Incoterms, HS codes, and quotes each week.

With experience, people move into:

- Team leader and supervisor roles.
- Key account management for major customers.
- Trade lane management, focusing on specific routes.

Later, branch, country, and regional leadership roles open up. These jobs combine staff management, profit and loss responsibility, and strategy. Many senior leaders in the forwarding industry started in operations as teenagers or in their early twenties.

10.3.2 Paths Upward: From Entry Level to Leadership

A simple forwarding career path might look like this:

Operations assistant → operations coordinator → senior coordinator or supervisor → operations manager → branch manager → country manager.

Along the way, people often:

- Specialize in certain cargo types, for example reefer or dangerous goods.
- Take on sales or pricing responsibilities.
- Spend time in different departments such as air, ocean, or customs brokerage.

Because forwarders operate globally, international postings are common. A coordinator in Manila might later run a branch in Dubai or Hamburg.

10.3.3 Working in Port Logistics

Ports employ a mix of technical, operational, and commercial staff.

Examples include:

- Vessel planners who decide how to load and discharge ships.
- Yard planners who manage container stacks and equipment.
- Gate supervisors who oversee truck flows.
- Commercial managers who negotiate contracts with shipping lines and terminal users.

Some roles are shift based and physically located at terminals. Others sit in planning offices, working with simulation models and performance dashboards.

Senior port and terminal roles can be well paid, especially at large global operators. They appeal to people who like visible, physical results and do not mind working in industrial environments.

10.4 Skills and Credentials That Drive Supply Chain Careers

10.4.1 Core Skills: Your Starter Pack

Several skills show up in almost every supply chain job description:

- Clear communication, written and spoken.

- Comfort with numbers and spreadsheets.
- Attention to detail in documents and data.
- Ability to stay calm and structured under time pressure.

You do not need to be a mathematician, but you do need to be comfortable with basic arithmetic, percentages, and reading charts and tables.

10.4.2 High Value Knowledge Areas

Knowledge that pays off across many roles includes:

- Incoterms and how they divide cost and risk.
- HS codes and the basics of customs classification.
- How to read freight quotes and calculate total landed cost.
- The main transport modes and how to compare them, from Chapter 3 and Chapter 6.

Learning these does not require a degree. Many people pick them up on the job or through focused short courses. What matters is that you can apply them in real situations, not just recite definitions.

10.4.3 Education and Credentials

Formal education helps, but there is no single required degree.

Common routes include:

- Bachelor's degrees in supply chain, logistics, operations management, business, or engineering.
- Short courses and certificates from industry bodies, such as APICS and CIPS.
- Specialized programs in customs brokerage, dangerous goods, or cold chain.

In many markets, experience and performance count more than titles. A coordinator who consistently solves customers' problems and learns quickly often advances faster than someone with more credentials but less initiative.

10.4.4 Logistics as a Dynamic, Global, Well Paid Career

Logistics and supply chain careers combine several advantages:

- They exist in almost every industry and country.
- They touch real products and real customers.
- They offer routes into leadership roles that shape corporate strategy.

Ecommerce keeps growing. Manufacturing shifts from country to country. Climate and regulation are forcing supply chains to adapt. Each of these trends creates demand for people who understand how goods move, what it costs, and how to keep flows resilient.

10.5 Chapter Wrap Up: Designing Your Own Supply Chain Career

The landscape is wide.

High paying roles sit at the top of supply chain management and logistics leadership in manufacturers, retailers, and technology companies. Freight forwarding offers its own ladder, from operations and documentation up to branch, country, and regional management. Specialized segments such as cold chain, project cargo, and dangerous goods reward deep technical knowledge with strong salaries. Ports, network design, and consulting add more options, each with its own mix of technical, operational, and strategic work.

If you are a student, you can test the waters through internships at freight forwarders, third party logistics providers, or port authorities. A summer spent in a warehouse or documentation office will teach you more about global trade than a year of reading headlines. Degrees in supply chain or related fields can help, but even a general business or engineering degree becomes more valuable if you aim it at this industry.

If you are early in your career, consider moving into operations, documentation, or customer service within a logistics setting. These jobs are not glamorous, but they are rich in learning. Set yourself a goal to master Incoterms, basic HS classification, and straightforward shipping cost calculations within your first year. Ask to sit in on rate negotiations or network planning meetings. Find mentors who work in the roles you admire and ask them what skills they wish they had built earlier.

If you run a small business, building your own logistics knowledge can change your bottom line. Understanding Incoterms and duty rates allows you to negotiate more confidently with freight forwarders and suppliers. Knowing how to read a freight quote, identify surcharges, and compare total landed costs can save meaningful money. These skills do more than cut your current bills. They become part of your personal toolkit, which you can carry into consulting, teaching, or a later corporate role.

Understanding supply chains is a bit like having an invisible superpower. You walk into a supermarket and see not just shelves, but paths: ships, planes, warehouses, customs screens, and spreadsheets behind each product. You notice that the "cheap" T shirt has already paid for port planners, freight forwarders, customs brokers, and logistics directors. You know where the money went, and you can see how to move that money more wisely.

Used well, this superpower lets you build a career that is both stable and varied. One year you might be cutting shipping costs. The next you might be helping launch a new product in a new market, or getting medical supplies into a crisis zone, or reducing the carbon footprint of a distribution network.

Supply chain, freight forwarding, and logistics are not just about boxes and trucks. They are about people who make the world's trade work reliably in the background while the rest of the world gets on with daily life. Many of them are paid very well to do so.

With the right mix of knowledge, practical skill, and curiosity, you can join them. The 5 dollar T shirt on the rack is not just the end of a journey. It can be the starting point of a career.

Field Guide: Building a Logistics Career

Key concepts

- Logistics, forwarding, and port roles exist in many industries and countries, from manufacturing and retail to tech and humanitarian work.
- The best paid professionals usually combine operational experience, technical knowledge of trade and transport, and comfort with financial and data tools.
- Career paths are flexible: people move between shippers, forwarders, brokers, ports, 3PLs, and consulting over time.
- Early exposure to real operations (warehouses, documentation, planning) builds credibility and insight that classroom work alone cannot match.
- Skills in Incoterms, HS codes, cost breakdowns, and network design travel well between employers.

Common mistakes

- Chasing job titles that sound prestigious but offer little real learning about how freight and supply chains work.
- Avoiding entry level operations roles because they seem repetitive, and then struggling later to understand practical constraints.
- Treating logistics as a temporary stop instead of investing in skills that compound across roles and employers.
- Ignoring the financial side of logistics decisions, such as landed cost and working capital, and focusing only on activity and volume.
- Assuming that only large, global companies offer interesting careers,

when many mid sized firms and forwarders provide faster responsibility growth.

Warning signs

- Job descriptions that mix many functions without clear priorities, suggesting a role that will struggle to make an impact.
- Employers that treat logistics purely as a cost center, with no interest in service quality, resilience, or careers for operations staff.
- A resume heavy on buzzwords but light on specific, measurable improvements or experiences.
- Hiring processes that never connect you with future colleagues in operations or planning roles.
- A career plan that depends on one narrow niche with no adjacent skills.

Practical shortcuts

- In your first logistics role, aim to master a small set of fundamentals within 12 months: Incoterms, basic HS classification, reading quotes, and mapping a shipment from door to door.
- When considering jobs, ask each employer how they train staff, move people between roles, and involve operations in decisions about customers and networks.
- Keep a simple log of projects where you reduced cost, improved reliability, or simplified a process; that log becomes evidence for promotions and future job searches.
- Use this book as a checklist for knowledge gaps and pick one chapter at a time to connect to your current work, whether that is ports, costs, or cold chain.

If You Only Remember Three Things

1. Logistics and freight forwarding offer broad, well paid careers for people who like concrete results, complex systems, and practical problem solving.
2. The combination of operations experience, trade and cost literacy, and clear communication puts you on the short list for leadership roles.
3. You do not need a perfect starting point; you do need to start somewhere, learn deliberately, and keep turning everyday shipments into lasting skills.

Chapter 11: Thinking Like a Freight Forwarder

11.1 Opening: The Day the Container Did Not Arrive

Think back to Maria's candle shipment in Chapter 7. Her first big export order to Europe should have been a win. Instead she met customs holds, unclear Incoterms, surprise charges at destination, and a missed promotion window.

In that chapter, you saw the story from Maria's point of view. Quotes that looked similar on the surface. An HS code copied from a blog. A casual "CIF" in a contract that nobody really unpacked. A moment when she realized her candles were physically in Europe but not in the right place, at the right time, or under the costs she expected.

This chapter is not about retelling that story. It is about looking at the same shipment through a different lens: how a competent freight forwarder or logistics planner would have thought about it before anything moved.

A good forwarder would look at Maria's shipment and immediately ask different questions:

- What is the business promise? Who needs what, where, by when, and at what acceptable total cost?
- How does the shipment actually flow, step by step, from her warehouse in Ohio to the retailer's distribution center in Germany?
- Which Incoterm makes sense for a small exporter selling to a large retailer, and what is the named place?
- Who is responsible for customs clearance, documentation, and HS classification on each side of the ocean?
- Where could delays, disputes, or surprise costs appear, and how can we design around them in advance?

Maria's pain points were not random. They came from skipping this kind of structured thinking and treating logistics like a black box you "book" with a single cheap quote.

This chapter is about the opposite mindset. You will turn the hidden machinery behind Maria's experience into a set of mental models and simple tools you can use yourself.

11.2 The Freight Forwarder Mindset in One Page

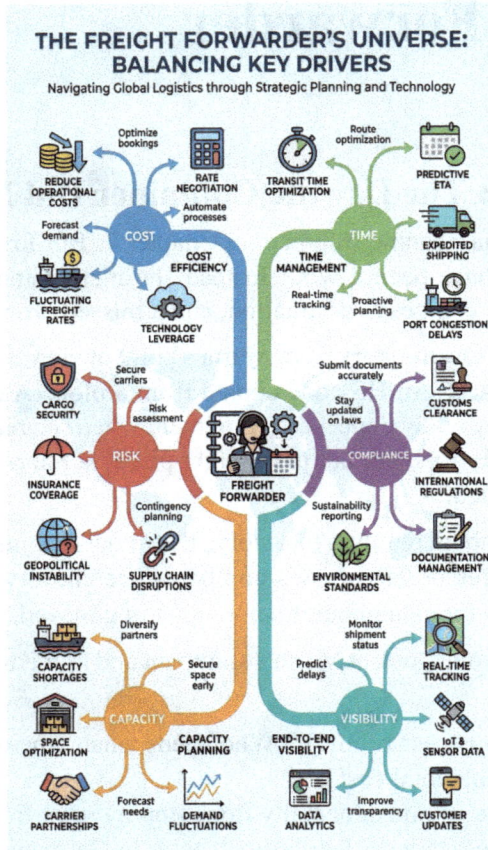

Figure 23: The Freight Forwarder Mindset

A freight forwarder does not own the ship, the truck, or the plane. The forwarder is the organizer in the middle, the one who turns a buyer's promise and a seller's product into a physical journey from origin to destination.

For a typical international shipment, that journey follows the seven steps you met in Chapter 2. Goods move from the factory to a warehouse at origin, clear export customs, are handled and packed into a container or unit, travel on a ship or aircraft, clear import customs, are handled again, and finally travel over land to the customer.

The forwarder makes those steps join up. They book trucks, arrange warehouses, file documents, and coordinate with shipping lines, airlines, customs brokers, and inland carriers.

Remember the school trip analogy from Chapter 2, with the freight forwarder as the teacher who organizes buses, tickets, and special requirements so everyone gets home safely. Keep that picture, but now pay more attention to how the teacher thinks than to the trip details.

Three simple mental models capture that thinking.

First, logistics as a flow. Think of goods as water in a pipe. The factory is the faucet. The customer is the sink. Every valve and bend in the pipe is a logistics step: export trucking, port handling, customs, ship schedule, inland delivery. If one valve gets blocked, the flow stops. A missing document, a closed highway, a congested terminal all have the same effect. Nothing moves.

Second, the forwarder as an orchestrator. Picture a conductor in front of an orchestra. The musicians know how to play, but someone has to set the tempo, cue entries, and hold the piece together. Each carrier, port, and warehouse is a section of that orchestra. The forwarder's work is not just booking one ship. It is sequencing all the players so that a box that left a factory in Ohio in September reaches a shelf in Munich in October.

Third, ports and ships as critical infrastructure. Ports are like global train stations and airports for goods. Ships are the long haul buses that connect continents. When Los Angeles or Rotterdam clogs up, that ripple spreads into factories in China, retailers in Europe, and small businesses everywhere. A forwarder watches those nodes closely, because that is where delays and extra costs often appear.

These mental models are useful in calm years and crucial in wild ones. They are how professionals made sense of 2020 and 2021, when ships waited outside ports, containers were in the wrong places, and rates spiked. When you read Chapter 12, you will see the same ideas, flow, orchestration, and nodes, playing out on a larger, noisier scale.

11.3 Designing a Simple End to End Shipping Plan

To think like a forwarder, you do not need complex software or a big team. You need a paper or digital page and some disciplined questions. Most professional forwarders now sit on top of transportation management systems, carrier portals, and APIs, but those tools only add value if someone is already asking the right questions about promises, routes, responsibilities, and costs.

11.3.1 Start with the Business Goal, Not the Container

Many people start planning with "how do I ship this pallet?" Forwarders start with "what is the business goal?"

For Maria's candles, the goal might be:

- Deliver 2,000 candles in time for a November promotion in Germany.
- Keep the total landed cost under a certain amount per candle.
- Avoid stock outs in the middle of the promotion.

This gives you a time window, a cost target, and a sensitivity to any delay.

11.3.2 Map the Physical Flow: The "Movie Timeline" of a Shipment

Next, you draw a simple timeline.

On one line, mark:

- Supplier or factory.
- Export warehouse.
- Origin port or airport.
- Vessel or flight.
- Destination port or airport.
- Destination warehouse or distribution center.
- Final delivery point.

Under each point, write who is responsible and what could go wrong. Is there a narrow river with draft limits? A congested port? A holiday that closes customs? A warehouse that only accepts deliveries on certain days?

This storyboard matches the seven step process from Chapter 2. You do not need a new list. Just keep that map in mind and check for blank scenes or mismatched responsibilities.

11.3.3 Choosing Modes of Transport: Speed, Cost, and Reliability

Forwarders constantly balance mode choices.

Air freight is fast and flexible but expensive. Ocean freight is slow but cheap per kilogram. Trucks and trains link inland points. Express couriers focus on parcels.

Chapter 3 walked through these tradeoffs. Here the point is how forwarders use them.

If you have a long lead time and stable demand, you might rely on ocean and rail, with a little air freight only for emergencies or product launches. If you have highly seasonal demand or unpredictable spikes, you might combine modes, shipping a base volume by sea and topping up with air or fast ocean services when needed.

Forwarders think in terms of value, urgency, volume, distance, and infrastructure. A pallet of high value electronics for a product launch justifies more speed and risk control than a pallet of low value spare parts with no fixed deadline.

11.3.4 Picking Ports and Routes: Why the Map Matters

Port and route choice is not just a geography question. It is a risk and cost question.

Two routes might look similar on a world map, but differ in:

- Port congestion patterns.
- Inland trucking and rail costs.
- Exposure to chokepoints such as Suez or Panama.
- Frequency of sailings and airline schedules.

Forwarders pay attention to these differences. They know, for example, that a slightly longer ocean leg to a less congested port with better rail links can beat a shorter leg to a crowded gateway that regularly generates storage and demurrage bills.

11.3.5 Selecting Incoterms to Match Your Business Model and Risk Tolerance

Incoterms are the shared rules that say who pays for what and who carries the risk at each point in the journey. Chapter 7 gave you a tour of codes such as EXW, FOB, CIF, and DAP. Here the focus is on choosing between them.

If you are a small exporter like Maria selling to a large retailer abroad, you might prefer to use FCA or FOB, handing control to the buyer at a known point, or DAP if your forwarder can give you door delivery at a predictable cost. If you are a large buyer with strong logistics expertise, you might insist on FOB or FCA so you control the main carriage and apply your own rates and routing.

The key is to match the Incoterm to your real capabilities. Do not offer DDP if you have no idea how to clear customs and pay taxes in the buyer's country. Do not accept EXW if you have no way to handle export filings where the seller is based.

11.3.6 Mapping Shipping Costs from Pickup to Final Delivery

From Chapter 6, you know that freight cost is a stack, not a single number. A forwarder level plan always includes a rough total landed cost.

On your shipment timeline, add:

- Origin trucking and handling.
- Export documentation and clearance.
- Main carriage by sea or air, with typical surcharges.
- Destination port or airport charges.
- Inland haulage and delivery.
- Duties, taxes, and insurance.

You do not need exact numbers at planning stage, but you do need an order of magnitude. That lets you see if a shipment is financially viable and how sensitive it is to rate swings or delay driven charges.

11.3.7 Special Cases: Cold Chain, Hazardous Goods, and Oversize Cargo

Some cargo types change the plan.

- Cold chain goods bring strict temperature requirements and more limited routing options.
- Hazardous materials demand special packaging, labeling, and carrier and port approvals.
- Oversize cargo constrains you to specific roads, ports, and equipment.

Forwarders treat these as separate "games" with their own rules and specialists. Recognizing when your cargo falls into one of these categories is the first step toward getting help early instead of scrambling late.

11.3.8 Pulling It All Together: A Mini End to End Plan for Maria

If Maria and a forwarder had applied this approach to her candle export, their plan might have looked like this:

- Business goal: candles arrive at the German retailer's distribution center two weeks before the promotion starts, with a maximum landed cost per unit that still leaves room for profit.
- Mode: ocean freight in a shared container for most of the volume, with a small air freight tranche as emergency backup if production slips.
- Route: truck from Ohio to an East Coast port with good Europe services and reasonable inland trucking from the destination port to the retailer's distribution center.

- Incoterm: DAP distribution center, with the retailer handling duties and taxes, clearly written on contracts and invoices.
- Documentation: HS code confirmed with a customs broker in both countries, labels checked for any European Union requirements on candles and fragrances, export filings assigned to the forwarder under power of attorney.
- Cost picture: rough total cost estimate including origin trucking, port fees, ocean rate, destination charges, and inland delivery, with a small buffer for inspections or minor delays.

A plan like this does not remove uncertainty, but it gives you a map. When the world lurches, as it did during the crises in Chapter 12, that map helps you steer instead of drift.

11.4 Avoiding Common Shipping and Compliance Mistakes

Maria's experience contained several classic errors. Forwarders see these patterns every week.

11.4.1 Story: One Container, Three Misunderstandings

Combine these real examples into one composite shipment.

An exporter in Asia agrees to sell machine parts "CIF Hamburg" but forgets to include the cost of insurance in the price and never actually buys a policy. A buyer in Europe assumes "CIF" covers door delivery, not just transport to port. A forwarder in between assumes the exporter has correctly classified the goods and files an HS code copied from an old shipment of a somewhat similar part.

Nothing goes wrong on the sea leg. The vessel arrives on time. At the port, customs flags the shipment. The HS code points to "electronic components" but the goods look more like "machined metal parts." The duty rate is higher. Customs orders an inspection. The container sits in the yard for a week, racking up storage and demurrage. The buyer's factory runs short of parts and loses production time. The exporter and buyer argue over who pays the extra costs and the lost output.

None of the problems are mysterious. They are the compounding result of fuzzy Incoterms, guessed HS codes, and undocumented expectations.

11.4.2 Compliance and Documentation Pitfalls

HS codes are the standard classification numbers that customs authorities use to decide which duty rate and rules apply to a product. Chapter 7 covered how they work in detail. Here the point is simple: if you guess or copy codes carelessly, you invite delays, extra duties, and fines.

The practical fix is to treat HS classification as a maintained reference, not a one off guess. Use official tariff databases, work with your customs broker or a knowledgeable forwarder, and create a product classification sheet for your main items so that everyone in your company uses the same, correct codes.

Incoterms get misused in a similar way. It is common to see "FOB" used for air shipments, even though FOB is designed for sea and inland waterway transport, or to see "CIF" written on a contract when the seller has not actually included insurance. The cure is discipline. Use official Incoterm abbreviations, pair each one with a clear named place, and make sure your operations match what your sales team writes.

Incomplete documentation is another frequent source of trouble. A commercial invoice that lacks a clear description, the correct Incoterm, or the buyer's details can slow customs. A packing list that does not match the physical shipment can trigger inspections. For United States exporters, missing the threshold that requires an AES filing can bring fines.

Think of documents as tickets and passports. The plane might be ready and your seat booked, but without a passport and boarding pass you are not going anywhere.

11.4.3 Underestimating Port Logistics and Inland Costs

Another trap is focusing on the headline freight rate and ignoring what happens at ports and on the road.

Suppose you receive two quotes. The first offers sea freight from Shanghai to Los Angeles for 1,000 dollars but says "destination charges as per tariff." The second offers 1,150 dollars but includes typical terminal handling charges and documentation fees in the destination line.

If you only compare the 1,000 and 1,150 figures, the first looks cheaper. In reality, the first quote might result in 600 dollars of extra terminal and handling fees, while the second might add only 300. By the time the container leaves the terminal, the "cheaper" option has cost you more.

Inland transportation can work the same way. A port that looks cheap on ocean rates may have higher trucking costs to your final destination, or more congestion, which raises storage bills.

The solution is to ask forwarders direct questions. What port and inland charges should I expect on this route? What is not included in this quote? Are there seasonal surcharges or congestion problems that might arise?

11.4.4 Misaligned Expectations Between Shipper, Forwarder, Broker, and Carrier

Global shipments involve several parties. Each has a different role.

- The shipper or exporter owns and sells the goods.
- The freight forwarder coordinates logistics and often handles documentation.
- The carrier operates the ship, plane, or truck.
- A customs broker specializes in getting goods through customs.
- A freight broker, as you saw in Chapter 9, may arrange trucking without ever physically touching the cargo.

Trouble starts when each party assumes someone else is handling a critical task.

An exporter might think, "My forwarder will classify my products and file customs paperwork correctly." The forwarder might think, "The exporter will give me the correct HS code and tell me if any licenses are needed." If no one checks, responsibility falls through the cracks.

One practical way to avoid this is to create a simple responsibility matrix. For each shipment, or at least for each major customer or supplier, note who is responsible for booking main freight, preparing commercial documents, filing export declarations, arranging insurance, handling import customs, and booking final delivery. Share that with your partners.

11.4.5 Simple Export and Import Checklists

You do not need a complex software system to reduce risk. A one page checklist, used consistently, can make a big difference.

For exports:

- Before you book, confirm the HS code with your broker or forwarder, select an Incoterm with a named place that fits your business, and think through mode and route with buffer time.
- Before cargo leaves your facility, check that the commercial invoice and packing list are accurate, that any required export declaration has been filed, and that special cargo such as hazardous goods is correctly documented.
- Before the vessel or plane departs, make sure you have a booking confirmation, that the details on the bill of lading or air waybill are correct, and that insurance is in place if you need it.

For imports:

- Before you buy, make sure you understand the Incoterm your supplier is offering, estimate duties and taxes based on the HS code, and clarify who will handle customs clearance.
- Before the shipment arrives, appoint a customs broker, send them the documents in advance, and arrange payment of duties and taxes so that release is not delayed.

11.4.6 The Value of Good Partners and Good Questions

Competent forwarders and customs brokers are worth their fees. They track changing regulations, know which ports are snarled or smooth, and see patterns across many clients.

They work best when clients ask informed questions and share clear information.

You do not have to become a customs lawyer. It is enough to ask, "How did you classify this product?" or "Which Incoterm would you recommend here, and what would that change in practice?" or "What are the top risks you see on this route in the next few months?"

11.5 Your Next Steps: From Informed Observer to Active Participant

11.5.1 Recap of Key Mental Models

By now, three ideas should feel familiar.

- Logistics is a flow of goods and information. Interruptions in one part of the pipe affect everything downstream.
- Freight forwarding is orchestration. It is about sequencing many players into a coherent journey, not pressing a single "book" button.
- Ports and ships are critical infrastructure. They shape how trade works, which routes thrive, and where bottlenecks appear.

These ideas tie together earlier chapters: the seven step flow from Chapter 2, the hardware and ports in Chapters 3 to 5, the cost and risk ideas in Chapters 6 and 7, and the crises in Chapter 12.

11.5.2 If You Run or Work in a Business: Three Immediate Wins

If you are involved in buying or selling goods, a few concrete steps can pay off quickly.

First, review the contracts you already use. Check that every sales and purchase agreement has an Incoterm, paired with a named place, that matches how you actually operate. If invoices say FOB but your team routinely arranges inland delivery at destination, paperwork and practice are out of sync.

Second, list your top products and confirm their HS codes with a broker or forwarder. Record those codes in a simple sheet. Make sure your sales, logistics, and finance teams all use the same references.

Third, take a recent shipment and reconstruct the total landed cost. Add freight, port fees, inland transport, insurance, duties, taxes, and surcharges. Compare that total with what you expected when you accepted the quote. The gap shows how much hidden cost is in your current process.

11.5.3 If You Are a Curious General Reader: How to Stay Informed

If you do not work directly in trade, you can still use these ideas to read the world differently.

When you see a headline about a blocked canal, a port strike, or a new warehouse opening near your city, ask:

- Which nodes in the network are affected?
- Which flows of goods are likely to slow or reroute?
- Who might bear the extra cost?

You do not need to track every ship and port. A few questions will turn vague news into understandable cause and effect.

11.5.4 If You Are Considering a Career in Freight Forwarding or Logistics

Logistics is a field full of real world puzzles. If you like figuring out how things fit together, it can be a rewarding path.

Entry level roles include operations assistants or coordinators at freight forwarders, documentation clerks, customer service staff at logistics firms, warehouse supervisor trainees, terminal assistants at ports, or junior analysts in supply chain departments.

A typical day might involve checking booking confirmations, emailing a shipper in one time zone and a carrier in another, updating shipment tracking, catching a discrepancy between an invoice and a packing list, or finding an alternative route when a vessel is delayed.

The skills that matter most are attention to detail, clear communication, comfort with numbers, and curiosity about how physical goods move.

To get started, you can look for internships or entry level jobs at forwarders, shipping lines, trucking companies, or logistics departments at manufacturers and retailers.

11.5.5 The Core Idea: Seeing and Shaping the System That Moves the World

If she had read this chapter before her big holiday order, Maria might have done several things differently. She would have sat down with the retailer and a forwarder to choose an Incoterm that matched both sides' expectations, and written it clearly. She would have asked a customs broker to confirm the HS code for her soy candles. She would have drawn the journey from Ohio to Germany as a timeline and checked who owned each segment. She would have compared quotes on total landed cost, not just the ocean rate.

Most importantly, she would have recognized that logistics is not a black box you drop a purchase order into. It is a system you can understand and influence.

Learning freight forwarding is like learning how the plumbing of the global economy works. Before, you turned on the tap by placing an order and hoped water came out. Now you can trace the pipes, spot where they might leak or clog, and even design better routes.

11.5.6 Final Section Takeaway

Pick one shipment you know, from your own work or from a story in this book. Draw its timeline. Label the Incoterm. Note every cost you can identify. Then circle one thing you would change next time.

When you read about blocked canals, drought hit rivers, overflowing ports, or sudden rate spikes in Chapter 12, try viewing those stories through the lens of this chapter.

- Where is the flow blocked?
- Which orchestrator is missing, or which decision was not made clearly?
- Which Incoterms, HS codes, or cost assumptions failed under pressure?
- What did the best prepared shippers and forwarders do differently before the crisis began?

If you can answer those questions for one or two of the crises in Chapter 12, you will have moved beyond simply knowing logistics vocabulary. You will be thinking like a freight forwarder, someone who understands the system well enough to design, question, and, when needed, redesign how cargo moves.

Field Guide: Thinking Like a Freight Forwarder

Key concepts

- Forwarder thinking starts with the business promise, not the container: who needs what, where, by when, at what acceptable total cost.
- Good plans make flows visible end to end, from supplier through ports and carriers to final delivery, with clear roles and Incoterms on each segment.
- Total landed cost, risk, and resilience sit alongside price and transit time in every serious routing decision.
- Documents, classifications, and contracts are design tools that shape outcomes, not clerical afterthoughts.
- Checklists and simple maps beat intuition alone when volumes, lanes, and rules multiply.

Common mistakes

- Treating logistics as a black box that someone else will "handle" once a purchase order is signed.
- Focusing narrowly on the lowest freight rate while ignoring port, inland, customs, and risk costs.
- Leaving HS codes, Incoterms, and export declarations to ad hoc decisions shipment by shipment.
- Assuming that a plan that worked once will work the same way under different volume, season, or policy conditions.
- Trying to manage complex flows entirely by memory or scattered email threads.

Warning signs

- Regular surprises in invoices from forwarders, carriers, or ports that nobody can explain clearly.
- Frequent arguments between sales, finance, and logistics about "who owns" certain costs or responsibilities.
- Shipments that reach the right country but sit at ports, terminals, or warehouses because the next step was never clearly assigned.
- A lack of any single, simple document that shows routes, Incoterms, costs, and roles for key lanes.
- People in your organization who use logistics vocabulary but cannot map a real shipment from door to door.

Practical shortcuts

- For each major lane, keep a one page "route card" with Incoterm, nodes, main carriers, typical costs, and known risks; use it as the default plan.
- Before launching a new product or promotion, walk one representative shipment through the full design process: promise, route, rules, cost, and

contingency.

- Reserve time each quarter to review one lane with your forwarder or broker, asking what has changed in costs, rules, or congestion since last year.
- When something goes wrong, document the chain of decisions and hand-offs rather than blaming individuals; use that timeline to adjust contracts and processes.

If You Only Remember Three Things

1. Thinking like a forwarder means seeing shipments as designed flows with clear roles, rules, and costs, not as boxes that somehow move on their own.
2. Simple tools such as lane maps, checklists, and basic cost stacks reduce surprises far more effectively than heroic last minute firefighting.
3. The same mental models that explain one painful shipment can be used to redesign your whole network, making future crises less damaging and routine business smoother.

Chapter 12: When the System Breaks - Real World Logistics Crises

12.1 Why Crises Matter to Freight Forwarders

Earlier in this book, disruptions appeared as bumps in the road: a late truck, a missed sailing, a customs inspection that adds a few days.

Sometimes, the road itself fails.

A ship blocks a canal. A virus shutters ports. A drought lowers water levels in a major canal or river. In those moments, even the best planned shipment can be trapped behind events that no single company controls.

If a normal week in logistics is like running the school trip from Chapter 2, booking buses, managing tickets, making sure everyone gets home, then the events in this chapter are what happen when the highway itself closes or the airport shuts down. The same mental models still apply. The stakes are higher and the scale is larger.

For freight forwarders and logistics managers, this is where the job becomes more than booking transport. It becomes risk management, damage control, and creative problem solving on a global scale.

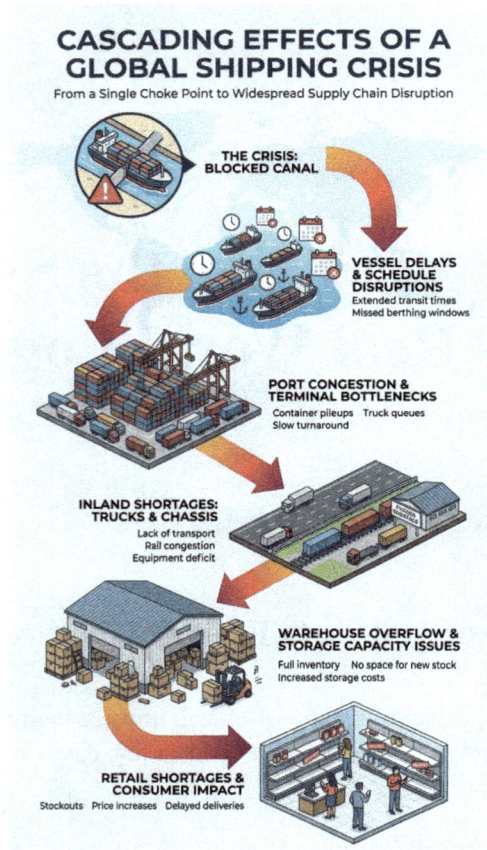

Figure 24: Cascade Effects

In this chapter, you will walk through several real world crises that shaped modern freight forwarding:

- The Suez Canal blockage by the Ever Given in 2021.
- COVID era port congestion and the Southern California backlog.
- The Yantian Port COVID shutdown in China.
- The container freight rate spike in 2020 and 2021.
- Drought related restrictions at the Panama Canal in 2023.
- Low water crises on the Rhine River in Europe.

For each one, we will focus on what happened, what it meant for freight forwarders and shippers, and what lessons you can take for your own planning.

12.2 Suez Canal Blockage: One Ship, Billions of Dollars

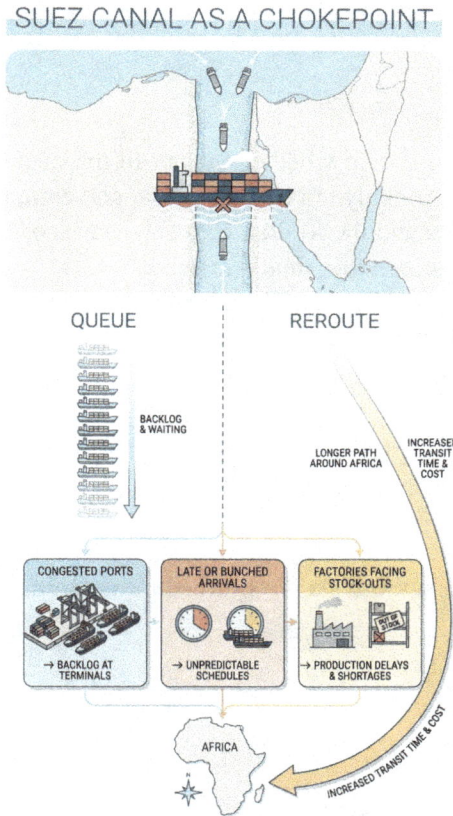

Figure 25: Global Supply Chain Vulnerability

In March 2021, a 400 meter container ship called the Ever Given ran aground in the Suez Canal.[15] Driven by strong winds and human error, it lodged sideways in a waterway that carries a significant share of global seaborne trade.

For nearly six days, no ships could pass.

By the time tugs and dredgers freed the vessel, more than 350 ships were stuck at both ends of the canal, waiting their turn. Analysts estimated that roughly 9 to 10 billion dollars of cargo per day was held up while the canal was closed.

---

[15] See the "Suez Canal / Ever Given Blockage (March 2021)" sources, including coverage in The Guardian, Trowers & Hamlins legal briefings, and Lloyd's List reporting in 2021.

The physical event was local. One ship in one place. The impact was global.

- Carriers had to decide whether to wait in the queues or reroute around Africa, adding roughly ten days of transit and extra fuel cost.
- Ports in Europe and the Middle East saw waves of late arrivals and then sudden peaks as convoys finally arrived.
- Manufacturers waiting on critical components, from auto parts to electronics, faced stock outs and production delays weeks after the canal reopened.

For freight forwarders, those six days turned into months of knock on effects:

- Schedules and estimated arrival times became moving targets.
- Importers asked whether to switch modes, pay for air on urgent items, or wait out the chaos.
- Questions surfaced about contracts and insurance and who pays when cargo misses delivery dates because of a canal blockage.

The key lesson is that highly optimized routes can still hinge on a small number of chokepoints. When one fails, no amount of planning inside a single company can fully shield you. What you can do is understand where your trade lanes depend on such points and build realistic contingency plans with alternative routes, buffer inventory, and flexible contracts.

12.3 COVID 19 Port Congestion and the Southern California Backlog

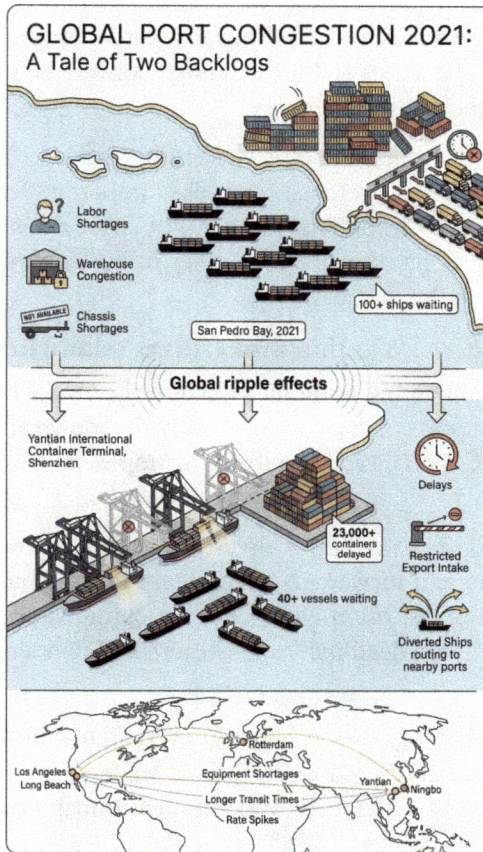

Figure 26: Port Congestion Overview

12.3.1 A Perfect Storm at Los Angeles and Long Beach

During the COVID 19 pandemic, consumer demand for goods surged while infrastructure strained under health restrictions and labor shortages. Nowhere was this more visible than in the twin United States ports of Los Angeles and Long Beach, which together handle a large share of United States containerized imports.[16]

---

[16] See the "COVID-Era Port Congestion – Los Angeles / Long Beach (2020–2022)" sources, including The Guardian, Journal of Commerce reports, and port authority throughput data.

By October 2021, more than 100 container ships were waiting offshore in San Pedro Bay, an armada that turned the coastline into a floating parking lot.

Behind those ships, terminals struggled with limited labor and COVID protocols. Containers piled up because trucking and warehouse capacity inland could not keep pace. Some boxes sat so long that ports considered penalty fees to push importers to move them faster.

For shippers and forwarders, the effects were immediate. Transit times from Asia to inland destinations stretched by weeks. Importers faced empty shelves or late product launches despite having paid for space on vessels. Routing decisions became a daily puzzle: divert to other ports, even if that meant longer inland legs, or wait in the queue.

12.3.2 Global Echoes: Yantian and Other Asian Hubs

In late May 2021, Yantian International Container Terminal in Shenzhen, one of the busiest container ports in the world, partially shut down after several workers tested positive for COVID 19.[17] Authorities imposed strict health measures, including temporarily halting export container intake.

Carriers began skipping Yantian or diverting ships to alternate South China ports. For exporters and forwarders, that meant last minute rerouting of containers to other terminals, often with scarce trucking, sudden shifts in cut off times and documentation deadlines, and extra risk of containers being rolled to later sailings.

The lesson is that a few key export hubs, from Yantian and Ningbo in China to Rotterdam in Europe, act as valves for global trade. When one closes, inefficiencies ripple outward in the form of equipment imbalances, rate spikes, and routing headaches for months.

12.4 The Pandemic Freight Rate Shock (2020 to 2021)

Before the pandemic, on major routes such as China to the United States West Coast, spot rates for a 40 foot container commonly sat in the range of roughly 1,500 to 2,000 United States dollars. They rose in peak season and fell in quieter months, but most shippers could plan around that band.[18]

---

[17]

See the "Yantian Terminal Partial Shutdown (June 2021)" sources, including Reuters coverage and Freightos market commentary.

[18]

Indicative rate ranges are based on historical data from the Freightos Baltic Index (FBX) and Drewry World Container Index for 2019–2020.

By mid 2021, those same routes saw spot rates above 15,000 dollars, with some shippers paying 20,000 dollars or more for urgent loads.[19]

Industry indexes such as the Freightos Baltic Index and Drewry's World Container Index recorded record highs. At the same time, major shipping lines and logistics firms reported strong profits, even as their customers complained about relentless cost increases.

For cargo owners, this produced a simple but brutal set of tradeoffs:

- Cancel orders, delay shipments, or adjust product launches.
- Accept higher prices and revise retail pricing or margins.
- Shift sourcing to nearer suppliers or different modes for some products.

For forwarders, the rate shock turned into daily work:

- Managing scarce space with allocations from carriers and deciding which customers to prioritize.
- Explaining to shippers why contracted rates no longer reflected reality or why allocations were cut.
- Advising on contract versus spot mix, alternative ports, and the merits of longer term agreements.

The lesson is that freight rates are not just a line on an invoice. They are a signal of imbalance between capacity and demand. In extreme cases they become a force that reshapes sourcing, pricing, and even which products remain viable.

12.4.2 Case Study: Blank Sailings and Empty Shelves

Not every disruption looks dramatic from a satellite image. Sometimes the key event is a sailing that never happens.

During the height of the rate spike, carriers began cancelling scheduled voyages, a practice known as "blank sailings." By skipping departures, they tried to realign ship positions, manage port congestion, and support higher rate levels on the sailings that did run.

A mid range fashion retailer in the United Kingdom discovered what this can mean at store level.

The retailer relied on six weekly services from major Asian ports to Felixstowe and Southampton. Its logistics team built delivery promises and inventory plans around those published schedules. Spring collections from Bangladesh and Vietnam were timed to hit stores in March and April.

---

[19] See the "Pandemic Freight Rate Spike (2020–2021)" sources, including LA Times coverage, Wolf Street analysis, and FBX and Drewry benchmarks.

One February, a vessel that was supposed to depart from a South China hub simply did not sail. The carrier had blanked the sailing to catch up with schedule delays elsewhere. The retailer's forwarder received notice only a few days before the planned departure.

The immediate impact:

- Several containers of new season stock were rolled to the next sailing, already heavily booked.
- The earliest realistic arrival for those goods shifted by nearly three weeks.
- The retailer's distribution centers had no buffer inventory of the specific styles affected, because buying had worked tightly against the original plan.

By late March, key stores in London and Manchester had gaps in their displays where new styles were supposed to be. Marketing had to pull back on campaign imagery showing items that customers could not actually buy yet.

The forwarder and retailer responded by:

- Reallocating some stock from slower selling lines and older collections to the worst affected stores to avoid completely empty racks.
- Pulling forward a portion of the next production batch and moving it by air freight into the main distribution center to close the most visible gaps.
- Pushing the carrier for better visibility of planned blank sailings and insisting, in future contracts, on notification lead times and minimum service levels.

In the next buying cycle, the retailer adjusted its sourcing and calendar:

- It placed a slightly higher share of volume on services from ports and carriers with a better track record of keeping published sailings.
- It added a modest buffer of extra weeks between factory ready dates and planned in store dates for high profile items.
- It negotiated with forwarders and carriers to understand which loops were most at risk of blankings and treated those as "amber" in planning tools.

From a customer's point of view, the story was simple: limited size ranges and missing colors on a few displays. From a logistics point of view, it was a case study in how a blank sailing can turn one missing departure into weeks of distorted sales and rushed air shipments.

12.4.1 Case Study: Surcharge Shock at a Mid Sized Importer

Consider a household goods importer based in Brazil that sourced most of its products from factories in southern China. Before 2020, its logistics budget assumed:

- Ocean freight of around USD 1,800 per 40 foot container on China to Santos services.
- Predictable terminal and handling charges.
- Occasional small surcharges for fuel or currency.

Products were priced for Brazilian retailers on the assumption that freight would remain in that general band. Margins were healthy but not extravagant.

When the pandemic rate spike hit, base ocean rates rose quickly. Within months, the importer began seeing offers of USD 6,000 to 8,000 per container, then USD 10,000 and above during peak periods. On top of that came new or higher surcharges:

- Equipment imbalance fees.
- Peak season surcharges.
- General rate increases rolled into "emergency" line items.
- Heavier bunker (fuel) and low sulphur surcharges.

For a time, the importer hoped this was temporary noise. They delayed re quoting prices to retailers and accepted lower margins. Then one particularly painful shipment arrived.

The invoice for a single 40 foot container showed:

- Base ocean freight: USD 9,800
- BAF and low sulphur fuel surcharges: USD 1,200
- Peak season surcharge: USD 1,000
- Equipment imbalance surcharge: USD 800
- Destination port congestion surcharge: USD 400

The all in sea leg for that container exceeded USD 13,000, more than seven times the pre pandemic level.

Spread over the 2,500 units of mixed household goods inside, freight alone was adding more than USD 5 per unit, in a category where retail prices for some items had been only USD 15 to 20. On some SKUs, the importer would lose money even before paying for inland transport, duties, and overhead.

The company reacted in three phases.

First, emergency triage. They:

- Prioritized containers with higher margin goods and essential retail commitments.
- Cancelled some low margin seasonal orders that would likely arrive too late and too expensive.

- Raised prices mid season on a subset of products, knowing that sales volume would drop but choosing that over selling at a loss.

Second, medium term adjustment. Over the next six months, they:

- Negotiated longer term contracts with a mix of carriers and forwarders to secure some capacity at less volatile rates, even if still higher than before.
- Shifted part of their sourcing to suppliers in closer countries such as Mexico and regional Brazilian manufacturers, reducing reliance on one long, expensive lane.
- Reviewed product mix, discontinuing some bulkier, low value items that could not support the new freight cost per unit.

Third, structural change. The importer built freight rate and surcharge scenarios into its product development and buying process. New items now required a "stress test" that asked, "If ocean rates double again, does this SKU still make sense?"

The spike hurt. It forced uncomfortable price increases and difficult conversations with retailers. But it also pushed the company to treat freight cost as a variable to be actively managed rather than a background number to be assumed.

For forwarders working with such customers, the ones who weathered that period best were those who could explain the components of the surcharge stack clearly, show alternative options, and help design contracts and sourcing plans that acknowledged that volatility instead of pretending it did not exist.

12.5 Climate and Waterways: Panama Canal and the Rhine

12.5.1 Panama Canal Drought (2023)

In 2023, the Panama Canal faced unusually low water levels in Gatun Lake, the reservoir that feeds its locks.[20] An extended dry season and high temperatures reduced available fresh water.

Canal authorities responded by:

- Capping daily transits below the usual number.
- Imposing draft restrictions that limited how heavy some ships could be.
- Using auctions for some transit slots, which pushed prices higher for certain vessels.

---

[20]

See the "Panama Canal Drought Restrictions (2023)" sources, including Reuters and The Guardian news reports and CarbonBrief analysis of Gatun Lake levels.

At one point roughly 140 vessels were waiting for a slot, compared with fewer than 100 in more typical conditions. Some ships waited two or three weeks.

For cargo owners, the effects included:

- Longer and less predictable transit times on routes that rely on Panama, such as Asia to United States East Coast or United States Gulf to Asia.
- Extra surcharges as carriers passed on the costs of delays and restrictions.
- A reminder that infrastructure relying on stable natural conditions, such as river levels or reservoir fed locks, is vulnerable to climate variability.

From a forwarding perspective, Panama's drought illustrates why natural risk is now a standard part of route planning. On some lanes, you must treat canal draft limits and transit caps as recurring constraints, not rare surprises.

12.5.1.1 Case Study: Routing Coffee Around a Dry Canal

A European coffee roaster imported green beans from producers in Colombia and Central America. For years, most shipments moved by container ship from Caribbean ports through the Panama Canal to Europe, then by truck and barge to roasting plants in Germany and the Netherlands.

When Panama's draft restrictions tightened, the roaster's forwarder noticed two problems at once:

- Vessels that used to transit on predictable schedules were queued or delayed.
- Carriers began adding Panama Canal surcharges on affected services.

On one key route, the forwarder saw estimated transit times stretch from about 18 days port to port to more than 30 days, with no guarantee that slots and drafts would stay stable.

Rather than simply accept longer, more expensive journeys, the roaster and forwarder explored alternatives.

Together they:

- Identified services that routed coffee via the Suez Canal or around the Cape of Good Hope, avoiding Panama entirely. These routes were longer in distance but, during the drought, sometimes offered more reliable schedules and fewer last minute restrictions.
- Tested a limited volume routing beans from some origins to East Coast United States ports, then by transatlantic services to Europe, trading one chokepoint for a more diversified path.
- Increased safety stock for critical blends in European warehouses so that a missed sailing or draft restriction would not immediately empty shelves

for supermarket customers.

For a few months, logistics staff had to manage more complexity: different services, different transshipment ports, and more varied arrival patterns. In exchange, the roaster reduced its exposure to a single canal's water level and a single set of auctioned transit slots.

The experience prompted a more permanent shift. Even after water levels improved, the roaster kept part of its sourcing on non Panama routes and embedded canal risk into its supply planning models.

The beans in a supermarket aisle still tasted the same. Behind the scenes, a routing change and some extra inventory had turned a climate driven constraint into a manageable, if ongoing, planning factor.

12.5.2 Rhine River Low Water Crises (2018 and 2022)

In Europe, the Rhine River is a backbone of inland waterway transport, feeding German, Swiss, and Dutch industry. In the second half of 2018, a severe drought caused parts of the Rhine to reach historically low levels.[21]

Consequences included:

- Barges forced to sail with less than half their normal loads, or not at all, on shallow stretches.
- Periods when large commercial traffic was effectively halted in some sections.
- Supply issues for industries dependent on barge transport, especially chemicals, oil, coal, and steel.

One major industrial firm declared force majeure because raw materials could not reach its plants. The German government estimated that the 2018 Rhine disruption shaved a measurable amount off the country's GDP.

A similar low water episode returned in 2022, again threatening traffic and forcing companies to scramble for rail and truck capacity.

For logistics planners, the Rhine story drives home that:

- Inland waterways are highly efficient but water dependent.
- Relying heavily on one mode without alternatives can turn a weather pattern into a business level crisis.
- Some companies have responded by investing in low draft barges, shifting part of their flows to rail or road, and adjusting safety stocks.

---

[21]

See the "Rhine Low-Water Events (2018, 2022)" sources, including Reuters, The Guardian, and German Federal Waterways and Shipping Administration bulletins.

In other words, climate trends are reshaping what used to be seen as reliable and boring transport routes.

12.6 What These Crises Teach Future Freight Forwarders

Looking across Suez, Los Angeles and Long Beach, Yantian, the rate shock, Panama, and the Rhine, a few patterns matter for anyone who wants to think like a freight forwarder.

1. Chokepoints amplify risk. Canals, narrow straits, and major hubs concentrate flows. A failure there affects many shipments at once. Mapping your dependence on these nodes is basic risk hygiene.

2. Port and inland capacity are inseparable. A ship can arrive on time, but if trucks, chassis, drivers, warehouses, or rail slots are short, containers will still sit. Watching inland congestion indicators is as important as watching vessel schedules.

3. Rates reflect system stress. When you see freight rates spiking many times above historical norms, it usually signals deeper imbalances: demand surges, capacity traps, or equipment shortages. A forwarder's job is not to guess the market, but to help clients adjust contracts, mode mix, and inventory strategies to survive those spikes.

4. Natural systems are part of your network diagram. Droughts in Panama and on the Rhine, storms that close ports, and floods that wash out rail lines are no longer edge cases. Climate related risk belongs in routing and inventory decisions.

5. Flexibility beats perfection. Many supply chains before COVID 19 were optimized for cost under stable conditions. These crises rewarded companies that had alternative ports, modes, and carriers already qualified, plus the financial and organizational flexibility to switch.

6. Communication is a core skill. During every one of these events, freight forwarders spent as much time explaining, updating, and renegotiating as they did booking space. Clear, honest communication about what is happening and what options exist is part of the value you provide.

As you build a career in logistics or design a supply chain for your business, you will not be able to prevent the next canal scale surprise. What you can do is:

- Understand where and how your routes are fragile.
- Use Incoterms, contracts, and service level agreements that share risk fairly.

- Design your network with enough slack and alternatives to keep moving when one link fails.

Crises test systems, but they also reveal which logistics strategies are truly robust. Freight forwarding, at its best, is the craft of keeping goods moving through a world that never stops throwing curveballs.

Field Guide: When the System Breaks

Key concepts

- Global trade relies on a small number of chokepoints such as canals, major ports, and big inland hubs.
- Port, inland, and equipment capacity are tightly linked; a problem in one often causes problems in the others.
- Extreme freight rate movements are signals of system stress, not random price noise.
- Natural systems such as river levels and rainfall patterns are now part of logistics planning, not background noise.
- Flexibility and clear communication are central risk management tools for forwarders and shippers.

Common mistakes

- Assuming that past average transit times and rates will hold during crises without building buffers.
- Relying on a single port, canal, carrier, or mode for critical flows with no qualified alternatives.
- Treating surcharges as an annoyance rather than as signals to revisit contracts, sourcing, and inventory strategy.
- Ignoring weak inland links such as limited truck and rail capacity while focusing only on ocean schedules.
- Waiting for official confirmation of every problem instead of acting on early, credible operational information.

Warning signs

- Growing queues of vessels at key ports or canals, or repeated notices of draft and transit restrictions.
- Carriers announcing large numbers of blank sailings, rolled containers, or sudden rate increases.
- Inland congestion indicators rising, such as increased truck and chassis turn times or full rail ramps.
- A sourcing portfolio heavily skewed to one distant region with long, fragile lanes.

- Internal reliance on "just in time" deliveries with no ability to hold extra stock of critical items.

Practical shortcuts

- For each critical lane, list at least one alternative port, mode, or carrier that could be used in an emergency, even if it is more expensive; qualify those options in advance.
- Build simple "what if" scenarios into planning: for example, what happens if transit time doubles, if rates triple, or if a canal becomes unusable for a season.
- Use early alerts from forwarders and carriers (for example congestion notices, low water bulletins, strike warnings) as triggers to review and, if needed, pre emptively reroute the most vulnerable shipments.
- Treat crisis periods as data gathering opportunities and record what worked and what did not so that your next crisis plan is based on experience, not theory.

If You Only Remember Three Things

1. Modern supply chains depend on a handful of chokepoints where failure can affect thousands of shipments at once, so mapping your exposure to those nodes is basic risk hygiene.
2. Crises turn hidden weaknesses into visible costs; companies that already have alternative ports, modes, and contracts in place suffer less than those that improvise from scratch.
3. A forwarder's value in turbulent times rests on clear communication and prepared options, not on predicting the next crisis perfectly.

Chapter 13: The Future of Freight

13.1 Opening: Planning Beyond the Next Sailing

Most of this book has lived close to the ground.

You have walked through quotes, bookings, containers, trucks, customs entries, invoices, and crises that have already happened. You have seen what goes wrong when Incoterms are fuzzy, HS codes are guessed, or ports clog up. That practical level is where most freight forwarding decisions are made day to day.

But the world that surrounds those decisions is shifting.

Customers now ask about emissions, not only rates. Ports and carriers face new rules on carbon. Software that once produced a simple schedule can now simulate whole networks. Trucks can steer themselves on long stretches of highway. Sensors report the temperature and location of cargo in real time. Trade lanes that used to feel fixed are bending as companies rethink where they make things.

The point of this chapter is not to predict the exact shape of freight in 2035 or 2050. Nobody can do that with precision. Instead, the goal is to show you the major forces already in motion and how they will change the work of shippers, forwarders, and logistics managers.

You will see:

- Why decarbonization is turning emissions into a design constraint, not a marketing slogan.
- How digital twins and simulation tools give small teams a view of networks that used to require whole departments.
- Where artificial intelligence can genuinely improve routing and planning, and where it still needs human judgment.
- How autonomous and highly automated trucking will change some links

in the chain before others.

- What cheap sensors and connected devices mean for predictive exceptions instead of late apologies.
- How ports are greening their operations and why that matters for cost and reliability.
- How trade lanes are already shifting through nearshoring and friend-shoring.

The details will change. The underlying skills will not. People who understand flows, costs, risk, and rules will be the ones who turn these trends into workable plans.

13.2 Decarbonization: Emissions as a Design Constraint

Freight has always burned fuel. For most of the industry's history, that fuel was cheap enough and the environmental cost distant enough that emissions were treated as someone else's problem.

That era is ending.

Regulators, investors, and customers are pushing carbon and other emissions into the center of logistics decisions. Several strands are coming together.

First, international rules are tightening. The International Maritime Organization has already forced cleaner marine fuels through regulations such as the 2020 sulphur cap.[22] New measures are adding pressure on overall carbon intensity for fleets. In Europe, the emissions trading system is starting to cover shipping, effectively putting a price on some ship emissions.[23] Other regions are experimenting with fuel mandates and reporting requirements.

Second, large cargo owners have made public commitments. Major retailers, manufacturers, and consumer brands have promised to cut emissions across their supply chains, not just inside their own factories and offices. That means they now ask freight providers tough questions about fuel type, vessel efficiency, aircraft choices, and route design.

Third, technology and fuel options are multiplying. Ship owners are testing and in some cases already ordering vessels that can run on methanol, ammonia,

---

[22]

See IMO greenhouse gas and fuel sulphur reports for details of the 2020 global sulphur limit and ongoing carbon intensity measures.

[23]

For example, the extension of the EU Emissions Trading System to maritime transport from 2024 onward, as described in EU climate policy notes.

liquefied natural gas, or future synthetic fuels. Trucking fleets are mixing in battery electric trucks on short, predictable routes and exploring hydrogen for some heavy long haul segments. Infrastructure for these options is uneven, but the direction is clear.

For a freight forwarder or logistics manager, this shows up in three practical ways.

You will see more line items on quotes linked to emissions and fuel. Some will be simple carbon surcharges. Others will be tied to low sulphur fuel, emissions trading costs, or green service tiers. You need to treat these not as random add ons but as signals of how a particular route and mode behave.

You will face more decisions that balance cost, time, and emissions. A slower steaming ocean service might cut fuel use and emissions but lengthen transit time. A rail option might offer lower emissions per ton kilometer than trucks on some corridors but require different handling. A nearshored supplier might reduce both emissions and risk even if unit prices are higher.

You will need to be able to explain emissions tradeoffs in plain language. Many shippers do not want a full life cycle assessment for every shipment. They want to know which of their options is dirtier or cleaner and by roughly how much. Simple comparisons between routes or modes, backed by credible data from carriers and reputable calculators, will become part of a forwarder's standard toolkit.

Decarbonization will not flip global freight from fossil based to zero emissions overnight. It will, however, steadily turn emissions from an externality into a constraint you design around, much like transit time or customs rules.

13.3 Digital Twins and Simulation for Freight Networks

For most of freight history, the best model of a network lived in a planner's head.

A senior logistics manager could sketch the main flows on a whiteboard, recite rough transit times and costs, and talk through what might happen if a port closed or a supplier moved. That intuition is still valuable, but it does not scale well when you must compare dozens of scenarios across multiple regions.

Digital twins are one response to that problem.

In logistics, a digital twin is a living model of a network that combines data about lanes, volumes, modes, transit times, constraints, and costs. It can represent a single warehouse, a port, or an entire global supply chain. The key is that the model can be updated with real data and used to simulate changes.

A shipper might use a digital twin to test what happens if they shift ten percent of sourcing from coastal China to inland Vietnam, or from East Asia to Mexico. A port authority might simulate how yard layout changes will affect truck turn times under different demand patterns. A carrier might explore how different schedules affect on time performance and utilization.

For freight forwarders and brokers, the most useful applications are often simpler.

You might not need a full company wide twin. Instead, you can use smaller models that compare route options on a few key lanes under different scenarios. What if the Panama Canal imposes stricter draft limits again? What if a new rail service between two inland hubs actually performs worse during peak season than it does in marketing material? How does a shift in manufacturing mix change the balance between ocean, air, and rail?

The important mindset shift is this: you can now test network changes before the world forces them on you.

In Chapter 12, you saw how companies scrambled when canals, rivers, and ports became bottlenecks. Digital twins and simulation do not remove those shocks, but they tilt the odds in favor of teams that have already explored alternatives on screen and in contracts rather than in panic when a crisis hits.

13.4 Artificial Intelligence in Routing and Planning

Routing and planning algorithms are not new. For decades, carriers and large shippers have used software to assign loads to trucks, plan vessel strings, and build airline schedules.

What has changed is the volume of data available and the tools that can learn patterns from it.

When people talk about artificial intelligence in freight, they often mean a mix of machine learning models and optimization engines that can:

- Predict transit times more accurately by learning from past performance.
- Suggest better routing options based on congestion, weather, and capacity.
- Flag shipments likely to run into trouble before they miss a key milestone.
- Recommend which bookings to prioritize when capacity is tight.

A forwarder's operations platform might use such models to rank loads by risk, highlight containers at elevated risk of detention, or suggest alternate ports for a new lane based on how similar cargo has behaved in the past. A trucking dispatch tool might suggest driver and truck assignments that cut empty miles and fuel consumption.

Used well, these tools can turn noisy data into practical prompts. Instead of scanning dozens of spreadsheets and dashboards, a planner can focus on a shorter list of decisions that actually matter today.

Used badly, they can become black boxes that nobody trusts.

The line between those outcomes is simple. Humans must still understand the basics of the network and keep authority over decisions. An algorithm that suggests routing a hazardous cargo through a port with stricter rules than the origin data implies needs human judgment. A model that predicts transit times should be checked against reality and explained in terms people can follow.

For your own career, the key is to become comfortable with these tools without surrendering your judgment to them. Learn enough to ask good questions about what inputs they use, how they are tested, and what kinds of decisions they are meant to support. The best forwarders in the next decade will not be those who ignore AI, but those who combine it with deep operational understanding.

13.5 Autonomous and Highly Automated Trucks

Road freight is where automation is most visible to the public. Images of self driving trucks on highways and tests of driverless yard tractors have become a regular feature in industry news.

The reality on the ground is more gradual.

Trucks are gaining advanced driver assistance features step by step. Lane keeping, adaptive cruise control, automatic braking, and improved stability systems are already common in many markets. Some routes, especially long highway segments between fixed hubs, are being tested with higher levels of automation, sometimes with a safety driver on board, sometimes in closely controlled corridors.

Yards and terminals are often the first places to adopt highly automated vehicles. A tractor that shuttles trailers between dock doors in a fenced, well mapped facility faces fewer unpredictable risks than one running in mixed traffic through a city.

What does this mean for freight planning and forwarding?

First, automation will change where human labor is most constrained. Local pickup and delivery in dense urban areas, cross border trucking with complex paperwork, and specialized moves that require on site problem solving are likely to keep human drivers in the loop longer. Middle distance corridor runs between hubs are more likely to see higher levels of automation earlier.

Second, it may alter cost structures over time. If automated highway runs can safely cut driver hours in some segments or reduce accidents, they can change the balance between long haul and rail on certain lanes. They might also shift where new distribution centers are built if automated routes favor specific corridors.

Third, it will change the skills demanded inside trucking and brokerage firms. Dispatchers may spend less time arbitraging small rate differences and more time managing exceptions, interpreting data, and coordinating between human and automated assets. Maintenance and safety teams will need new technical skills.

Autonomous trucks will not erase the need for forwarders or brokers. They will show up as new kinds of capacity with different constraints. People who understand how those constraints interact with customer promises, regulations, and infrastructure will remain essential.

13.6 IoT and Predictive Exceptions

In earlier chapters, you saw exceptions the old fashioned way. A container did not show up. A temperature logger inside a pallet of pharmaceuticals showed a violation after delivery. A truck missed a time window and nobody could reach the driver.

Cheap sensors and connected devices are changing that pattern.

Today, a shipper can attach a tracking device to a high value pallet that reports location, temperature, humidity, and even shock events in near real time. Containers can carry built in telemetry. Reefer units can report their status to central platforms. Trucks, trailers, and even individual packages can be tracked at varying levels of detail.

Most of the value from this data does not come from watching dots move on a map. It comes from acting before a small problem becomes a large one.

If you know that a reefer container's temperature has drifted out of range while it is still in port, you can intervene before it leaves on a long ocean leg. If you see that a shipment is late leaving a consolidation warehouse, you can warn the customer and discuss alternatives while there is still time to change a downstream booking. If movement data shows that a particular cross dock consistently introduces delays, you can raise that issue with the provider or redesign the route.

Predictive exception management is the discipline of using these signals to act early.

For forwarders and shippers, adopting it means agreeing on what really matters. You do not need alerts for every minor delay. You do need clear rules for which exceptions require a call, an email, or a change in plan. You need simple dashboards that highlight the few shipments that are at real risk today rather than a long list that everybody learns to ignore.

Over time, companies that treat connected data as a planning tool instead of a marketing gimmick will deliver more reliable service with fewer unpleasant surprises.

13.7 Greener Ports and Logistics Corridors

Ports and freight corridors are also being reshaped by environmental and community pressures.

Residents near major ports care about local air quality, noise, and traffic. Regulators care about emissions and fuel use. Port authorities and terminal operators balance those concerns with the need to move cargo efficiently.

Several trends are emerging.

First, ports are investing in cleaner equipment. Yard tractors, cranes, and other terminal vehicles are being upgraded to electric or hybrid models where feasible. Shore power systems allow ships at berth to plug into the electrical grid instead of running auxiliary engines, cutting local emissions. Some ports are experimenting with on site renewable power generation.

Second, port community systems are improving coordination. Better data sharing between terminals, truckers, rail operators, and warehouses can reduce idle time and unnecessary trips. Appointment systems for trucks, coupled with digital gate passes, can smooth peak flows and cut queues outside terminals.

Third, green corridors are being piloted. These are routes where ports, carriers, and shippers agree to use cleaner fuels, more efficient vessels, or better coordination to cut emissions on specific lanes. They often start as small, focused projects on high volume corridors and then expand if they work.

For shippers, these efforts may show up as new service offerings that combine environmental and reliability benefits. For forwarders, they create another dimension to consider when choosing routings and partners. A port that invests in clean equipment and better coordination may be worth a slightly higher handling charge if it delivers fewer delays and lower emissions.

13.8 Shifting Trade Lanes: Nearshoring and Friendshoring

Even before recent crises, companies were experimenting with shifting parts of their production closer to customers or to a broader mix of countries. Trade policy tensions, pandemic era disruptions, and rising wages in some manufacturing hubs have accelerated that trend.

Nearshoring is the move to bring production closer to major end markets. For a United States focused brand, that might mean more manufacturing in Mexico or Central America. For a European company, it might mean greater use of suppliers in Eastern Europe, North Africa, or Turkey.

Friendshoring is the idea of concentrating production in countries that are seen as politically or economically aligned, to reduce the risk of sudden tariffs, sanctions, or export controls.

These shifts do not mean that China or other existing manufacturing giants suddenly disappear from supply chains. They do mean that networks become more diverse.

A company that once sourced 80 percent of its products from coastal China might now blend production across Vietnam, Indonesia, India, Mexico, and domestic plants. That changes freight patterns. Some lanes to West Coast ports may shrink while Gulf and East Coast volumes grow. Cross border trucking between Mexico and the United States may become more important. Intra regional shipping within Asia or within Europe may gain volume as suppliers cluster in new places.

For freight forwarders and brokers, this means three things.

First, you will see more complex mix and match networks. A single brand may need support on ocean lanes from Asia, cross border trucking from Mexico, and regional distribution within Europe. That rewards providers who can manage multi region flows without treating each lane as an isolated contract.

Second, origin and destination pairs that used to be niche might suddenly matter. A corridor that handled low volumes a decade ago might become a strategic lane if a major customer shifts production. Paying attention to early signs from customers and trade statistics can help you prepare.

Third, customs and regulatory knowledge becomes even more valuable. New sourcing locations mean new tariff schedules, trade agreements, and compliance rules. The ability to design supply chains that make smart use of trade agreements while staying compliant will be a real advantage.

13.9 What This Means for Your Career

If you are early in your logistics career, it is easy to feel that trends like decarbonization, digital twins, AI routing, and autonomous trucks are distant from your daily work of chasing bookings and resolving exceptions.

They are not.

The shipments you manage in the next few years will increasingly sit inside networks shaped by these forces. You may be the one explaining a green service option to a customer, reviewing an AI generated routing suggestion, or helping a client design a nearshored supply chain.

A few practical implications follow.

First, deepen your grasp of fundamentals. No amount of software can replace a clear understanding of Incoterms, HS classification, cost breakdowns, port and carrier constraints, and the physical realities of moving goods. The more the tools change, the more valuable those basics become.

Second, build data and technology literacy. You do not need to become a programmer. You do need to be comfortable reading dashboards, asking where data comes from, and spotting when a model's suggestion violates common sense. Learn enough about emissions metrics, routing tools, and exception systems to use them confidently.

Third, stay curious about policy and geography. Trade agreements, sanctions, canal rules, climate regulations, and infrastructure projects all shape the landscape you operate in. A forwarder who can connect a news headline about a new trade corridor or a carbon rule to concrete advice for clients will stand out.

Fourth, invest in communication and trust. As networks become more complex and the future less predictable, customers will rely even more on advisors who can explain, not just execute. Clear explanations of options, risks, and tradeoffs will matter at least as much as clever use of technology.

The future of freight is not a separate topic from the rest of this book. It is the same craft, practiced in a world with new constraints and new tools. If you can combine the habits you have built in earlier chapters with an eye on these emerging trends, you will be well placed to help your customers and employers navigate the next decades.

Field Guide: The Next Decade in Freight

Key concepts

- Emissions are becoming a core design constraint in freight, not an afterthought.
- Digital twins and simulation let teams test network changes before crises force them.
- Artificial intelligence can improve routing and exception prediction, but it needs human oversight.
- Autonomous and highly automated trucks will change some corridors and roles faster than others.
- Nearshoring, friendshoring, and greener ports are already reshaping trade lanes and logistics corridors.

Common mistakes

- Treating decarbonization as a marketing project instead of a constraint that affects routes, modes, and sourcing choices.
- Accepting AI or optimization outputs without checking them against basic operational reality and rules.
- Ignoring new trade patterns and continuing to design networks as if sourcing and demand were frozen in place.
- Collecting sensor and tracking data without building processes to act on early warning signs.
- Assuming that new technology will automatically cut costs without revisiting contracts, training, and workflows.

Warning signs

- Customers asking detailed questions about emissions while your organization has no consistent way to answer.
- Repeated surprises when crises expose overreliance on a single supplier region or corridor.
- Operations teams overloaded with manual exception handling despite heavy investment in tracking tools.
- Key partners lagging on port, fleet, or systems upgrades while competitors move ahead.
- Internal resistance to experimenting with new routes, modes, or tools even on a small scale.

Practical shortcuts

- Add a simple emissions and resilience check to your standard lane and sourcing reviews, alongside cost and transit time.
- Pilot one or two focused digital tools, such as a predictive delay alert or a simple network simulation, and measure whether they actually reduce fire drills.

- Map your top ten product families or lanes against emerging trade corridors and nearshoring options to spot where early moves could help.
- Build relationships with carriers, ports, and tech providers that are clearly investing in cleaner operations and better data, and use their expertise as part of your planning.
- Set aside regular time, even once a quarter, to review how news about climate, trade policy, and technology might affect your specific network, and turn the most relevant items into concrete questions for your forwarders and brokers.

If You Only Remember Three Things

1. Decarbonization, data driven planning, and automation are already reshaping freight; they are constraints and tools you must work with, not distant theories.
2. The fundamentals of good forwarding, from clear Incoterms to solid cost models and realistic routes, remain the base that makes new tools useful rather than confusing.
3. Staying curious about technology, trade policy, and climate while deepening your operational craft is the most reliable way to keep your skills valuable over the next decade.

Appendix A: Glossary of Essential Logistics Terms

3PL (Third Party Logistics Provider) A company that manages logistics functions such as warehousing, distribution, and transportation on behalf of shippers. It may include forwarding and brokerage activities under one roof.

AES (Automated Export System) The electronic system United States exporters use to file export declarations (EEI) before goods leave the country.

AMS (Automated Manifest System) A United States Customs and Border Protection system for transmitting cargo manifest data before arrival.

Arrival Notice A document sent by the carrier or forwarder to inform the consignee that a shipment is due to arrive and to list any charges owed before release.

AWB (Air Waybill) The transport contract for air freight. Functions as a receipt, tracking reference, and agreement of carriage between shipper and airline or forwarder.

BAF (Bunker Adjustment Factor) A fuel surcharge that carriers add to base freight rates to account for changes in marine fuel costs.

Bill of Lading (B/L) Issued by an ocean carrier or forwarder to acknowledge receipt of cargo. Serves as a receipt, contract of carriage, and in some cases a document of title.

Bonded Warehouse A secured storage facility where imported goods can be held without paying duties until they are released for consumption, re exported, or destroyed.

Cargo Insurance Insurance that protects shippers from financial loss due to damage, loss, or theft during transit.

Carrier The company physically transporting goods by sea, air, road, or rail.

CBM (Cubic Meter) A measurement of volume (length x width x height) used for calculating freight rates, especially for LCL and air cargo.

Chassis A wheeled frame used to carry containers behind a truck. In some markets, chassis are owned separately from trucks and containers, which can create availability constraints.

Commercial Invoice The primary sales document issued by the seller. Used by customs to determine value, HS codes, duties, and taxes.

Consignee The party receiving a shipment, usually the buyer or its designated warehouse.

Country of Origin The country where a product is manufactured or substantially transformed. Origin drives duty rates, trade agreement eligibility, and some regulatory rules.

Customs Broker A licensed professional or firm that files import declarations, coordinates duty and tax payments, and helps ensure compliance with customs regulations.

DAP (Delivered At Place) An Incoterm where the seller arranges and pays for carriage to a named place at destination, but the buyer handles import customs, duties, and taxes.

DDP (Delivered Duty Paid) An Incoterm where the seller handles almost everything, including main transport, import customs clearance, and payment of duties and taxes, delivering to a named place at destination.

Demurrage Fees charged by shipping lines or terminals when a full container stays inside the terminal beyond the agreed free time.

Detention Fees charged by shipping lines when a container, empty or full, is kept outside the terminal beyond the free time before it is returned.

Drayage Short distance trucking moves, typically between a port or rail terminal and a nearby warehouse, depot, or factory.

FCL (Full Container Load) Cargo that uses an entire container for one shipper. Pricing is per container, regardless of whether it is completely full.

FEU (Forty Foot Equivalent Unit) A capacity measure equal to one 40 foot container. Two TEU (twenty foot equivalent units) equal one FEU.

Freight Forwarder (Forwarder) A logistics provider that arranges transport, routing, documentation, and customs coordination on behalf of shippers, often across multiple modes and countries.

Free Time The number of days a container or shipment can sit at a terminal or in the consignee's possession before demurrage or detention charges begin.

HS Code (Harmonized System Code) The international product classification number used by customs to set duty rates, apply controls, and compile trade statistics.

Lead Time The time between placing an order and receiving goods, including production, transport, and handling. Longer lead times usually require more inventory or more flexible customers.

Dimensional Weight (Volumetric Weight) A billing weight used mainly in air and parcel freight that converts shipment volume into a weight figure using a standard divisor; carriers charge based on whichever is higher, actual or dimensional weight.

Incoterms (International Commercial Terms) Standard three letter trade terms, published by the International Chamber of Commerce, that define who pays for transport and insurance and where risk transfers between seller and buyer (for example EXW, FOB, CIF, DAP, DDP).

Intermodal Transport The movement of a container or trailer by more than one mode of transport (for example truck, rail, barge) without unpacking the cargo in between.

ISF (Importer Security Filing) Also known as "10+2." A mandatory United States pre arrival filing for most ocean imports, containing shipper, buyer, and cargo details.

LCL (Less than Container Load) Cargo that does not fill a container and is consolidated with other shippers' cargo into a shared container.

LTL / TL (Less than Truckload / Truckload) In road freight, LTL refers to shipments that share trailer space with other shippers. TL refers to loads that fill most or all of a trailer.

Manifest The carrier's complete list of all cargo on board a vessel, aircraft, train, or truck, usually including HS codes, weights, and consignees.

Packing List A document that details how a shipment is packed: number of cartons, pallet counts, dimensions, and weights. Used by warehouses and customs.

Port Congestion When vessel, truck, or rail traffic exceeds a port or terminal's capacity, causing queues, delays, and longer dwell times.

Pre carriage / On carriage Pre carriage is inland transport from the shipper to the port or airport at origin. On carriage is inland transport from the port or airport at destination to the final consignee.

Reefer (Refrigerated Container or Trailer) A temperature controlled container or truck body used to ship chilled or frozen goods, such as food and pharmaceuticals.

Seal Number The unique identification number on a container's door seal. If the seal is broken or the number does not match the documents, it can indicate tampering.

Spot Rate / Contract Rate Spot rates are prices for one off shipments in the current market. Contract rates are agreed for a period and often for a committed volume or lane.

TMS (Transportation Management System) Software used by shippers, forwarders, and 3PLs to plan, execute, and track freight movements, manage carrier contracts and quotes, and analyze transport performance and cost.

WMS (Warehouse Management System) Software that manages inventory locations, receiving, picking, packing, and shipping processes inside warehouses and distribution centers.

PCS (Port Community System) A shared digital platform that connects port authorities, terminals, carriers, customs, and inland transport providers so they can exchange arrival notices, clearances, and status updates for cargo moving through a port.

Dwell Time The time a container, trailer, or pallet spends waiting at a terminal, yard, or warehouse between transport legs. High dwell times are often early warnings of congestion or process problems.

Blank Sailing A scheduled vessel voyage that a carrier cancels, usually to manage capacity or because of low demand, reducing available sailings on a lane.

TEU (Twenty Foot Equivalent Unit) A standard measure of container capacity based on a 20 foot container. A 40 foot container equals 2 TEU.

Total Landed Cost The full cost of getting a product to its final warehouse or store, including production, freight, duties, taxes, insurance, and handling.

Transshipment When cargo is transferred from one vessel or flight to another at an intermediate port or airport, typically at a hub on the way to final destination.

Final Thoughts

A ceramic mug on your desk, a packet of frozen berries, a vial of insulin in a hospital fridge. By now you know that none of these items simply "showed up."

Each one depended on a chain of ships, trucks, data messages, inspections, and human decisions that stretched across countries and oceans. Freight forwarding is the craft of making that chain work, day after day, even when the weather turns, a port goes on strike, or a regulation changes overnight.

You have seen how forwarders coordinate carriers, customs, warehouses, and paperwork so that trade can move. You have walked through ports and terminals, decoded quotes and surcharges, unpacked Incoterms and HS codes, peeked inside the cold chain, and met the people and jobs that keep this system alive. Global logistics can look chaotic from the outside, but inside it is a web of rules, habits, and relationships that experienced practitioners learn to navigate.

None of this is abstract. In March 2021 the container ship Ever Given blocked the Suez Canal for six days. About 12 percent of global trade normally passes through that narrow channel. Freight forwarders and logistics teams around the world stayed up through the night, rebooking vessels, finding alternate routes around the Cape of Good Hope, and warning customers that shipments would arrive weeks late. Some companies had resilient supply chains and absorbed the shock. Others had no backup plans and paid dearly. The same knowledge you have just worked through, applied in practice, is what separates those two outcomes.

Whether you ship a few pallets a year or are thinking about a career in this field, you now have the language and mental models to ask better questions, catch expensive mistakes early, and spot opportunities others miss. You know what is inside a quote, what a forwarder actually does, how risk and cost pass between buyer and seller, and why a delay in one port can ripple into store shelves half a world away. Hold on to that curiosity. The infrastructure of trade is changing fast, but the fundamentals you have learned here will continue to guide smart decisions.

Key Concepts

Below are the central ideas from the book, with brief reminders of why each one matters in real shipments and real careers.

Freight Forwarding and the Bigger Picture

- **Freight forwarder as "orchestrator"** A freight forwarder is a company that plans and manages the movement of goods for shippers, usually across borders and often across several transport modes. The forwarder does not normally own the ship, plane, or truck. Instead, it books space with carriers, prepares documentation, and coordinates customs, storage, and delivery. Shippers rely on forwarders because the forwarder understands routes, regulations, and risks better than they do.

- **Logistics versus freight forwarding versus supply chain** *Logistics* is the movement and storage of goods. *Supply chain* is the broader system that includes sourcing, production, logistics, and distribution. *Freight forwarding* sits inside logistics. It focuses on arranging transport and clearance, especially for international moves. Keeping these levels separate helps you see where a delay or cost really comes from.

- **End to end supply chains** The mug in Chapter 1 passed through factories, consolidation warehouses, ports, a container ship, a rail hub, a regional distribution center, and finally a delivery truck. Only by tracing the entire path can a business calculate true cost and risk, or decide whether paying extra for faster or more reliable transport is worth it.

Modes of Transport and Infrastructure

- **Four main transport modes** The book covered road, rail, air, and sea. Each has its strengths. Trucks are flexible and can reach most locations directly. Trains move heavy cargo efficiently over land. Air is fast but expensive and best for high value or urgent goods. Ocean shipping is slow yet cost effective for large volumes. Most international supply chains combine several modes, which is why forwarders talk about *multimodal* or *intermodal* transport.

- **Containerization** Standard shipping containers, most often 20 foot and 40 foot units, transformed global trade after the 1960s. They made it possible to move goods from a factory in Shenzhen to a warehouse in Chicago without unpacking at each step. Containers reduced theft, cut handling time, and slashed shipping costs. Much of modern freight forwarding is built around container flows.

- **Types of ships** You learned the major ship types:
  - *Container ships* for boxed consumer goods, machinery, and many manufactured products.
  - *Tankers* for liquids, such as crude oil, refined fuels, and chemicals.
  - *Bulk carriers* for unpackaged dry goods, such as iron ore, coal, and grain.
  - *Roll on roll off ships (Ro-Ro)* for vehicles. Each ship type serves different cargo and ports, which shapes routes and pricing.

- **Ports, terminals, and inland ports** A port is not just a pier. It is a complex system of berths, cranes, yard space, customs offices, and transport links. Within a port, *terminals* are specialized areas that handle containers, bulk cargo, vehicles, or passengers. *Inland ports* and *dry ports* extend this infrastructure inland, often by rail or barge, to relieve congestion at coastal ports and bring customs and storage closer to factories. Knowing which terminals and inland links a port offers helps forwarders design better routes.

Costs, Quotes, and Surprises

- **Ocean freight rates and their building blocks** A freight quote is more than a single price. It has several layers:

  - The *base ocean freight* that the carrier charges for moving a container between two ports.
  - *Origin* and *destination* charges at ports and terminals, such as handling and documentation fees.
  - *Surcharges*, for example, bunker adjustment factor (fuel), currency adjustment factor, low sulfur fuel surcharges, or congestion charges.
  - *Accessorials*, which are extra services like chassis rental, pre pull, or detention and demurrage fees for late pickup or return of containers. Understanding these components helps you compare quotes and avoid "cheap" offers that hide costs until the final invoice.

- **Total landed cost** Total landed cost is the full cost of getting a product into your warehouse or store. It includes production, freight, duties, taxes, insurance, handling, and sometimes even damage and loss. A freight rate that looks low might raise your total landed cost if it causes delays or higher inventory holding costs. Good logistics decisions focus on total landed cost, not just one line on the quote.

- **Service levels and trade offs** Fast, cheap, reliable: in shipping you rarely get all three at once. Companies like Zara and H&M use faster and more expensive modes so they can keep fashion cycles short. Commodity producers often choose slow but cheap options. Forwarders help shippers find the right balance among speed, price, reliability, and risk.

Rules, Codes, and Compliance

- **Incoterms and transfer of risk** Incoterms are standard three letter trade terms, such as FOB, CIF, or DAP, published by the International Chamber of Commerce. They define who arranges and pays for transport and insurance, and where the risk passes from seller to buyer.

  - Under *FOB Shanghai*, the seller covers local costs and export clearance in China, and responsibility shifts when goods are loaded on the vessel.

   – Under *DAP Chicago*, the seller pays for almost the entire transport and delivers to the buyer's door, but the buyer handles import customs and duties. Misunderstanding Incoterms can leave a small exporter paying for costs it never budgeted or carrying risks it cannot manage.

- **HS codes and classification** The Harmonized System (HS) is a global coding system for goods, maintained by the World Customs Organization. Each product receives a numeric code that determines duty rates, import restrictions, and statistical tracking. For example, ceramic tableware has a different HS code than plastic cups, and many countries tax them at different rates. Getting the code wrong can mean fines, shipment holds, or back payment of duties for years.

- **AES filing and export data** In the United States, exporters above certain value thresholds must file shipment data electronically through the Automated Export System, often called AES filing. Many other countries have similar systems. These filings track trade flows, support security checks, and create a legal record of what left the country. Freight forwarders often submit this data for their customers, but the exporter is still legally responsible for accuracy.

- **Customs as a process, not a single event** Customs clearance depends on advance data, correct paperwork, accurate HS codes, and compliance with special rules for items like food, medicine, or electronics. Customs officials look at risk profiles. A business with a strong history of accurate filings and clean audits usually moves faster. Those with repeated errors attract more inspections.

Special Chains and Special Roles

- **Cold chain logistics** Cold chain logistics is the temperature controlled supply chain that serves products such as vaccines, frozen food, blood, and some chemicals. It uses refrigerated containers, trucks, and warehouses, along with calibrated sensors that record temperature throughout the journey. A single break in the cold chain can ruin a shipment or threaten patient safety. That is why companies like DHL, Kuehne + Nagel, and UPS built dedicated pharma logistics networks with backup power, generator fueled warehouses, and strict handling procedures.

- **Freight broker versus freight forwarder** A freight broker, most common in road transport in countries like the United States, matches shippers with carriers and earns a margin on the spread between what the shipper pays and what the carrier receives. The broker usually does not take responsibility for cargo or offer full international services. A freight forwarder arranges more complex, often cross border moves and may issue its own transport documents. In practice, forwarders and brokers often work together, especially on the trucking legs of international shipments.

- **Key careers and roles** The book highlighted several important jobs in this field:

    - *Freight forwarding operations*: coordinate bookings, documents, and daily problem solving.
    - *Customs brokers*: specialize in tariff classification, duty calculation, and customs clearance.
    - *Logistics analysts and supply chain planners*: use data to design networks, set inventory levels, and choose routes.
    - *Port and terminal managers*: run the infrastructure where goods transfer between sea and land.
    - *Sales and account managers in logistics*: translate complex shipping options into clear proposals for customers. Many of these roles pay well because they demand a mix of analytical skill, regulatory knowledge, and the ability to stay calm when things go wrong.

Thinking Like a Freight Forwarder

- **Anticipation and contingency planning** Experienced forwarders do not just react to problems. They think ahead. If a winter storm threatens Chicago, they warn customers and may reroute cargo through Houston. If they see congestion building at a major transshipment hub, they shift bookings before delays become obvious. The habit of asking "what could go wrong here?" and acting early is central to this profession.

- **Route design and carrier selection** Two routes with similar transit times can have very different risk profiles. One may rely on a congested port such as Los Angeles in peak season. Another might use a smaller but more reliable port such as Oakland or Prince Rupert. A forwarder weighs factors like carrier reliability, transshipment points, seasonal patterns, and political risk, not just published schedules.

- **Visibility and data** Tracking tools, from online container tracking to satellite based ship monitoring, have changed expectations. Companies now want end to end visibility. Forwarders who can combine multiple data sources and explain delays clearly to customers have a strong edge. This makes basic data skills, such as working with spreadsheets or simple analytics, increasingly valuable.

- **Relationships and communication** Many of the stories in the book came down to people: a dispatcher who found an extra truck before a factory line stopped, a port contact who squeezed in an urgent container, a customs officer who flagged a repeated error and helped fix it before it became serious. Strong relationships with carriers, terminals, and officials increase flexibility and resilience. Clear, honest communication with customers builds trust when things go wrong, which they inevitably will.

- **Ethics and compliance as long term assets** Cutting corners on documentation or misclassifying goods to save duty might offer short term gains. Over time it usually destroys reputations, triggers fines, and can even lead to criminal charges. In a sector built on trust and long term partnerships, a reputation for clean, compliant operations is an asset that keeps paying back.

Further Exploration

Freight forwarding and logistics are deep fields. The goal of this section is not to overwhelm you, but to point you toward sources that practitioners and serious students actually use. Pick one or two areas that match your interests and go from there.

Books and Long Form Reading

- **"The Box: How the Shipping Container Made the World Smaller and the World Economy Bigger" by Marc Levinson (2006, updated editions)** This is the definitive story of containerization. Levinson traces how Malcom McLean's idea of putting truck trailers on ships reshaped ports, labor, and trade patterns. It gives valuable context for why modern freight forwarding looks the way it does.

- **"Logistics and Supply Chain Management" by Martin Christopher (latest edition)** A clear overview of supply chain thinking, from demand forecasting to inventory and transport strategy. It helps connect what you learned about freight forwarding to broader business decisions on sourcing and customer service.

- **"Port Economics, Management and Policy" by Theo Notteboom, Thanos Pallis, and Jean-Paul Rodrigue (2022)** More advanced, but very readable if you are serious about ports. It explains how ports compete, how terminal concessions work, and why some regions attract more maritime traffic than others.

- **"International Logistics: The Management of International Trade Operations" by Pierre A. David (latest edition)** Focused on the nuts and bolts of moving goods across borders. Covers documentation, Incoterms, transport modes, and risk management in detail, which is useful if you plan to work in forwarding, exporting, or importing.

- **Annual "Review of Maritime Transport" by UNCTAD** A free report that comes out each year. It tracks freight rates, fleet sizes, port through-put, and new regulations. Professionals use it to understand trends such as consolidation among carriers or shifts in trade routes.

Data, Indices, and Market Insight

- **World Bank Logistics Performance Index (LPI)** This index, released periodically, ranks countries on customs efficiency, infrastructure quality, logistics competence, tracking, and timeliness. It helps you see which trade lanes are likely to run smoothly and where to expect delays.

- **UN Comtrade and WTO trade data** These databases show what countries trade with each other and in what volumes, broken down by HS codes. They are useful for spotting growth markets or understanding the cargo mix that flows through particular regions.

- **Freight rate indices**

  - *Freightos Baltic Index (FBX)*, which tracks container freight rates on major routes.
  - *Drewry World Container Index*, another respected benchmark. Even if you are not buying space directly from carriers, following these indices will help you understand why your forwarder's quotes rise or fall.

- **Port authority statistics** Many port authorities publish annual reports and throughput data on their websites. For example, the Port of Rotterdam and the Port of Singapore both offer detailed breakdowns by cargo type. These documents show how ports invest and adapt, which is useful if you care about infrastructure or policy.

Industry Tools and Resources

Beyond books and data, practitioners rely on a small set of recurring tools.

- **Transportation Management Systems (TMS)** help shippers, forwarders, and 3PLs plan loads, choose carriers, compare rates, and track shipments across modes. Even simple versions can replace dozens of email threads and spreadsheets.
- **Warehouse Management Systems (WMS)** drive inventory accuracy and order fulfillment inside warehouses and distribution centers. Under-

standing what your WMS can and cannot do is as important as knowing a carrier's service levels.

- **Port community systems and customs portals** connect carriers, terminals, customs, and inland transport around major gateways. Examples include port community platforms in Rotterdam or Singapore and national customs single window systems. Learning how to read and use their status messages is part of modern forwarding.

- **Tariff and trade tools** such as online HS code search engines, national tariff databases, and rules of origin calculators are essential for getting duties and trade agreement benefits right.

- **Tracking and visibility tools** range from carrier portals and parcel tracking pages to AIS ship tracking sites and specialized visibility platforms that aggregate data from many providers. Used well, they support early exception detection rather than just post hoc storytelling.

Hands On Ways to Learn More

You do not need a job in logistics to keep learning. Simple, practical exercises can bring the concepts from this book to life.

- **Track a container in real time** Websites such as MarineTraffic and the tracking tools of carriers like Maersk or MSC let you follow ships and containers as they move. Pick a service from Shanghai to Los Angeles or from Antwerp to New York and watch the pattern of port calls and transit times. Compare what you see with the schedules carriers publish.

- **Study a real freight quote** If your company imports or exports, ask to see an anonymized freight quote and final invoice. Identify the base rate, surcharges, origin and destination terminal charges, and any accessorial fees. Match them to the concepts in Chapter 6. This one exercise will make future negotiations far more informed.

- **Visit a port, terminal, or distribution center** Many ports organize public tours or open days. Some large distribution centers and parcel hubs occasionally host visitors, especially for students. Standing on a quay beside a 18,000 TEU container ship or watching automated cranes stack boxes in a yard makes the scale of global trade very tangible.

- **Map your own supply chain** Choose a product you use daily, such as your smartphone, breakfast cereal, or running shoes. Try to trace its journey back through retailers, distribution centers, ports, and factories. Note which parts likely moved by air, sea, road, or rail. This exercise trains you to think in terms of flows, not just items on a shelf.

In 2015, a university student in Mumbai attended a port tour at Nhava Sheva, then took a short online course in supply chain basics. Within a year she had landed an internship in operations at a mid sized freight forwarder. She did not start with deep technical knowledge. She started with curiosity and a willingness to follow the trail of goods from factory gate to store shelf. You now have a much richer toolkit than she did on that first port visit.

Use it. Ask shrewder questions. Demand clearer quotes. Design more resilient supply chains. Or build a career in a field that, quietly but decisively, keeps the modern world stocked, fed, and connected.

Appendix B: Frequently Confused Concepts

This reference pairs terms that readers and even professionals often mix up, with a short reminder of the differences.

Freight Forwarder vs Freight Broker vs Carrier vs 3PL - A *freight forwarder* designs and manages international shipments, booking carriers and handling documentation and customs coordination. - A *freight broker* matches individual road freight loads with trucking companies and usually does not touch the cargo. - A *carrier* operates the physical vehicle, such as ships, trucks, aircraft, or trains. - A *3PL* manages broader logistics functions such as warehousing and transport planning and may run forwarding and brokerage activities internally.

Demurrage vs Detention vs Storage - *Demurrage* is charged when a full container sits too long inside a port or terminal beyond free time. - *Detention* is charged when a container is kept too long outside the terminal before being returned. - *Storage* is a terminal or warehouse fee for goods or containers occupying space beyond the free period, separate from demurrage or detention.

FCL vs LCL; TL vs LTL - *FCL* (full container load) is one shipper using a whole container, even if not literally full. *LCL* (less than container load) is cargo from multiple shippers consolidated into one container. - *TL* (truckload) is a road shipment that uses most or all of a trailer. *LTL* (less than truckload) shares trailer space with other shippers and moves through carrier terminals.

Parcel vs LTL vs Palletized Freight - *Parcel* is small, usually boxed shipments handled by package carriers with hub and spoke networks and many delivery stops. - *LTL* moves larger freight, often on pallets, and uses trucking terminals but still combines multiple shippers' cargo. - Full palletized freight at higher volumes usually moves as TL or in containers.

HS Code vs Schedule B vs ECCN vs HTS - The *HS code* is the six digit base under the Harmonized System used worldwide. - *HTS* (Harmonized Tariff Schedule) codes extend HS digits for import duty and statistics in a given country. - *Schedule B* codes are export classification numbers used by the United States for export statistics. - *ECCN* (Export Control Classification Number) is a separate export control code used to identify items subject to United States export licensing rules.

Country of Origin vs Country of Export vs Country of Destination - *Country of origin* is where the product is manufactured or substantially transformed. - *Country of export* is where the goods are shipped from. - *Country of destination* is where the buyer or final consignee receives the goods. Origin, not export country, usually determines duty rates and eligibility for trade agreements.

Incoterms vs Payment Terms - *Incoterms* define who pays for transport and where risk passes (for example FOB, CIF, DAP). - *Payment terms* state when and how the buyer pays the seller (for example net 30 days, letter of credit, advance payment). You can have the same Incoterm with very different payment terms, and vice versa.

FOB vs EXW vs FCA - Under *EXW* (Ex Works), the buyer handles almost everything from the seller's door onward, including export formalities in many cases. - Under *FOB* (Free On Board), the seller delivers goods onto the vessel at the origin port and clears export customs, after which risk transfers to the buyer. - Under *FCA* (Free Carrier), the seller delivers goods to a named place such as a terminal or forwarder's warehouse and clears export customs; it is often a better fit than FOB for containerized shipments.

Customs Broker vs Freight Forwarder - A *customs broker* focuses on import and sometimes export declarations, duty, tax, and compliance. - A *freight forwarder* arranges the physical movement of goods and often hires customs brokers or has them in house. In some firms, one legal entity holds both roles, but the underlying functions remain distinct.

Commercial Invoice vs Pro Forma Invoice - A *commercial invoice* records an actual sale and is used by customs to assess duties and taxes. - A *pro forma invoice* is a preliminary or indicative document, often used for quotations or for applying for licenses or financing, not for customs valuation.

Booking Confirmation vs Bill of Lading / AWB - A *booking confirmation* shows that space has been reserved with a carrier for a planned shipment. - A *bill of lading* or *air waybill* confirms that the carrier has actually received the cargo and states the terms of carriage.

Appendix C: Sample Documents

The following simplified samples show the key fields that appear on common shipping documents. Real formats vary by company and country, but the structure is similar.

Sample 1: Commercial Invoice (Export from United States)

Seller (Exporter): Maria's Candle Studio LLC 123 Warehouse Road, Austin, TX 78701, USA

Buyer (Consignee): Lumière Boutique SARL 45 Rue de Turenne, 75003 Paris, France

Invoice Number: 2025 0115 Invoice Date: 15 January 2025 Purchase Order: PO 7843 Incoterm and Place: DAP Paris, Incoterms 2020 Currency: USD

Line Items: 1. Scented soy candles in glass, "Winter Cedar" HS Code: 3406.00 Quantity: 2,000 units Unit Price: USD 6.50 Line Value: USD 13,000.00

Total Invoice Value: USD 13,000.00 Country of Origin: United States Terms of Payment: Net 30 days

Declaration: I declare that the information on this invoice is true and correct. Signature, Name, Title, Date

COMMERCIAL INVOICE

SELLER / EXPORTER	INVOICE NUMBER:
Maria's Candle Studio LLC	2025 0115
123 Warehouse Road, Austin,	**INVOICE DATE:**
TX 78701, USA	15 January 2025
	PURCHASE ORDER:
	PO 7843
BUYER / CONSIGNEE	**INCOTERM AND PLACE:**
Lumière Boutique SARL	DAP Paris, Incoterms 2020
45 Rue de Turenne, 75003 Paris,	**CURRENCY:**
France	USD

DESCRIPTION	HS CODE	QUANTITY	UNIT PRICE	LINE VALUE
Scented soy candles in glass, 'Winter Cedar'	3406.00	2,000 units	USD 6.50	USD 13,000.00

| COUNTRY OF ORIGIN: | TOTAL INVOICE VALUE: | USD 13,000.00 |
| United States | | |

TERMS OF PAYMENT:
Net 30 days

I declare that the information on this invoice is true and correct.

SIGNATURE: _____

NAME: _____

TITLE: _____

DATE: _____

Figure 27: Commercial Invoice Sample

Sample 2: Packing List (Linked to the Invoice Above)

Exporter: Maria's Candle Studio LLC Consignee: Lumière Boutique SARL Invoice Number: 2025 0115

Packaging Details: - 100 cartons, each 20 units of candles - Carton Dimensions: 40 cm x 30 cm x 25 cm - Carton Gross Weight: 12.5 kg

Totals: - Total Cartons: 100 - Total Units: 2,000 - Total Gross Weight: 1,250 kg - Total Volume: 3.0 CBM (approximate)

Marks and Numbers on Cartons: "MC WINTER CEDAR", Carton 1 of 100 to 100 of 100

"PACKING LIST"

EXPORTER	CONSIGNEE	
Maria's Candle Studio LLC 123 Warehouse Road, Austin, TX 78701, USA	Lumière Boutique SARL 45 Rue de Turenne, 75003 Paris, France	INVOICE NUMBER: 2025 0115

PACKAGING DETAILS

- 100 cartons, each containing 20 units of candles
- **Carton Dimensions:** 40 cm x 30 cm x 25 cm
- **Carton Gross Weight:** 12.5 kg

TOTALS

Total Cartons:	100
Total Units:	2,000
Total Gross Weight:	1,250 kg
Total Volume:	3.0 CBM (approximate)

Maria's Candle Studio LLC
45 Rue de Turenne, 75003 Paris, France, USA

MARKS AND NUMBERS

"MC WINTER CEDAR, Carton 1 of 100 to 100 of 100"

Figure 28: Packing List Sample

Sample 3: Ocean Bill of Lading (Key Fields Only)

Shipper: Maria's Candle Studio LLC Consignee: Lumière Boutique SARL Notify Party: Lumière Boutique SARL (or forwarder in France)

Vessel / Voyage: MV Atlantic Star / VOY 105W Port of Loading: Houston, TX, USA Port of Discharge: Le Havre, France Place of Delivery: Paris, France

Container Number / Seal Number: ABCU1234567 / Seal 987654

Cargo Description: 1 x 20 foot container 100 cartons scented soy candles in glass HS Code: 3406.00 Gross Weight: 1,250 kg Measurement: 3.0 CBM

Freight and Charges: Freight: As per agreement (prepaid / collect)

Number of Original Bills of Lading: 3 Place and Date of Issue: Houston, 20

January 2025 Signed for the Carrier: (authorized signature)

Bill of Lading   **Bill of Lading**

Shipper	Consignee	Notify Party
Maria's Candle Studio LLC	Lumière Boutique SARL	Lumière Boutique SARL (or designated forwarder)

Transport Details

Vessel / Voyage	Port of Loading	Port of Discharge	Place of Delivery
MV Atlantic Star / VOY 105W	Houston, TX, USA	Le Havre, France	Paris, France

Container and Seal Information

Container Number	Seal Number
ABCU1234567	987654

Cargo Description Section

1 x 20 foot container
100 cartons scented soy candles in glass
HS Code: 3406.00
Gross Weight: 1,250 kg
Measurement: 3.0 CBM

Freight and Charges Section

Freight
As per agreement (prepaid / collect)

Document Control and Legal Section

Number of Original Bills of Lading	Place and Date of Issue	Signed for the Carrier:
3	Houston, 20 January 2025	_____ (authorized signature)

Figure 29: Bill of Lading Sample

Sample 4: Arrival Notice (Import into France)

To: Lumière Boutique SARL From: OceanBlue Shipping France SAS (local agent for carrier)

Vessel / Voyage: MV Atlantic Star / VOY 105W Port of Discharge: Le Havre ETA: 3 February 2025

Container: ABCU1234567 Bill of Lading: OBL HOU PAR 2025 0115

Charges Due Before Release (Summary): - Destination THC: EUR 210 - Documentation / Delivery Order Fee: EUR 65 - Security Fee: EUR 25 Total: EUR 300 (plus VAT where applicable)

Instructions: Please arrange customs clearance and payment of above charges. Once completed, contact our office to schedule pickup or delivery.

Arrival Notice

To:	From:
Lumière Boutique SARL	OceanBlue Shipping France SAS (local agent for carrier)

Shipment and Vessel Details

Vessel / Voyage:	Port of Discharge:	ETA:
MV Atlantic Star / VOY 105W	Le Havre	3 February 2025

Container and Document References

Container Number:	Bill of Lading:
ABCU1234567	OBL HOU PAR 2025 0115

Charges Due Before Release

• Destination THC	EUR 210
• Documentation / Delivery Order Fee	EUR 65
• Security Fee	EUR 25

Total Charges: EUR 300 (plus VAT where applicable)

Instructions Section

Please arrange customs clearance and payment of the above charges. Once completed, contact our office to schedule pickup or delivery.

Figure 30: Arrival Notice Sample

Appendix D: Incoterms Quick Reference (Incoterms 2020)

The table below summarizes commonly used Incoterms from Incoterms 2020. It is a quick reminder of who pays for what, where risk transfers, and who handles customs. For full legal definitions, always consult the original ICC Incoterms 2020 rules.

Incoterm	Main Modes	Seller Pays For	Buyer Pays For	Risk Transfers At	Export Customs	Import Customs
EXW (Ex Works, named place)	Any	Making goods available at seller's premises	All transport, export and import formalities, duties, and insurance	When goods are placed at buyer's disposal at named place (often seller's warehouse)	Usually buyer, depending on local law	Buyer
FCA (Free Carrier, named place)	Any	Export packing, loading and delivery to named place, export clearance	Main carriage, insurance, import charges	When goods are handed to carrier or another person at named place	Seller	Buyer

Incoterm	Main Modes	Seller Pays For	Buyer Pays For	Risk Transfers At	Export Customs	Import Customs
FAS (Free Along-side Ship, named port of shipment)	Sea / inland waterway	Export packing, delivery alongside vessel at origin port, export clearance	Loading on vessel, ocean freight, insur-ance, import charges and inland delivery	When goods are placed alongside the vessel at origin port	Seller	Buyer
FOB (Free On Board, named port of shipment)	Sea / inland waterway	Export packing, delivery to port, loading on vessel, export clearance	Ocean freight, insur-ance, import charges and inland delivery	When goods are on board the vessel at port of shipment	Seller	Buyer
CFR (Cost and Freight, named port of destination)	Sea / inland waterway	Export costs and main carriage to named port of destination	Insurance (if any), import charges and inland delivery	When goods are on board vessel at port of shipment	Seller	Buyer

Incoterm	Main Modes	Seller Pays For	Buyer Pays For	Risk Transfers At	Export Customs	Import Customs
CIF (Cost, Insurance and Freight, named port of destination)	Sea / inland waterway	Export costs, main carriage to named port of destination, minimum insurance	Import charges and inland delivery	When goods are on board vessel at port of shipment	Seller	Buyer
CPT (Carriage Paid To, named place of destination)	Any	Export costs and main carriage to named place of destination	Insurance (if any), import charges and inland delivery	When goods are handed to first carrier	Seller	Buyer
CIP (Carriage and Insurance Paid To, named place of destination)	Any	Export costs, main carriage to named place of destination, insurance meeting ICC requirements	Import charges and inland delivery	When goods are handed to first carrier	Seller	Buyer

Incoterm	Main Modes	Seller Pays For	Buyer Pays For	Risk Transfers At	Export Customs	Import Customs
DAP (Delivered At Place, named place of destination)	Any	Export costs, main and inland carriage to named place	Import duties, taxes, and customs clearance	When goods are ready for unloading at named place	Seller	Buyer
DPU (Delivered At Place Unloaded, named place of destination)	Any	Export costs, main and inland carriage to named place, unloading at named place	Import duties, taxes, and customs clearance	When goods are unloaded at named place	Seller	Buyer
DDP (Delivered Duty Paid, named place of destination)	Any	Almost all costs: export and import formalities, duties, taxes, main and inland carriage to named place	Unloading at named place (unless otherwise agreed)	When goods are ready for unloading at named place	Seller	Seller

Notes:

- Incoterms allocate transport cost and risk between seller and buyer. They do not by themselves specify payment method (for example letter of credit, open account).
- Some terms are designed for sea and inland waterway transport only (FAS, FOB, CFR, CIF) and are not appropriate for container shipments under other modes. For containerized cargo, FCA, CPT, or CIP are usually better fits.
- Always pair an Incoterm with a clearly named place (for example FCA Shanghai terminal, DAP Munich warehouse) to avoid ambiguity about where responsibilities change.

Sources

U.S. Section 301 Tariffs on China

- **Office of the United States Trade Representative (USTR)**, "China Section 301-Tariff Actions and Exclusion Process" , https://ustr.gov/issue-areas/enforcement/section-301-investigations/tariff-actions, various years.
- **Congressional Research Service (CRS)**, "Section 301 Tariffs on Chinese Imports: Recent Developments," various reports 2018–2021.
- **U.S. Customs and Border Protection (CBP)**, informed compliance publications on tariff classification and country-of-origin / "substantial transformation" guidance, various years.

Suez Canal / Ever Given Blockage (March 2021)

- **The Guardian**, "Suez canal blocked after giant container ship runs aground," March 24, 2021.
- **Trowers & Hamlins**, "Ever Given: The Suez Canal Blockage and its legal implications," legal briefing, 2021.
- **Lloyd's List**, coverage of the grounding, refloating, and subsequent arbitration, March–July 2021.

COVID-Era Port Congestion – Los Angeles / Long Beach (2020–2022)

- **The Guardian**, "More than 100 container ships wait to dock at southern California ports," October 2021.
- **Journal of Commerce (JOC)**, multiple reports on vessel queues, dwell times, and chassis shortages, 2020–2022.
- **Port of Los Angeles / Port of Long Beach**, monthly TEU throughput reports and press releases, 2020–2022.

Yantian Terminal Partial Shutdown (June 2021)

- **Reuters**, "China's Yantian port congestion approaches normal after COVID outbreak," June 2021.
- **Freightos**, market commentary on rate impacts from Yantian, June 2021.

Pandemic Freight Rate Spike (2020–2021)

- **LA Times**, "How high can shipping rates go? Pandemic keeps pushing prices to new records," November 2021.
- **Wolf Street**, "Freight costs skyrocket: Container rates from China to US hit $20,000," July 2021.
- **Freightos Baltic Index (FBX)**, historical spot rate data, 2019–2022.
- **Drewry World Container Index**, weekly rate benchmarks, 2020–2021.

Panama Canal Drought Restrictions (2023)

- **Reuters**, "Panama Canal extends transit restrictions due to drought," September 2023.
- **The Guardian**, "Panama Canal drought forces severe restrictions on shipping," August 2023.
- **CarbonBrief**, analysis of climate factors behind Gatun Lake water levels, 2023.

Rhine Low-Water Events (2018, 2022)

- **Reuters**, "Rhine water levels halt barge traffic, German industry feels pinch," October 2018.
- **The Guardian**, "Rhine at 'historic' low level as drought bites," August 2022.
- **German Federal Waterways and Shipping Administration (WSV)**, water level bulletins, 2018 and 2022.

General Sources and Further Reading

The "Further Exploration" section earlier in this book provides additional resources, including textbooks, industry reports, freight indices, and professional associations. Together with the crisis-specific sources above, they give readers a solid foundation for continued learning.

Additional Data Sources Used in the Book

Port Throughput, Fleet Size, and Container Ship Capacities

- **UNCTAD**, *Review of Maritime Transport*, various annual editions – container ship size classes, global fleet composition, and leading port throughput ranges (for example Shanghai, Ningbo, Rotterdam, Antwerp, Los Angeles/Long Beach, and New York–New Jersey).
- **Alphaliner** and **Drewry**, fleet and port rankings, various years – typical TEU capacities of ultra large container vessels and major port throughput bands.
- **Port of Los Angeles**, **Port of Long Beach**, and **Port of New York and New Jersey**, annual statistics and fact sheets, various years – approximate TEU volumes and rail/truck shares.

Modal Emissions and Energy Use

- **International Maritime Organization (IMO)**, *Fourth IMO GHG Study* and related greenhouse gas reports – relative carbon intensity of international shipping.
- **International Energy Agency (IEA)**, *The Future of Rail* (2019) and transport sector overviews – energy efficiency comparisons between rail, road, and air freight.
- **European Environment Agency (EEA)**, "Greenhouse gas emissions from transport" and modal comparison briefs, various years – indicative emissions per ton-kilometre by mode.
- **IPCC**, *Climate Change* assessment reports, transport chapters – overview of transport's role in global emissions.

Trucking Regulation and Capacity

- **U.S. Federal Motor Carrier Safety Administration (FMCSA)**, "Electronic Logging Devices and Hours of Service Supporting Documents" final rule and guidance materials – ELD enforcement and driver hour constraints.
- **American Trucking Associations (ATA)** and **Bureau of Transportation Statistics (BTS)**, selected reports and data tables – driver shortages, capacity cycles, and freight volumes in North American trucking.

Cold Chain Practices and Temperature Ranges

- **World Health Organization (WHO)**, guidelines on the international packaging and shipping of temperature-sensitive pharmaceutical products – typical vaccine and biologic temperature bands.
- **Food and Agriculture Organization (FAO)** and national food safety

agencies, cold chain and perishable logistics guidance – common temperature ranges and shelf-life considerations for chilled and frozen foods.